The Gospel and Its Meaning

The Gospel and Its Meaning

A Theology for
Evangelism and Church Growth

Harry L. Poe

ZondervanPublishingHouse
Grand Rapids, Michigan

A Division of HarperCollinsPublishers

The Gospel and Its Meaning
Copyright © 1996 by Harry L. Poe

Requests for information should be addressed to:

 Zondervan Publishing House
Grand Rapids, Michigan 49530

Library of Congress Cataloging-in-Publication Data

Poe, Harry L. 1950–
    The gospel and its meaning : a theology for evangelism and church growth
/ Harry L. Poe.
      p. cm.
    Includes bibliographical references and index.
    ISBN: 0–310–20172–1
    1. Evangelistic work.   2. Church growth.   I. Title.
BV3790.P57   1996
269'2'01—dc20   96–1033
                                                                          CIP

Edited by Verlyn D. Verbrugge

Printed in the United States of America

---

96 97 98 99 00 01 02 / ❖ DH / 10 9 8 7 6 5 4 3 2 1

For
Rebecca
and
Mary Ellen,
who slept peacefully while this book was being written,
with the prayer that as they grow older
they will find this gospel
sweeter than all else in life.

Contents

Preface

The completion of this book comes with a surprising sense of disappointment. What I hoped to accomplish could not be done in a reasonable amount of space. I could not go into depth; as a result, the book will suggest rather than prove its thesis about the gospel: the different elements of the gospel speak to different levels of spiritual concern in different cultures at different times. Sometimes the death of Christ speaks most meaningfully to a people, while at other times the resurrection of Christ speaks more powerfully.

The concern that prompted the writing of this book stems from the evangelistic ministry of the church in the latter days of the twentieth century. Christians have a tendency to proclaim the gospel *from* the perspective of their own spiritual issues rather than *to* the perspective of their audience. Furthermore, Christians tend to speak of the gospel in terms of the aspect of the gospel that means the most to them, rather than in terms of the aspect of the gospel that might offer the most good news to another person. This habit creates the oft observed situation in which the church answers questions people are not asking.

This book is written to provide Christians with a way to begin to think about the extent of the good news of Jesus Christ and how this good news touches different levels of human experience. The writing of the book has only demonstrated to me the extent to which I represent the same habit of minimizing the gospel. I discovered things in writing that I did not expect to find. Likewise, I have found myself in the distasteful position of realizing I was wrong. I have even come to appreciate the perspectives of church traditions vastly different from my own. Rather than attempt to perpetuate the mythology of scholarly detachment, I should say that I write from a faith perspective as an evangelical Southern Baptist, concerned about an issue that affects Christ's whole body.

My methodology will please few, for I have committed one of the unpardonable sins of academia: I have crossed disciplines. This study necessarily involves a biblical treatment of the gospel, but it also includes a theological treatment in historical perspective. In order to do justice to these, however, I have also borrowed from cultural anthropology, pastoral care, and sociology. This study cannot stand as a legitimate study within any of these disciplines, though I would argue that at some point an effort at integration of disciplines must take place in order to arrive at an adequate theology for ministry. In this case I am concerned with developing a foundation upon which ministries in different settings may understand a theology for evangelism.

The first chapter of the book revisits C. H. Dodd's "quest for the historical kerygma."[1] It concludes that the early church understood the good news to include the existence of a Creator, the fulfillment of Scripture, the incarnation of Jesus Christ as Son of God and Son of David, his death for sins, his resurrection, his exaltation, the gift of the Holy Spirit, and the return of the Lord. The good news was also offered with the expectation that humans would respond. The rest of the book devotes one chapter to each of these elements of the gospel. Every chapter contains a biblical treatment, a discussion of the historical/theological development of an element over the past two thousand years, and the implication of the discussion for evangelism.

I did not construct the biblical treatment in the way I thought I would. I originally began by using several of the tools of New Testament research, but I found that they were not answering my questions. The atomizing of texts and traditions and theological perspectives tends to obliterate the larger mosaic created by the nuances. I have looked for how each book of the New Testament uses the elements of the gospel, some with an evangelistic (*kerygma*) purpose while others have a discipleship (*didache*) purpose. Regardless of the purpose, the same elements have been used. What startled me is the surprising similarity of gospel themes common to the variety of books and writers. In microcosm, however, the books use the themes in particular ways to address the spiritual issues of particular cultural contexts.

The historical/theological sections explore how the various elements of the gospel have played a dominate role in the life of the church. Each element became the basis for the development of entire doctrines. Eventually, the church developed dogma and systematic theology through defining, explaining, qualifying, expounding, and speculating on the elements of the gospel as the church lived out the faith in response to specific cultural, political, economic, social, and religious forces. At different times and in different cultures, different elements of the gospel have provided the point of orientation for the church or for systems of theology. While this approach speaks powerfully to its context, the church has also tended to cling to the answers of past generations, which, over time, can distort or veil the gospel that lies hidden under all of the contextualization.

The brief application section at the end of each chapter provides a more personal interaction with the material. It suggests how some of the dominant themes of the gospel address some of the spiritual issues people face in different contexts. One of the implications of this study is that the presentation of the gospel may not be reduced to a single formula of presentation that addresses all people in all cultures. While I argue that the gospel contains fixed affirmations of faith, it is not a formula, for its implications are truly astounding in their complexity.

I did not write this book under the most conducive of circumstances. The research and writing took place in the context of a heavy administrative load in addition to teaching responsibilities. It was written in airports, motel rooms, airplanes, cars, vans, and buses as well as at home and in my office. It was written in Louisville, St. Paul, San Diego, San Francisco, Boston, Denver, Chicago, Orlando, Atlanta, Pawley Island, River Falls, The Cove, Arrowhead Springs, Memphis, Glorietta, Greenville, Fort Collins, North Platt, Estes Park, Boulder, and Moscow. Most of the writing took place between ten o'clock at night and one o'clock in the morning. While this schedule does not commend itself as a standard for writing projects, it actually allowed me to observe the gospel dynamics in a variety of cultural and ethnic contexts.

Throughout the five years of this study, I have grown aware of the extent to which other people have influenced me or provided me with insight through our interaction.

I was first introduced to the question of what is the gospel almost thirty years ago in a Bible study for teenagers led by Fern Christman. My supervisory professor in my doctoral studies, Lewis A. Drummond, introduced me to the work of C. H. Dodd. Barrie

White, with whom I read church history at Oxford, introduced me to the changing concerns of the Puritans and the way their focus shifted as the circumstances of England shifted. Timothy George, now of Beeson Divinity School, spurred me to examine different emphases of the gospel when he insisted that all English churchmen of the late sixteenth and early seventeenth centuries agreed about the gospel. George R. Beasley-Murray demonstrated during my doctoral studies how to engage in critical scholarship from a faith perspective, but he should not be held responsible for the idiosyncrasies of my approach. Richard Cunningham guided me through a seminar on the philosophy of history that incubated my interest in the relationship between history and Scripture.

This study has provided many topics of conversation with colleagues in various disciplines over the past five years. In the context of those conversations the study has taken shape. I owe particular gratitude to Herb Klem, Ralph Hammond, Dennis Phelps of Bethel Seminary in St. Paul, Minnesota, and to David Dockery of The Southern Baptist Theological Seminary in Louisville, Kentucky. Marvin Anderson and Jill Bierwirth offered guidance through some less well-known periods of history. This study has also taken shape in the classroom through teaching and dialogue with students. I wish to acknowledge the stimulation and insight generated by students in my theology of evangelism seminars at Bethel Seminary and The Southern Baptist Theological Seminary: David Harkreader, Ben Thomas, Michael Eldridge, Tim Harris, John Pate, Liz Radic, Scott Wiggins, David Elks, Gregory Qualls, Irene Myhro, Leeland Stevenson, John Able, Al Shuck, Raymond Daines, Gary Marshall, Jon Dainty, William Shrader, David Jones, Paul Fife, Tracie Pogue, Aaron Mockley, Kip Smith, Rodman Williams, Kory Tedrick, Brian Jones, Allen Raub, David Murphy, Cher Moua, Cottrel Carson, and Peter Vogt.

The following students in my Ph.D. colloquium at Southern also rendered valuable assistance in proofing the final draft of the book: Don Cox, Tommy Ferrell, Scott Guffin, Charles Lawless, Ron McLain, and Rob Jackson (my Garrett Fellow at Southern Seminary). Nick Matchefts, my teaching assistant at Bethel Seminary, also helped with early proofreading. The staffs of the libraries at Bethel and Southern patiently helped with my research and made my hours in the libraries a joy. The manuscript was prepared by Gloria Metz, faculty secretary at Bethel, and JaRhonda Staples, Brenda Wessner, Bev Tillman, Laura Allen, Carmen Faison, and Winnie Reed, who serve as faculty secretaries at Southern.

This project could not have been completed without the help of Lea Andra Foster, secretary for the Research Doctoral Studies Office at Southern Seminary, and Joyce Durham, secretary for the Professional Doctoral Studies Office. During a time of institutional reorganization that coincided with the final revisions to the manuscript, these ladies rendered extraordinary service in putting the manuscript into final form. Chuck Lawless did the work of compiling the indexes. Ed van der Maas and Verlyn D. Verbrugge of Zondervan Publishing House have been not only helpful but delightful to work with in the production of this book.

Most of all, I thank my closest colleague in the ministry, Mary Anne, who has helped me think through this project from beginning to end. Her insights as a minister have helped me keep this book grounded in the purpose for which Christ came.

Harry L. Poe
Moscow
September 1995

NOTE

1. Portions of chapter 1 originally appeared as "Renewing the Quest for the Historical Kerygma," *Journal of the Academy for Evangelism*, 9 (1994): 59–71.

Chapter 1

Renewing the Quest for the Historical Kerygma

The world is approaching a significant anniversary. The Christian faith has made itself known for almost two thousand years. To say it rose from humble origins hardly describes the unlikeliness of its beginnings. The first followers of Jesus represented a diverse group: fishermen, tax collectors, prostitutes, members of the Sanhedrin, revolutionaries, Pharisees, adulteresses, respectable women. Jesus had only a brief ministry of about three years before his execution by the Romans on a charge of sedition. When the uncertain political circumstances of the day turned against him, the crowds and closest associates of Jesus turned their backs on him. One of his intimates sold him into the hands of his opponents, and all but a handful of the other closest followers scattered.

THE PROBLEM OF CHRISTIAN FAITH

One can readily understand how a successful, charismatic leader might have left a powerful legacy by gathering a great following over the course of many years and by creating a movement to carry on the mission, as Mohammed did. Likewise, one can appreciate how a teacher like Buddha prepared a generation of disciples who stood committed to carry on his teachings. In a rarer case, when the message of the thinker gains recognition as being of such value to the culture that the entire political/cultural system appropriates it, a philosophical position may form the basis for society, as happened with Confucius.

As one accounts for the presence of the Christian faith after two thousand years, all of the foregoing dynamics have played a part in its survival at various stages in different places and times. The difficulty comes in appreciating how the Christian faith survived the death of Jesus. Unlike Mohammed, Jesus did not overthrow the political/religious power of his day. Unlike Buddha, Jesus did not leave a group of disciples committed to carrying on his teachings. On the contrary, at his death the disciples fled. Unlike Confucius, Jesus did not enjoy the approval and sanction of his culture and its power structure.

Quite candidly, the Christian faith comprises a collection of assertions about Jesus, any one of which would render it ridiculous, and the cumulative effect seems utter foolishness. Saul of Tarsus, one of the earlier persecutors of the followers of Jesus, who after his conversion became one of the primary proponents of Jesus, acknowledged that he asked people to believe foolishness (1 Cor. 1:18–25). When Porcius Festus, Roman Procurator of Judea (ca. 60–62), heard Saul's account of his faith (by then known as Paul), he declared him a madman (Acts 26:24). Two thousand years later, the Christian faith seems even more absurd.

Remarkably, the early followers of Jesus had already rejected the absurdities of his teaching before his death. They excised whatever did not conform to their expectations and theological presuppositions. They liked Jesus as a faith healer and preacher who drew large crowds. They liked Jesus as the embodiment of the long frustrated national hope for the revival of the kingdom of Israel. They liked his talk about heaven and his victory over demons. On the other hand, they did not like his talk about dying. Neither did they understand his talk about the resurrection. They accepted the concept of resurrection, but it was supposed to happen at the end of time. Like most religious people, they expressed a preference for the supernatural as long as it happened in a different time and a different place. When Jesus died, their faith in him as a leader also died.

The twentieth century has witnessed an earnest and deliberate effort on the part of Christian theologians to make the Christian faith conform to a modern worldview that has no place for what cannot be explained through scientific observation. A variety of theories for the origin of religions and the interpretation of biblical literature has developed from the point of view of faith as well as skepticism. The understanding of Scripture at the hands of different schools of thought presents a variety of conceptions: for example, a record of God's saving acts, a reflection about an encounter with God, a literary construction to meet the needs of a particular group of people, and a projection of psychic need. Such approaches have developed in order to make the Christian faith acceptable to the twentieth century mind and relevant to the contemporary situation.

To an amazing degree, the modern mind with its disdain for the supernatural shows a common methodology with the ancient mind and its love of the supernatural. Both share an emotional inability or unwillingness to deal with what does not conform to preconceived notions of how things should be. The misdirected faith of the first followers of Jesus had to die before a faith could emerge that saw life and reality from a new perspective. In that sense, modern theology has not performed a particular service to the world by helping people maintain their own preconceived notions about the nature of life and reality. The Christian faith must begin with the honest confession that it is total foolishness from the perspective of everyone's worldview. Only then can one proceed to an assessment of whether this foolishness is true. As the world approaches the two-thousandth anniversary of Jesus' death, any examination of the Christian faith must come to grips with the absurd message that the followers of Jesus began to spread after his execution. Then one must wonder why a reasonable person would believe such things.

To begin, the apostles declared that Jesus had risen from the dead. The idea of resurrection had common acceptance in the ancient world. Many Jews, especially the Pharisees, expected a general resurrection at the end of time, though this expectation differed from themes of rising in other Near Eastern religions. The resurrection theme in the ancient nature and fertility religions accounted mythologically for the changing seasons, from the death of winter to the new life of spring. The Baal cult of ancient Canaan featured the death of Baal at the hand of Mot and his subsequent rising through the efforts of his consort/sister Anath, who mutilated Mot and scattered his parts on the fields. Tammuz and Ishtar played the same role in Babylonia. Osiris and his consort Isis carried out the same fertility myth in Egypt. The theme of resurrection also figured prominently in the mystery religions of the Roman Empire, in the mythic accounts of the regional and popular deities, particularly of

Asia Minor. Though they shared the idea of resurrection, these cults described dramatic episodes that happened "once upon a time."

Instead of a primordial setting in conflict with a monster like Mot, Jesus "suffered under Pontius Pilate." The Romans executed him publicly outside the walls of Jerusalem. The events surrounding Jesus took place in a historical setting with which the people of his day were familiar. J. R. R. Tolkien, scholar of Norse mythology and writer of fanciful tales, readily admitted the mythic elements surrounding Jesus, but added that in the case of Jesus, the myth really happened.[1] He reasoned that the universal presence of the dying/rising myth served a divine purpose in preparing the world to receive such a fanciful idea when it happened in a particular place and time.

What the world knows of Jesus comes from those followers who, in the moment of crisis, fled from him because the Jesus they believed in was lost. Jesus left no written records. Instead, he charged his disciples with the responsibility of bearing testimony to what they knew, like witnesses in a court trial. Those who heard the testimony played the part of judge. They believed the testimony of the witnesses, or they did not. What the early followers of Jesus told people when they gave testimony, then, comprises a helpful key to understanding why people then, or at any other time and place, would choose to believe and follow Jesus.

The followers of Jesus prefaced their testimony by calling it *good news*. In the vernacular Greek of the first century, the term used was *euangelion*, which, when anglicized, becomes *evangel* (from which the word "evangelism" comes). Literally, then, evangelism means telling good news. The expression entered the English language as the Old English word *godspel* and survives today as *gospel*. The gospel is the good news about Jesus that his followers told people.

Why did the story of Jesus have the status of good news? More importantly, why would someone receive it as good news personally so as to change his or her worldview and become a follower of Jesus? To answer these questions, one must determine what the followers of Jesus included when they gave testimony of what they had heard and seen and of what this gospel meant. The remainder of this study proposes to identify the elements of the gospel and their meaning. Two thousand years later, however, one cannot ignore a related question. In a highly organized, technological world, which looks to science for the verification of all knowledge and adheres to a value neutral morality, does the gospel still mean anything?

In searching for the central elements of the gospel, a distinction appears between the Christian faith and the actual form Christianity has taken in different places and times. The gospel precedes the development of tradition, dogma, or even church organization and hierarchy. All of these grew out of the gospel, and they immediately began to appear in the early church. But these elements exist only as servants of the gospel. When Peter preached the first gospel sermon on the Day of Pentecost (Acts 2), he did not hold the office of Bishop of Rome, he had no vestments, and he had no liturgical calendar or prescribed color for the season of Pentecost. He certainly did not subscribe to the idea of celibacy, if the presence of a wife bears any evidence in that regard.

On the Day of Pentecost, fifty days after the ancient Feast of the Passover, when Jesus had been executed, Peter publicly declared why the scattered disciples of Jesus had come back together. He explained why the ones who had feared any association with Jesus fifty days before now identified themselves openly and publicly as followers of Jesus. The occasion for the speech or sermon leaves modern commentators with the embarrassment of dealing with yet another supernatural setting. After forty days of appearing to the disciples in resurrected form, Jesus told his followers to remain in Jerusalem until the Holy Spirit came upon them. After this parting word, he vanished out of their sight. Ten days later, as the group of gathered disciples met, the promise of Jesus happened. Luke describes a sound like a rushing wind, accompanied by tongues like fire that rested on everyone as a visible manifestation of their possession by the Holy Spirit. In contrast to the torment of those poor wretches described as "demon possessed," these followers of Jesus were "God possessed."

No doubt the experience of Pentecost sealed the faith of the disciples in Jesus. With his resurrection, they still wondered whether Jesus might now restore the ancient kingdom of Israel (Acts 1:6). This view of the Messiah and his work saw salvation as a possession or commodity to which someone held title. With the coming of the Spirit, however, the disciples entered the new age they had not anticipated. Salvation meant incorporation into the kingdom of God, which occurred as the Holy Spirit swallowed them. They understood that incorporation into the kingdom meant incorporation into the King. Until Pentecost, Jesus and the resurrection were wondrous events outside them. At Pentecost, however, the followers of Jesus became a part of the body of Christ. All of these ideas found expression in the writings of the New Testament.

Luke described the phenomenon of the disciples speaking "in other tongues" as a result of the Spirit's coming. The rushing sound and the noise of the speaking drew a large crowd of holiday visitors to Jerusalem who, according to Luke, could understand the disciples in the native languages of the countries throughout the empire from which they had come. In this setting, Peter delivered the first gospel message (Acts 2:14–40). Significantly, Luke mentions that the explanation of the disciples' experience came in response to the question, "What does this mean?" The subsequent discourse by Peter explained what the events of the gospel meant for the crowd in Jerusalem.

THE QUEST FOR THE HISTORICAL KERYGMA

In this century, C. H. Dodd set the agenda for analyzing Christian evangelism in New Testament times. His 1935 lectures, later published as *The Apostolic Preaching and Its Development*, sought to identify the essential elements of a gospel formula that he believed the apostles commonly proclaimed.[2] Dodd began by examining Paul's writings, based on his interpretation of 1 Corinthians 1:21: "It pleased God by the foolishness of *preaching* to save them that believe" (KJV). Dodd demonstrated that the *kerygma*, the word rendered "preaching" in the King James Version, signifies the content of preaching or the message preached, not the act of delivering a sermon.

Dodd equated *kerygma* with the gospel and made a radical distinction between it and the teaching of the early church, which he designated as *didache*. To those outside the church the apostles proclaimed *kerygma*; to those inside the church they proclaimed *didache*. In more contemporary terminology, Dodd attempted to demonstrate an apostolic distinction between evangelism and discipleship.

In order to find the most primitive form of the apostolic message, Dodd went to the writings of Paul, but immediately he met an obstacle. As writings to his churches, the letters of Paul constituted *didache*. Nonetheless, Dodd found support for his thesis in the distinction Paul drew between foundational precepts and matters of deeper maturity (1 Cor. 1:23; 2:2–6; 3:10ff.). In his letters, Paul addressed the implications of the gospel that lead to maturity; thus, fragments of the *kerygma* appear throughout the Pauline writings as the basis for specific instruction.

The most obvious of these passages is 1 Corinthians 15:3b–5, where Paul reminded the Corinthians in what terms he preached the gospel to them:

> that Christ died for our sins according to the Scriptures,
> that he was buried,
> that he was raised on the third day according to the Scriptures,
> and that he appeared to Peter. . . .

Paul went on to catalogue a series of resurrection appearances. Having stated enough of the gospel to remind the Corinthians of the centrality of the resurrection for their faith, he then proceeded in the remainder of this long chapter to elaborate the doctrine of resurrection. As far as Paul was concerned, the gospel included, at the least, the facts related to the death of Christ for our sins and his resurrection. But did it include more?

As he further explored the writings of Paul, Dodd concluded that the gospel Paul proclaimed also included as major themes:

> the return of Christ as Lord and Son of God who intercedes for
>   us (Rom. 10:8–9; 14:9; 2 Cor. 4:4; Eph. 1:20; Col. 3:1)
> the return of Christ for judgment (Rom. 2:16; 14:10; 1 Cor. 4:5;
>   2 Cor. 5:10; 1 Thess. 1:9–10)
> the fulfillment of Scripture (Rom. 1:2)
> Christ as Son of God and Son of David (Rom. 1:3–4; 8:31–34)

Dodd made it clear, however, that his treatment of the gospel revolved around his concern for realized eschatology.[3] Thus, he was working to establish an eschatological formula sanctioned by the early church.

In searching for actual examples of how the apostles preached, Dodd naturally turned to the book of Acts. In the first four speeches of Peter from Acts 2–4, Dodd identified six major points and several subpoints to Peter's message:

1. The age of fulfillment has dawned (Acts 2:16; 3:18; 3:24).
2. This has taken place through the ministry, death, and resurrection of Jesus, which was described with proof from the Scriptures to attest:
   a. His Davidic descent (Acts 2:30–31; cf. Ps. 132:11)
   b. His ministry (Acts 2:22; 3:22)
   c. His death (Acts 2:23; 3:13–14)
   d. His resurrection (Acts 2:24–31; 3:15; 4:10).
3. By virtue of the resurrection, Jesus has been exalted at the right hand of God, as messianic head of the new Israel (Acts 2:33–36; cf. Ps. 110:1; Acts 3:13; 4:11; cf. Ps. 118:22; Acts 5:31).
4. The Holy Spirit in the church is the sign of Christ's present power and glory (Acts 2:33; cf. Joel 2:28–32; Acts 5:32).
5. The messianic age will shortly reach its consummation in the return of Christ (Acts 3:21; 10:42).
6. The *kerygma* always closes with an appeal for repentance, the offer of forgiveness and of the Holy Spirit, and the promise of "salvation," which Dodd interpreted as "life of the Age to Come" for those who enter the new community (Acts 2:38–39; cf. Isa. 62:9; Joel 2:32; Acts 3:19, 25–26; cf. Gen. 12:3; Acts 4:12; see also Acts 5:31; 10:43).[4]

Dodd argued that this summary of the apostolic preaching formed the outline for the preaching of Jesus as described by Mark in Mark 1:14–15. That outline had three parts:

1. The time is fulfilled—referring to prophecy and fulfillment of Scripture.
2. The kingdom of God has drawn near—referring to the ministry, death, resurrection, and exaltation of Christ.
3. Repent and believe the gospel—referring to the appeal for repentance and the offer of forgiveness.[5]

Without commenting on whether the apostles based their preaching on the model of Jesus or whether Mark had modeled the preaching of Jesus on the apostles, Dodd saw the similarity as supportive of his view that the gospel circulated as a formula in the early days of the church.

Dodd noted several differences between the preaching of Peter, which he called the Jerusalem Kerygma, and the preaching of Paul, which he called the Pauline Kerygma. The Jerusalem Kerygma did not refer to Christ as the Son of God, nor did it assert that Christ died for our sins or that the exalted Christ intercedes for us. Dodd speculated on how the shift of emphasis may have arisen and whether the changes represented a change in theology or merely a change in terminology. This line of thought fit well with his theory of the development of the gospel away from its apostolic origins.

Though laying out all the elements of his reconstructed gospel, Dodd fell into the same path as generations of his predecessors. He singled out the aspect of the *kerygma* that appealed to him the most, arguing that his study of the apostles' preaching drives one to think of "resurrection, exaltation, and the second advent as being, in their belief, inseparable parts of a single divine event."[6] The apostles were not so much concerned with an "*early* advent" as with the "*immediate* advent" experienced through the Holy Spirit. Dodd's discussion formed a forum for expounding realized eschatology.

Dodd has come under severe criticism for several major features of his argument. (1) He assumed the reliability of Acts as a faithful example of the primitive preaching, rather than as a literary creation of Luke. (2) He argued for a fixed formula for the *kerygma*, which took on a creedal dimension. (3) He argued for a rigid distinction between *kerygma* and *didache*. On these points, scholars have argued for over fifty years, but a proper understanding of the ministry of evangelism requires yet another examination of the subject. (4) In his discussion another issue requires attention: the role of the Holy Spirit in the formulation of the gospel.

RELIABILITY OF ACTS

Martin Dibelius argued that the speeches in Acts were compositions by the author, but that they represent what the author understood the apostolic message to be.[7] The apostles' message did not concentrate on the biographical details of the life of Christ. Instead, they emphasized "what faith longed to hear and . . . what was likely to impress and convert unfaith, vis. that here it was God who spoke and who was at work."[8]

Bo Reicke argued that the similarity between sermons in Acts rests on a real tradition rather than on later constructions by Luke.[9] According to this scholar, the preaching of Jesus fell into four basic form traditions shared in common with the Jewish community. The apostles then adopted the forms of preaching they had learned from Jesus. One of these forms, missionary preaching, followed a form designed to persuade, which included thesis, proofs, and conclusion. Jesus provided the primary topics that comprised the early apostolic preaching that followed this pattern:

1. Thesis: Jesus was the Servant and the Lord.
2. Proofs
   a. His life showed him to fulfill these titles.
   b. Scripture bore witness to him.
   c. He was raised from the dead.
   d. The miracles demonstrated the power of his resurrection.
3. Conclusion: Everybody must turn to the Lord, including the Gentiles.[10]

Because of the similarity in form of the apostolic sermons but the slight differences in theology and development, Reicke suggested that these early sermons preserved the original tradition of the apostles rather than the creativity of Luke.[11]

Bertil Gärtner took strong exception with Dibelius over the reliability of Acts as historically substantial of the early preaching. He maintained that the church still living at the time of the writing of Acts, which had heard the apostolic preaching, would have insisted upon reliability.[12] Furthermore, any similarity between the sermons does not rest on Lucan composition, but on Peter and Paul's having the same message to deliver. Gärtner believed that shades of difference among the sermons reflect particular theologies, such as, the "older" Christology of Peter or concern for justification with Paul.[13] Gärtner discounted Dibelius's categorization of ancient historiography and suggested that the latter's failure to understand ancient historiography led to a flawed understanding of Acts as a literary creation by Luke.

C. S. C. Williams joined Gärtner's criticism of Dibelius. He accused Dibelius of failing to take seriously the extent of disagreement among scholars over the degree to which ancient historians freely composed or relied on factual material in their reports of speeches.[14] The position of Dibelius assumed a monolithic approach to writing history by the ancient historians. Michael Green has identified the variety of approaches pursued by Thucydides, Lucian, Livy, Cicero, and Philostratus, suggesting how unsafe it is "to argue from other writers as to what Luke could or could not have done in his speeches."[15] Rather than a Gentile approach to history, Williams argued that Luke would more likely have followed a Jewish model for history. Such an approach would have included the rabbinic method of memorization to preserve important words or sayings.[16] By regarding Acts as simply a literary-theological document without historical substance, Dibelius and others presumed that the ancient historians had no interest in presenting the content of what would have been said on significant occasions.

Dibelius does not stand alone in viewing the sermons in Acts as literary creations of Luke. Hans Conzelmann credited Luke on this account with being "the first Christian author consciously to try to conform to the standards of Hellenistic literature."[17] He believed the sermons in Acts represent Luke's attempt to imitate the style of Thucydides.

C. F. Evans insisted that Luke had greater freedom to write as he pleased in composing Acts since a model did not yet exist in the church for writing that kind of book.[18] This argument falls, however, in a comparison with the four Gospels. Though they were a different kind of book, speeches comprised a major part of them. Evans also held that the speeches of Acts must be Luke's composition rather than the preserved tradition of what was said by the apostles because Evans had difficulty envisioning the *Sitz im Leben* of the church that would have preserved and repeated the apostles' words. He further argued that no one would remember a speech twenty, thirty, or forty years after it was heard unless it was repeated, and he found no evidence for such repetition in the church.[19]

Evans therefore followed Dibelius in his method. In assessing the individual sermons, one must view them as part of one large composition, *The Acts of the Apostles*. Luke composed the speeches to illustrate his overall theme. As examples of this kind of composition, Evans referred to the commissioning by Christ (Acts 1:8) and Paul's sermon in Athens (17:22–31). The commissioning of Christ would not have been preserved by any of the fragmentary traditions that Luke used, because Evans could not imagine a case calling for the preservation of such material. The presence can only be explained, in his judgment, as a composition by Luke.[20] Evans makes a similar case for Lucan composition of Paul's sermon in Athens. While Paul may be speaking in character for Athens, the words do not seem appropriate for him.

Though he had no knowledge of Aramaic, Evans undertook to refute C. C. Torrey's theory of the Aramaic background of the speeches in Acts. Evans compared passages in Acts said to come from Aramaic sources with passages from Luke's Gospel with similar form and structure in his attempt to prove that the Aramaisms were not present.[21] In actuality, however, this strange approach tends to confirm rather than refute the theory of Aramaic backgrounds, since the speeches in the Luke all have an Aramaic context. R. A. Martin's subsequent analysis of the passages has demonstrated that the poor Greek of these passages translates into good Aramaic, suggesting that Luke relied on preserved Aramaic sermons for the early speeches in Acts.[22]

Rather than supporting the idea of a common *kerygma*, Evans' other presuppositions led him to conclude that the similarity between sermons in Acts resulted from Luke's literary style. A comparison of Peter's sermon on Pentecost with Paul's sermon at Antioch of Pisidia suggested to Evans that "Luke is operating with a stereotyped form which is current as the apostolic preaching in his own day, rather than with historical reminiscences of what the apostolic church in Jerusalem actually preached."[23]

THE ROLE OF THE HOLY SPIRIT IN THE FORMULATION OF THE GOSPEL

Critical study of the New Testament in the twentieth century has tended to neglect at best or deny at worst God's role in the composition of the books that became the New Testament. This attempt to avoid the transcendent arises from a legitimate concern to maintain objectivity in study, but such concern collapses in the face of the enormity of subjective presuppositions scholars bring to their study concerning what could or could not have happened two thousand years ago. Even worse cases of subjectivity arise when scholars attempt to reconstruct a life situation in the early church that would have called for the church to construct miracle stories or ascribe claims to divinity by Jesus.

In the case of the Acts of the Apostles and the effort to reconstruct the gospel as the apostles preached it, one school of scholarly thought has concluded that Acts cannot reveal how the apostles preached because Luke constructed it as a literary work to express his own theological concerns. Others argue for the acceptance of the material in Acts as the legitimate tradition of the church and an accurate representation of how the apostles would have preached. Neither approach seems entirely satisfactory, however, since neither grapples with the place of God in the development and preservation of the gospel. Historians, scientists, political scientists, grammarians, musicians, and the full range of academic disciplines have the luxury of pursuing their research with respect to the finite world. By positing the existence of God, however, the disciplines of theology cannot with integrity study their areas without thinking about God.

The Role of the Witness

The role of the witness plays a critical part in the Gospel of Luke and the Acts of the Apostles. Luke's Gospel begins by attributing his and other Gospel narratives to the testimony of witnesses (Luke 1:1–4). It concludes by describing the instructions of Christ to his followers that they should be witnesses to the fulfillment of Scripture, his death, his resurrection, the call for repentance, and the offer of both forgiveness of sins and the Holy Spirit (24:44–49). The Acts of the Apostles begins with Jesus' final instructions to his followers in which he promised them the power of the Holy Spirit and charged them to be his witnesses (Acts 1:8). The book closes with Paul in Rome declaring to the Jews "the kingdom of God and [trying] to convince them about Jesus from the Law of Moses and from the Prophets" (28:23), while the preaching and teaching go on unhindered. In other words, the substantial internal evidence of Luke's writings indicates his methodology, which concentrates on preserving the testimony of witnesses.

Furthermore, Luke, more than any other New Testament writer, paid attention to details of setting and confirmation. These details add credibility to his witness. He dated the birth of Christ "while Quirinius was governor of Syria" (Luke 2:2). He set the beginning of John's ministry "in the fifteenth year of the reign of Tiberius Caesar—when Pontius Pilate was governor of Judea, Herod tetrarch of Galilee, his brother Philip tetrarch of Iturea and Trachonitis, and Lysanias tetrarch of Abilene—during the high priesthood of Annas and Caiaphas" (3:1–2). Only Luke gave the age of Jesus when he began his ministry as "about thirty years old" (3:23). Luke also had a habit of including names of people: Mary, called Magdalene; Joanna, the wife of Cuza, Herod's steward; and Susanna (8:2–3); Simon the Pharisee (7:40); Zacchaeus (19:1–10); and Cleopas (24:18), in addition to names also cited in the other Gospels.

In the Acts of the Apostles, Luke's citation of names increases dramatically in relation to the enlargement of the field in which the story unfolds. The life of Jesus from birth to ascension took place in a small geographical area with a small number of followers. In Acts the story spreads throughout the Hellenistic world to the very capital of the empire. All along the way Luke documents names and "addresses" of people who heard the testimony and believed. The internal evidence of Acts indicates how Luke would have come by so many sermons and sermon fragments years after their delivery.

The Conversion Testimony

C. F. Evans and other skeptical critics can imagine no situation in the life of the church that would have led to the preservation of the sermons in Acts. The experience of the church from the time of Paul to this very day, however, suggests why the sermons would have been remembered and repeated. At one place Luke described Paul's conversion (Acts 9:1–30). In two other places Luke described how Paul gave testimony of his conversion experience: first before the crowd in Jerusalem (22:1–21), then before Agrippa (26:1–23). Converts to faith in Christ remember the circumstances of their conversion until they die. What is more, converts tend to obey the command of Christ to be his witnesses. External evidence of this phenomenon fills volumes of Christian devotional literature of the last two thousand years, including such classics as Augustine's *Con-*

fessions, Bunyan's *Grace Abounding* (which he allegorized as *The Pilgrim's Progress*), and C. S. Lewis's *Surprised by Joy*.[24]

While Peter, Paul, Philip, and certainly Stephen would not likely have remembered what they preached precisely on a given occasion, they would have known generally that they had preached Christ. With only that to go by, Luke would have had to resort to literary license. Luke had no such handicap, however, when writing his account of how the church fulfilled its commission to bear witness to Christ. Just as the apostles remembered the words of Christ, the converts would have remembered the words they heard from the apostles (cf. 1 Cor. 15:1). Of the three thousand converts on the Day of Pentecost who returned to the corners of the empire after their pilgrimage to Jerusalem, Luke undoubtedly encountered many in his travels who shared their testimony of how they had met Christ through the gospel on Pentecost when Peter preached.

The church did not preserve the debates, sermons, or discussions that accompanied the appointment of the seven deacons, the election of a twelfth apostle, or the Jerusalem Council. Only brief statements by the participants survive. If Luke's writing pattern had exercised freedom in constructing speeches, he would surely have fortified those episodes with some Thucydidean monologues. But he does not. This suggests that the speeches and sermons in Acts do have a historical base in Luke's research.

The concept of the witness that Luke forthrightly accentuates explains both the preservation of the sermons of the apostles and the origin of the apostolic *kerygma* tradition. But witness alone does not fully explain it. The disciples witnessed many things Jesus said and did during his ministry, but they understood little or none of what happened in their midst. They did not understand the parables, the Transfiguration (Mark 9:6), talk about a resurrection of Jesus (Matt. 17:9; Mark 9:9; John 11:24), talk about the coming passion (Matt. 17:23; Mark 9:31–32; Luke 9:22, 44–45; 17:25; 18:31–34), or their place in the kingdom (Luke 22:24–27). What they had witnessed of Jesus did not have meaning nor did it meet with understanding among the disciples until after the resurrection.

All four Gospels bear testimony to the fact that the disciples had not expected the resurrection. Though singled out for his articulation of the denial of Jesus, Peter spoke for most of the other disciples whose absence from the crucifixion and burial belied the disappointment of their expectations. Prior to the resurrection the disciples had more expectation than faith. Luke described how understanding commingled with faith as they met their risen Lord. In his description of the resurrection appearances, Luke explained the origin of the apostolic *kerygma* tradition.

When Cleopas and the other unnamed disciple met Jesus on the road to Emmaus, they recited the basic events in the ministry and death of Jesus (Luke 24:19–24). They knew of his teachings and miracles and of how the power structure of the establishment had conspired his death. They even knew the stories of the resurrection that had begun to circulate that day. They had information, but they did not know the meaning of it. After the two disciples told Jesus the news of the crucifixion and the rumors of the empty tomb, Jesus replied, "How foolish you are, and how slow of heart to believe all that the prophets have spoken! Did not the Christ have to suffer these things and then enter his glory?" (Luke 24:25–26). Luke then adds that "beginning with Moses and all the Prophets, he explained to them what was said in all the Scriptures concerning himself" (24:27).

Luke makes clear at the end of his Gospel that the message the apostles declared in Acts had its origin in the teaching of Jesus between the resurrection and the ascension. The teaching that occurred during the resurrection appearances also reiterated what he had taught during his ministry, but what the disciples had not comprehended. The passion predictions by Jesus stand as ironic examples of the disciples' inability to understand what was happening. The Synoptic Gospels record three such episodes:

Episode	Matthew	Mark	Luke
1.	16:21–23	8:31–33	9:22
2.	17:22–23	9:30–32	9:44–45
3.	20:17–19	10:32–34	18:31–34

At the empty tomb, the Synoptic Gospels contain an angelic message to recall what Jesus had said:

"He is not here; he has risen, just as he said." (Matt. 28:6)

"But go, tell his disciples and Peter, 'He is going ahead of you into Galilee. There you will see him, just as he told you.'" (Mark 16:7)

"Remember how he told you, while he was still with you in Galilee: 'The Son of Man must be delivered into the hands of sinful men, be crucified and on the third day be raised again.'" (Luke 24:6–7)

In all three cases, the evangelists emphasize that the disciples had not grasped the meaning of Jesus' death nor anticipated the resurrection, even though they had heard of it from him. Confused by many things their master had said, the death and resurrection predictions seem to have passed out of their thoughts until something happened to make them remember.

Luke wrote that Jesus did not leave the work of preserving his Gospel to memory guided by chance. Instead, Jesus taught his disciples during his resurrection visits the meaning of all that had happened concerning him.[25] Luke gave the substance of this teaching in the last verses of his Gospel:

> He said to them, "This is what I told you while I was still with you: Everything must be fulfilled that is written about me in the Law of Moses, the Prophets and the Psalms."
>
> Then he opened their minds so they could understand the Scriptures. He told them, "This is what is written: The Christ will suffer and rise from the dead on the third day, and repentance and forgiveness of sins will be preached in his name to all nations, beginning at Jerusalem. You are witnesses of these things. I am going to send you what my Father has promised; but stay in the city until you have been clothed with power from on high." (Luke 24:44–49)

In other words, Luke clearly describes a gospel tradition that originated with Jesus during his resurrection appearances. The command to be witnesses came as a command to be witnesses "of these things" that Jesus recapitulated and the meaning he ascribed to them.

Before undertaking the responsibility of a witness, however, the disciples received the further instruction to wait in Jerusalem for the promise of the Father, who would clothe them with power (Luke

24:49). The Holy Spirit forms the final critical link in the origin and preservation of the Gospel. While Luke emphasizes this dimension of the gospel, he does not stand alone. In the Great Commission recorded by Matthew, the activity of going, making disciples, baptizing, and teaching is framed by (1) the declaration of Christ's supreme authority in heaven and on earth, and (2) his promise to always be with his disciples as they fulfilled this command (Matt. 28:18–20).

The origin and preservation of a gospel tradition by the early church has been described as a sociological phenomenon by many critical scholars during the twentieth century. Efforts to reconstruct the life situation of the church focus on the survival needs the church would have had that might have prompted a particular tradition. Efforts at analyzing the mind of the authors focus on the attempt to discover the creative theological contribution of that author as he responded in faith to the situation in the church. In contrast to this approach, the New Testament seems to present the Holy Spirit as the dominant "life situation" of the church out of which the gospel witness emerged.

In the Gospel of John, Jesus told the disciples that the Holy Spirit "will teach you all things and will remind you of everything I have said to you" (John 14:26). This concept of the role of the Holy Spirit in the witness to Christ finds a parallel in Luke, where Jesus said,

> When you are brought before the synagogues, rulers and authorities, do not worry about how you will defend yourselves or what you will say, for the Holy Spirit will teach you at that time what you should say. (Luke 12:11–12)

These passages acknowledge both creativity in the gospel message and the preservation process while ascribing both processes to the Holy Spirit. By calling to remembrance the circumstances related to Christ, the Holy Spirit maintains the objective basis for good news, rooted in what Christ said, what he did, and whom he represented himself to be. On the other hand, the teaching ministry of the Holy Spirit takes the truth of Christ expressed by the gospel to impact each person, culture, and age in a creative, personal way.

A GOSPEL FORMULA

Martin Dibelius, who had examined the subject before Dodd, agreed generally that a formula or formulas preserved the gospel in the early church. He declared that regardless of which sermon one reads in Acts, "the work of Jesus is presented in brief formulas testifying to the divine plan of salvation."[26] The nature of early Christian preaching would have sounded like Peter's message to Cornelius. It began with the baptism of John as signaling the new era and went on to include the death of Christ, his resurrection, details about his deeds and works to substantiate who Jesus was, the fulfillment of prophecy, the forgiveness of sins, the exaltation, and the return for judgment.[27]

A. M. Hunter argued that the *kerygma* had three main headings: the fulfillment of the prophecies of Scripture, a presentation of the life, death, resurrection, and exaltation of Jesus, and a summons to repent and accept the forgiveness of sins in Jesus.[28] Hunter allowed that the presentation of the second point would also include such matters as the dawning of the new age, the Davidic descent, good deeds and works of power, and the return of Jesus as Judge and Savior. Hunter found this *kerygma* in the Gospels and the letters of the New Testament, though it was often restated, as Hebrews does with Platonic imagery, for a particular audience.[29] Hunter believed that the gospel must "be restated in terms intelligible to modern men and women for whom the technical terms of Jewish eschatology— the conceptions of the Kingdom and the Messiah and the Two Ages—mean little or nothing."[30]

T. F. Glasson proposed a *kerygma* containing five points:

1. Fulfillment of Scripture
2. The death of Christ
3. The resurrection of Christ
4. Forgiveness of sins
5. Apostolic witness[31]

In this construction, he deliberately omitted any reference to the return of Christ in glory to judge the world. To support his view, he pointed out that Acts 2, 3, 5, and 13 do not make reference to the judgment.[32] At most, the coming of Christ is part of the promise of what God will do. Since the apostles could not bear witness to a future event, they could not preach the return of Christ as part of their message. Glasson also deleted the Holy Spirit from the gospel because reference to the Spirit does not appear with the frequency of reference to the apostolic witness sighted five times in Acts (2:32; 3:15; 5:32; 10:40–41; 13:30–31).[33] Glasson defined the *kerygma* as a "proclamation of certain facts about Jesus, particularly the Resurrection; and this was certified by witnesses."[34]

Bertil Gärtner held that the missionary preaching contains recurring ideas that seem to reflect a formula "embodying the salient features of God's redeeming action through Jesus Christ. . . ."[35] He went on to identify seven elements of this formula:

1. The ministry of Jesus, his suffering, death, and resurrection
2. Prophecies being fulfilled
3. Jesus as the Lord and Messiah, exalted to the right hand of God and bestowing the Holy Spirit
4 The apostolic message directed also to the Gentiles
5. The expectation of the advent and the judgment of the Lord (the eschatological motif)
6. The exhortation to conversion
7. The bearing of witness[36]

Gärtner drew his conclusions in the context of a study of Paul's sermon in Athens, a sermon Dodd had oddly ignored in his study. In Athens, Paul's sermon included four elements that Dodd did not treat: natural revelation, God, idolatry, universalism and the divine plan of salvation.[37] Nonetheless, Gärtner agreed with Dodd's categories enough to say that only the latter part constituted *kerygma* and offended the sensibilities of the Athenians.[38] Gärtner did offer the observation that Acts holds four different kinds of missionary sermons, including preaching to Jews, preaching to Gentiles, the type of Stephen's defense, and Paul's farewell speech at Ephesus.[39]

Ethelbert Stauffer contended that missionary preaching represented the liveliest and most original form of preaching for the early church, but that for all its freedom of expression, it had a "dogmatic center" with the *kerygma*. In his preaching, Paul labored to reproduce this "official" version of the gospel formula "word for word."[40] Stauffer also pointed out that the relationship between Christ and the one and only God received attention in the early preaching (Acts 14:15; 17:23ff.; 22:14; 24:14; cf. Rom. 3:30; 16:27; 1 Cor. 8:4; Gal. 3:20; 1 Thess. 1:9; Phil. 2:11; 1 Peter 4:19; Jude 25).[41] This observation by Stauffer, combined with Gärtner's identification of the elements of the Athens speech, raises serious question about the need to include another element about the one God in the *kerygma*, a question to be addressed later.

Floyd Filson's list of elements for inclusion in the *kerygma* only numbered four, but his third point about the historical Jesus had nine subpoints! For the most part Filson mentions items already introduced, though he makes it a special point to emphasize the importance of the historicity of Jesus.[42] A point he adds focuses attention on John the Baptist as preparatory to the coming of Christ as a common feature of early preaching (Acts 10:37; 13:24–25).[43] The crucial matter Filson insisted upon was the resurrection, as the title of his study suggests.

In a later study, Filson distanced himself from Dodd though still holding basic agreement about the gospel message in the first decades of the church. Filson moved away from using the term *kerygma* because in it one loses sight of the kingdom of God as the focus of preaching, seen in how God has established his rule through Christ. Filson held that the use of an esoteric Greek term that never occurs in Acts as the "algebraic x which vaguely points to the gospel" did not help clarify matters.[44] H. J. Cadbury had even less regard for the technical use of *kerygma* in his remarks, "When a term from a foreign language is employed in such matters it often seems to the simpleminded to give the concept a validity even greater than if plain English was used."[45]

With Rudolf Bultmann, the question of the historical origin of the preaching became irrelevant for he only cared that the preaching of the death and resurrection of Christ were the word of God. In rejecting the "quest for the historical *kerygma*," he did not reject the idea of an apostolic message so much as the discipline of modern historical research as a tool for evaluating the Bible. In a sense his radical approach to criticism is a rejection of any form of criticism. He argued that the resurrection cannot be proven or accepted on historical grounds; it can only be appropriated by faith.

Bultmann recognized a basic *kerygma* similar to that identified by other scholars of his generation, but he argued that it was shrouded in the mythological worldview of the first century.[46] The idea of a preexistent divine Being appearing on earth as a man, atoning for sin in a sacrificial death, abolishing death, vanquishing demonic forces through a resurrection, and returning to the right hand of God as Lord and King only to return one day soon to complete redemption and judge the world all smacked of mythology. Though he viewed the *kerygma* as a mythological construction that spoke to the needs of its day, he would not abolish it with Harnack and the older liberals; rather he sought to interpret it.[47] Furthermore, he criticized the philosophers for thinking that humanity can do anything about its fallen condition because it is total.[48]

Bultmann further criticized liberalism and the history of religions school for disregarding the person of Jesus, whom the New Testament presents as "the decisive event of redemption."[49] The love of God is only an abstract idea unless God reveals that love. That is why, for the Christian, faith means faith in Christ, for God demonstrated his love in Christ.[50] Bultmann declared that "he who formerly had been the *bearer* of the message was drawn into it and became its essential *content*."[51] The first preachers of the gospel were concerned to show that the cross had meaning because of the significance of Jesus; thus, they told about the Jesus they had known. The cross had meaning for Bultmann, however, because of its inseparable unity with the resurrection.[52] Yet, Bultmann declared that "an historical fact which involves a resurrection from the dead is utterly inconceivable!"[53]

Thus, Bultmann disagreed with Glasson, Gärtner, and others who had made the apostolic witness an element of faith, since the apostles could not have witnessed what did not happen. More importantly for his approach, however, faith can never come as a result of proof; otherwise it would not be faith. In his existential system, "Christ meets us in the preaching as one crucified and risen."[54]

Ernst Käsemann followed Bultmann's lead and asserted that those who hoped to demonstrate a unity of early *kerygma* and tradition are "trying to maintain that the *kerygma* includes the recital of facts as mediated by the tradition."[55] Käsemann held that the church modified the tradition to meet the challenges represented in changes of time and place, which led in turn to variations in the *kerygma*, though the early church held fast to the same profession of faith throughout the changes.[56] While the Gospels tell the life of Christ, Käsemann insisted that only the "Cross and the Resurrection" had any real importance for the early church.[57]

Käsemann concluded that neither miracles, nor the tradition of the church found in the canon of accepted Scripture, nor the historical Jesus sought by scholarly criticism can give security to faith. Instead, only the Holy Spirit can enable a person "to come to Christ and believe in him as Lord."[58] When he looked at the New Testament, he saw so wide a variability in the form and content of the *kerygma* that the evidence compelled the recognition "not merely of significant tensions, but, not infrequently, of irreconcilable theological contradictions."[59] This variability demonstrated for Käsemann that primitive Christianity had a variety of confessions by the time of the writing of the New Testament, which constantly replaced one another in dialectic fashion, mutually delimiting one another.[60] Though he recognized that the gospel serves as the foundation for the church, he declared that "the question, 'What is the Gospel?' cannot be settled by the historian according to the results of his investigations but only by the believer who is led by the Spirit and listens obediently to the Scripture."[61]

In his comparative study of 1 Corinthians 15:3–5 and 1 Timothy 3:16, Edward Schweizer examined the passages as "creeds" or kerygmatic formulas. He suggested that 1 Corinthians 11:23–25 has the same creedal concern as 1 Timothy 3:16 and that Philippians 2:6–11 has the same creedal concern as 1 Corinthians 15:3–5.[62] He further suggested that both strands could have emerged from an even earlier creed like one he identified as beginning with Romans 1:3. Both passages concern what God did in Christ, but 1 Corinthians 15:3–5 stresses the death and resurrection, while 1 Timothy 3:16 stresses the incarnation and exaltation.[63] Schweizer resolved the discrepancy by citing the cultural context in which the gospel found expression. The death and resurrection of Christ spoke to the problem of the Palestinian Jew: "How may I get rid of my sins, how shall I get through doomsday?" The incarnation and exaltation spoke to the problem of the Gentiles in the Hellenistic world: "How may I be freed from the powers of a blind fate? How may I obtain access to the heavenly, divine world?"[64]

Schweizer's study suggests that different elements of the gospel speak to different issues of human existence. The elements of the gospel an evangelist might employ in presenting Christ and the message of salvation depend, to a great extent, on the kinds of fundamental questions that plague a person or culture. This conclusion has profound implications not only for New Testament criticism, but more immediately for how a Christian presents Christ to a nonbeliever anywhere in the world on the eve of the twenty-first century. Schweizer asked pointedly,

> ... since the Japanese people do not think in ontological terms, must we convert them first to our Greek thinking or to Western thinking as a whole in order that the gospel might be preached in these terms?[65]

Alternatively, in preaching the gospel, Christians ought to present Christ as the answer to the problem of a person who does not understand that problem as one of sin. The loneliness and meaninglessness of modern life represent nothing else than a contemporary nomenclature for the old biblical term "sin."[66]

The Christians of the New Testament church spoke specifically to the particular issues of life and expressed the gospel in terms that communicated with their audience, regardless of the cultural context within or beyond the Roman empire.[67] When the evangelists moved outside the context of a Jewish community, they no longer bound themselves to the language of the people of the covenant, wrapped up as it was with a remote time, place, and tradition. Instead, they employed language that communicated the same message, but to a people who never knew the Law or the Prophets.[68] Nonetheless, they retained the basic elements of the *kerygma*, even where they did not have the same meaning. For the modern church, Schweizer warned of the danger associated with only retaining those elements of the gospel that suit her. Different elements of the *kerygma* speak with different power in different ages. The church does not have the liberty to discard what it considers out of date or difficult to understand.[69]

C. F. D. Moule took a similar track to Schweizer. He proposed that Christianity in apostolic times took many forms throughout the empire and beyond. Factors such as geography, socio-economic standing, educational background, cultural setting, religious environment, and local politics played a part in shaping the way Christianity expressed itself in a given locale. Though the New Testament writings reflect a wide variety of theological perspectives, the *kerygma* gives "coherence to all the diversity within the New Testament."[70] Particularly, the affirmation of the incarnation of Jesus and his resurrection maintain this coherence.

The New Testament letters reflect the strong sense of responsibility the church felt for receiving, preserving, and handing on the authentic gospel message (cf. 1 Cor. 11:23; 15:1; Gal. 2:2; Col. 1:5–6; 1 Thess. 2:2–4; 1 Tim. 2:7; 2 Tim. 2:8; Heb. 2:3; James 1:18, 21; 1 Peter 1:23–25; 1 John 2:20, 27–28; Rev. 2:25).[71] In spite of the variability observed by such commentators as Käsemann, the various writings of the New Testament "speak with a remarkably unanimous voice of a single Gospel and of one Lord."[72] In fact, Moule argues, this *kerygma* became the basis for evaluating the legitimacy of writings for inclusion in the canon:

> Judged by this standard, any estimate of Jesus which did not acknowledge his historical existence and his real death would be out; so would any which did not acknowledge the resurrection and the decisiveness of his fulfillment of God's plan of salvation outlined in the Old Testament.[73]

This standard excludes the writings of Gnostic dualism as well as a variety of other unorthodox views that emerged in the first centuries of the life of the church. Moule contends that the application of this test may be found in 1 and 2 John.[74]

Ralph P. Martin carried even further the idea that the one gospel found multiple expressions. As the church spread into the Hellenistic world, the bearers of the gospel faced the problem of translating the message of Christ into terms with which the common person could identify and understand, while clearly demonstrating how Christ met the deepest needs of life.[75] Martin identified what he considered the greatest needs of the Hellenistic age:

1. freedom from evil spirits
2. freedom from the bondage of archons (spiritual powers) and the rule of "destiny" and "necessity"
3. deliverance from sin, mortality, and finitude[76]

In 1 Corinthians 15:3–4, the forgiveness of sins was a burning issue for the community in Corinth. In Philippians 2:6–11, however, the problem that demanded attention was the "purposelessness of existence and the conquest of those agencies which tyrannized over Hellenistic man."[77] In Philippians the gospel provides the basis for explaining how God in Christ has all authority and power, thereby assuring the meaningfulness of life.[78] Martin contended that interest in prophecy and the concern over estrangement from God have little appeal today, but the questions that lie behind the fears of the ancient world persist into the modern age.[79]

While Dodd's critics appear to be correct that the *kerygma* did not exist as a fixed formula, Dodd was correct to the extent that the *kerygma* existed as a fixed content upon which the early Christians drew when proclaiming their faith in Christ.

PREACHING AND TEACHING IN CONTEXT

When C. H. Dodd began "the quest for the historical *kerygma*," he sought to identify a gospel creedal formulation acknowledged by the apostles. Any deviation from this formulation constituted "development" or the introduction of new theological views by an author. The primary theological idea he attacked as a new development was the idea of a future return of Christ. Dodd wrote from what many would call a conservative point of view to establish a tradition that went back to the early church. Rudolf Bultmann wrote from what many would call a liberal point of view, in order to free the gospel from tradition altogether. Both shared a presupposition, however, one that is common to many who study the New Testament, that the New Testament is a human book full of traditions about what people believed or taught about Jesus long ago. From this perspective, any differences in the gospel message or nuances in theological formulation occur as a result of the personal quirks of the authors of the New Testament books.

If, on the other hand, the Holy Spirit actually guided the apostles in what they said and how they said it, one might expect a change in the expression of the message without an alteration in its substance. Rather than reciting a creedal formula, the apostles presented Jesus Christ, the Savior. They said enough about him to set him apart, to indicate in what sense he is the only Savior, and to explain from what and to what he saves. Presenting Jesus in the Hellenistic world required the translation or transformation of terminology wed to the Jewish context, such as the substitution of "Christ" for the term "Messiah."[80]

In moving beyond the Jewish context to the nations, more than terminology needed attention. The gospel had assumed several fundamental elements that Peter did not have to elaborate in Jerusalem. He could assume a common understanding and belief in the Creator God, who upheld the universe by his power. This represented not only the religion of the Jews, but also their worldview. The Creator God had taken the initiative to provide salvation for his creatures. To this end, God had spoken by the prophets to prepare Israel for the appearing of the Messiah. Floyd Filson has criticized C. H. Dodd's study of the apostolic preaching in Acts for concentrating his analysis on the messages that appear in a Jewish context while ignoring Paul's messages in the pagan settings of Lystra (Acts 14:15–17) and Athens (17:22–31).[81] In these settings, Paul first had to proclaim the Creator God who made the heavens and the earth. Filson observed:

> In a world of polytheism and idolatry it was necessary to present the basic message of monotheism, the one God who is Creator, Lord, and Judge, and under whom all life is lived. It was necessary to state clearly man's moral responsibility before God, and in doing this the Resurrection and the final judgement were proclaimed.[82]

This theme forms the prologue to John's Gospel as well as to Hebrews. It figures prominently in Paul's letters, particularly in Romans 8, Ephesians 1, and Colossians 1.

In Jerusalem Peter spoke of Jesus as Lord (Acts 2:36). He never referred to him as "Son of God" the way Paul did in Damascus after his conversion (9:20). Though Paul used the terminology "Son of

God" in his writings (Rom. 1:4; 1 Cor. 1:9; 2 Cor. 1:19; Gal. 2:20), he more frequently used the term of preference of Peter in Jerusalem, which had constituted the confession of Thomas: "My Lord and my God" (John 20:28). Rather than a "theological development," the "Son of God" terminology constituted the effort to express to the Gentiles what "Lord" meant to the Jews.

For centuries, the Jews had refrained from speaking the holy name of Yahweh, the Lord God Almighty, who redeemed Israel from Egypt and declared his name to Moses. When the rabbis came to the holy name in Scripture, rather than speak it, they substituted the word *Adonai*, the Lord. Modern translations of the Hebrew Scriptures maintain this tradition by writing the name Yahweh as "Lord." Instead of a low Christology, by using the divine title when referring to Jesus, Peter expressed the highest of Christologies.[83] The title "Lord" ascribed to Jesus had its origin in Palestine in the Jewish community, as the ancient Aramaic prayer *Maran atha*, "Lord, come" (1 Cor. 16:22), indicates.[84] The confession "Jesus is Lord" meant something to those who understood what Lord meant. The Gentile world, however, had many lords. The term "Son of God" expressed for the Gentile the divine relationship that "Lord" conveyed to the Jews.

In Jerusalem, Peter never stated specifically that Christ died for our sins. Paul stressed this meaning of the death throughout his writings. Instead of a theological development in the understanding of the atonement, the difference between Peter and Paul reflects the cultural difference of their audiences. In Jerusalem on the Day of Pentecost, Peter could assume a common understanding of sin and its remedy. In the shadow of the temple, the pilgrims that day understood better than any that the Law of Moses prescribed that forgiveness of sin only came through sacrifice. Peter proclaimed the death of Jesus that took place at Passover, and he proclaimed forgiveness of sins in Jesus' name. The details did not require explanation, for the understanding of an atoning sacrifice had formed over a thousand years of the consciousness of Israel.

In the Gentile world, however, Paul had a formidable problem. The Gentiles offered sacrifices to their gods, but sacrifices served as bribes to enlist the aid of a god or to pacify an offended deity. Paul had to explain the moral demands of a holy God and the significance of the death of Jesus with respect to the problem of human sin. Without the preparation of the Law and the Prophets, the Gentile world required explanation that the Jewish community did not need.

Paul indicated in the strongest of terms that the apostles felt no freedom to alter the terms of the gospel. His manner of presenting the gospel to Gentiles came to him by way of revelation from Jesus Christ (Gal. 1:6–12). Peter also claimed divine revelation as the basis for his message to the Gentiles when he had his vision in Joppa before witnessing to Cornelius (Acts 10:9–16, 19–20, 28, 34–35). Philip received similar guidance in witnessing to the Ethiopian eunuch as he expounded the fulfillment of Scripture in Christ (8:26–29). Likewise Ananias received divine counsel before witnessing to Saul when he demonstrated the power of the Holy Spirit (9:10–17). By divine revelation, Stephen of all the apostles bore witness to the exaltation of Christ to the right hand of the Father and the freedom his reign has given to those in persecution (7:56). In each case, however, the revelation did not alter what the witness had received of the gospel. Rather, the revelation amplified and gave deeper meaning to particular aspects of the gospel.

Instead of the rigid distinction C. H. Dodd drew between *kerygma* and *didache* expressed by evangelism and discipleship, the New Testament seems to imply that the gospel cannot be separated from the meaning ascribed to it in the apostles' teaching. The gospel simply declares that Christ died for our sins, but the meaning of this declaration includes deliverance, redemption, cleansing, forgiveness, and justification. Those who have faith receive the gift of the Holy Spirit, but the meaning of this declaration includes regeneration, adoption, assurance, sanctification, and empowerment.

Salvation comes through faith in Jesus Christ who has the power to save. The gospel is God's instrument of revealing Jesus Christ (Rom. 1:16–17). The evangelist does not have the freedom to conform the gospel to the expectations of any person or culture. Rather, the evangelist has the responsibility to demonstrate what the gospel of Jesus Christ means to each individual and culture. For Paul it meant freedom from the curse of the law, but to the Gentiles he addressed in Colosse it meant freedom from the "elemental spirits of the universe" (Col. 2:8 NRSV). For Stephen the gospel offered hope to die, but to the Philippian jailer it offered hope to live (Acts 16:29–31).

As the church prepares to enter the third millennium of its mission on earth, the same Holy Spirit that guided the apostles moves in its midst to bring the gospel to a world suffering from the consequences of sin. The challenge now as then involves presenting Christ as the Savior to a world of different people and cultures. Whether the message focuses on the fulfillment of Scripture in Christ as it did when Philip witnessed to the Ethiopian, the Creator God as it did when Paul spoke at Lystra and Athens, the challenge to faith as it did when Paul witnessed to the Philippian jailer, or the gift of the Holy Spirit as it did when Paul taught in Ephesus, the message addresses the gospel to the world's experience of the effects of sin and presents Christ as the only Savior.

CONCLUSION

Jesus Christ formed the sum and substance of the apostolic message. People who joined themselves to the fledgling band of disciples did so because they had joined themselves to Jesus Christ. The message presented Christ as the one who answered life's deepest questions; thus, he came through the message as a Savior. In presenting Christ, the apostles told the significant aspects of Christ and demonstrated their saving import. Though the apostles used different terms in different settings, they spoke about the same basic matters, telling of Christ from eternity, through earthly ministry, to eternity.

When the apostolic *kerygma* focused on the death of Christ, the apostolic *didache* for that person related the significance of the other saving activity of Christ. When the apostolic *kerygma* focused on the fulfillment of Scripture in Christ, then the apostolic *didache* for that person related the significance of the other saving activity of Christ. Thus, the New Testament contains no single formula of the gospel, though the many instances of gospel proclamation and teaching form a consistent pattern.

In 1 Corinthians 15, Paul's discussion of resurrection indicates the relationship between gospel proclamation and teaching about the implications of the gospel. Paul began by reminding the Corinthians of the terms in which he preached the gospel and cited the death for sins, the burial, and the resurrection, all according to

Scripture. Instead of a declaration of the definition of the gospel, however, the passage shows how the gospel formed the foundation for all apostolic teaching. Paul laid out only enough of the gospel to lay a foundation for the subject he had to address. Resurrection was the issue in Corinth that required addressing.

The good news of Christ requires both *kerygma* and *didache*. The *kerygma* establishes Christ concretely as the decisive act of God for the salvation of the world and preserves the historical and eternal claims of Christ. The *didache* unfolds the significance of the *kerygma* for salvation. Thus, while the apostles "preached" the gospel, the New Testament describes their methodology in terms of "teaching." This ministry of presenting Christ revolved around several basic elements:

1. The Creator God	Salvation came as a work of the Creator who has the right to all creation and who exercises authority over all creation.
2. The fulfillment	Jesus came to fulfill Scripture rather than to abolish the faith of Israel, and stands in continuity with all God had spoken by the prophets as the culmination point of Israel's relations with the God of Creation.
3. Son of God/ Son of David	Jesus stood uniquely related to God and humanity, which suited him alone to be the Savior, as demonstrated by his teaching and demonstrations of power.
4. Death for sins	The death of Christ came as the plan of God for salvation from sin, rather than as an unfortunate mishap.
5. Resurrection	God raised Christ from the dead as a demonstration of his Lordship and victory over sin and death, revealing his power to save.
6. Exaltation	Christ reigns at the right hand of God, providing immediate access to God for all who abide in him.
7. Gift of the Holy Spirit	Christ sends the Holy Spirit to live within all who have faith in him.

| 8. Return for judgment | Christ will return to bring this age to an end, judge the nations, and complete redemption. |
| 9. Response | The good news always expected the decisive response of repentance and faith. |

Throughout the centuries, these simple foundational elements of the faith have grown into the body of systematic theology and dogma. By the third century, the church had begun to develop a gospel formula in the form of creeds. In their earliest form the creeds summarized the basic teachings about Christ, but over time they grew longer as the church added to them in response to theological controversies. The final form of the Nicene Creed was twice the length of the final form of the Apostles' Creed as the church sought to clarify, amplify, define, and set the boundaries for the orthodox faith.

The Apostles' Creed reads like many of the twentieth-century reconstructions of the *kerygma*. It does indicate how the emphasis of teaching had shifted. In the early apostolic preaching, the apostles stressed the descent of Christ from King David. The Apostles' Creed of a church now long removed from Palestine and the Jewish world did not speak of the Davidic descent and all its messianic implications. Instead, it stressed the virgin birth. Both the Davidic descent and the virgin birth, however, struck at the human nature of Jesus in counterpoint to his relationship to God the Father Almighty.

The Apostles' Creed

I believe in God the Father Almighty, Maker of heaven and earth: and in Jesus Christ his only Son, our Lord; Who was conceived by the Holy Ghost; born of the virgin Mary, suffered under Pontius Pilate, was crucified, dead and buried; He descended into hell; the third day He rose again from the dead; He ascended into heaven and sitteth on the right hand of God the Father Almighty; from thence He shall come to judge the quick and the dead. I believe in the Holy Ghost, the holy catholic church; the communion of saints; the forgiveness of sins; the resurrection of the body; and the life ever-lasting. Amen.[85]

The Nicene Creed follows the Apostles' Creed in basic outline, but devotes a major exposition to what is meant by Son of God. The development of the creeds illustrate how the church has added the theological discussions, speculations, and debates to the gospel in each successive generation.

The Nicene Creed

I believe in one God the Father Almighty, Maker of heaven and earth, and of all things visible and invisible. And in the Lord Jesus Christ, the only-begotten son of God, Light of Light, very God of very God, begotten, not made; being of one substance with the Father, by whom all things were made: Who for us men and for our salvation came down from heaven, and was incarnate by the Holy Ghost of the virgin Mary, and was made man; and was crucified also for us under Pontius Pilate. He suffered and was buried; and the third day He rose again according to the Scriptures, and ascended into heaven, and sitteth on the right hand of the Father. And He shall come again, with glory, to judge both the quick and the dead, whose kingdom shall have no end.

And I believe in the Holy Ghost, the Lord and Giver of life, Who proceedeth from the Father and the Son, Who with the Father and the Son together is worshipped and glorified: Who spake by the prophets.

And I believe in one Christian and apostolic church. I acknowledge one baptism for the remission of sins, and I look for the resurrection of the dead, and the life of the world to come. Amen.[86]

Each element of the gospel became the foundational element for the major doctrines of the church over time as the church attempted to address the issues of life and culture through the centuries. The basic elements of the gospel identified above have their corollary doctrine in the body of systematic theology:

Gospel Element	Doctrine
Creator God	God, Providence, Creation, Grace, Humanity, Natural revelation
Fulfillment of Scripture	Inspiration/Specific revelation
Son of God/Son of David	Incarnation, Christology, Ethics
Death for sins	Justification, Atonement
Raised from the dead	Resurrection
Exaltation	Lordship, Ecclesiology
Gift of the Holy Spirit	Regeneration, Sanctification, Adoption
Return for judgment	Eschatology, Theodicy
Response	Conversion

Throughout the centuries theologians have tended to organize their theological systems either around one of these elements or around a related group of these elements (see Fig. 1-A). Thomas Aquinas, for example, oriented his theology around the Creator God and the doctrine of natural revelation. Martin Luther oriented his theology around the death of Christ for our sins and the doctrine of justification. John Wesley oriented his theology around the gift of the Holy Spirit and the doctrines of sanctification and regeneration. Karl Barth and Carl F. H. Henry oriented their theologies around Christ as the fulfillment of Scripture and the doctrine of specific revelation. Reinhold Niebuhr oriented his theology around the Creator God and the doctrine of humanity. Walter Rauschenbusch oriented his theology around Christ as Son of God and Son of David and the doctrine of the incarnation. Rudolf Bultmann oriented his theology around the response to the gospel and the doctrine of conversion. Dietrich Bonhoeffer oriented his theology around the exaltation and the doctrine of the Lordship of Christ. C. I. Scofield oriented his theology around the return of Christ and the doctrine of eschatology. John Calvin oriented his system around the Creator God and the doctrine of grace.

Though most of these figures would acknowledge the truth and reality of most of the elements of the gospel here identified, their theological agenda gives entirely different nuances to the meaning of the gospel. Each approach has tended to explain the entire gospel in terms of one particular doctrine. In the past century, Protestant evangelicals have tended to equate preaching the gospel with explaining the doctrine of justification with the parallel tendency to equate salvation and justification. Salvation certainly includes justification, but it also includes regeneration. The twentieth century has witnessed the strange phenomenon of evangelical gospel presentations inquiring if someone is "born again" or would like to have eternal life. Rather than explaining how to be born again or receive eternal life, however, the presentation explains how to receive forgiveness of sins and the imputed righteousness of Christ. This theological abridgment of the gospel has emerged as evangelical Christians have avoided reference to the Holy Spirit for fear of Pentecostal or charismatic expression.

If the gospel is the good news of salvation in Jesus Christ, it must be free to address more than the issue of justification.[87] For the person experiencing the conviction of sin as guilt, which includes a significant number of people in the United States, justification is the issue and the death of Christ should be stressed. People experience conviction of sin, however, in other terms than guilt over transgression. This experience is particularly true for those who have never known the law. The gospel demonstrates how salvation extends to whatever way the Holy Spirit is convincing of sin, righteousness, and judgment.

The remainder of this study will explore each element of the gospel described here from a biblical as well as historical/theological perspective, in order to demonstrate how the gospel has addressed the ultimate spiritual issues of people in different times and cultures. The study will suggest how each element of the gospel addresses ultimate issues of life concerning which the Holy Spirit convinces people of sin. In this regard, bearing witness to Christ by proclaiming good news to people laboring under sin will always be a spiritual exercise. It involves the willingness to care about people as Christ cared, to listen for how the Holy Spirit is convincing them of sin, and to rely on the Holy Spirit to give guidance

FIGURE 1-A

Kerygma	Doctrines	Theologian or Movement	Evangelistic Issue
Creator God	God Creation Humanity Providence	Augustine Aquinas Calvin Process Theology	Purpose Grace Identity Value Ecology
Fulfillment of Scripture	Revelation Inspiration	Justin Martyr Hus Tertullian Luther Origen Evangelicalism Wycliff	Continuity Authority Faithfulness Epistemology of God Nature of God
Son of God/Son of David	Incarnation Christology	Irenaeus Barth Athanasius Brunner The Early Councils Black Church Theology The Social Gospel Liberation Theology	Reliability of God Example Compassion of God Physical Need Identification of God Reconciliation Acceptance Love
Death for Sins	Atonement Justification [The Lord's Supper]	Celtic Church Anselm Transubstantiation Protestantism	Redemption New Beginning Relationship Purification Love Substitution
Raised from the Dead	Resurrection [Baptism]	Early Christian Worship Eastern Orthodoxy	Hope Personhood Victory Eternal Life Freedom

Exaltation	Ecclesiology Lordship	Martyrdom Monasticism Church Government Bonhoeffer	Prayer Signs and Wonders Worthiness Personal Relationship	Martyrdom Tradition
Gift of the Holy Spirit	Pneumatology Sanctification Regeneration Adoption	Filioque Controversy Eastern Orthodoxy Western Mysticism Protestant Awakenings	Transformation Holiness Empowerment Guidance Application of Salvation	
Return of Christ	Eschatology Theodicy	Montanus Sibylline Literature Savonarola Joachim of Fiore Münster Anabaptists Fifth Monarchy Men The Third Rome Dispensationalism	Chaos Accountability The Problem of Evil Rescue Justification Perseverance and Reward	
Human Response	Conversion Election Predestination Grace Faith Repentance	Baptism Erasmus Penance Reformed Theology Sola Fide Bultmann Pelagius Revivalism	Jesus Christ	

in demonstrating how Christ saves from the manifestation of sin in a person's life. Finally, suggestions will be made as to the kind of ministries that best address the issues each element of the gospel satisfies.

NOTES

1. C. S. Lewis, *They Stand Together*, ed. Walter Hooper (New York: Macmillan, 1979), 425.

2. C. H. Dodd, *The Apostolic Preaching and Its Development* (New York: Harper & Row, 1964), 14–15.

3. Ibid., 13, 31, 36ff.

4. Ibid., 21–24.

5. Ibid., 24.

6. Ibid., 33.

7. Martin Dibelius, *The Message of Jesus Christ*, trans. Frederick C. Grant (New York: Charles Scribner's Sons, 1939), 129.

8. Ibid., 128.

9. Bo Reicke, "A Synopsis of Early Christian Preaching," in *The Root of the Vine*, ed. Anton Fridrichsen, et al. (New York: Philosophical Library, 1953), 129.

10. Ibid., 138–39.

11. Ibid., 140.

12. Bertil Gärtner, *The Areopagus Speech and Natural Revelation* (Uppsala: C. W. K. Gleerup, 1955), 33.

13. Ibid.

14. C. S. C. Williams, *A Commentary on the Acts of the Apostles*, Harper's New Testament Commentaries (New York: Harper & Row Publishers, 1957), 37.

15. Michael Green, *Evangelism in the Early Church* (Grand Rapids: Eerdmans, 1970), 67.

16. Williams, *Commentary on the Acts*, 38.

17. Hans Conzelmann, *The Theology of St. Luke*, trans. Geoffrey Buswell (London: Faber and Faber, 1961), 218.

18. C. F. Evans, "The Kerygma," *Journal of Theological Studies*, n.s. 7 (April 1956), 27.

19. Ibid., 28.

20. Ibid., 30.

21. Ibid., 37–38. See C. C. Torrey, *Documents of the Primitive Church* (New York: Harper, 1941) and *The Composition and Date of Acts* (New York: Kraus, 1969).

22. R. A. Martin, "Syntactical Evidence of Aramaic Sources in Acts i–xv," *New Testament Studies* 11: 1 (October 1964), 38–59.

23. Evans, "The Kerygma," 41.

24. For a recent overview of some of the more prominent conversion testimonies, see Hugh T. Kerr and John M. Mulder, eds., *Conversions* (Grand Rapids: Eerdmans, 1983).

25. F. F. Bruce, *The Acts of the Apostle*, 2d ed. (Grand Rapids: Eerdmans, 1952). C. H. Dodd reached a similar conclusion to account for the early church's way of using Old Testament texts to support their claim that Jesus was the Messiah: "But the New Testament itself avers that it was Jesus Christ Himself who first directed the minds of His followers to certain parts of the scriptures as those in which they might find illumination upon the meaning of His mission and destiny. . . . To account for the beginning of this most original and fruitful process of rethinking the Old Testament we found need to postulate a creative mind. The Gospels offer us one. Are we compelled to reject the offer?" C. H. Dodd, *According to the Scriptures* (London: Nisbet & Co., Ltd., 1953), 110.

26. Dibelius, *The Message of Jesus Christ*, 129.

27. Ibid., 130–31.

28. Archibald M. Hunter, *The Message of the New Testament* (Philadelphia: Westminster, 1944), 29–30.

29. Ibid., 35.

30. Ibid., 36.

31. T. F. Glasson, "The Kerygma: Is Our Version Correct?" *The Hibbert Journal* 51 (October 1952–July 1953), 129, 132.

32. Ibid., 131.

33. Ibid., 129.

34. Ibid., 130.

35. Gärtner, *The Areopagus Speech*, 30.

36. Ibid., 30–32.

37. Ibid., 72.

38. Ibid., 47.

39. Ibid., 35.

40. Ethelbert Stauffer, *New Testament Theology*, trans. John Marsh (New York: Macmillan, 1955), 235–36.

41. Ibid., 243.

42. Floyd V. Filson, *Jesus Christ: The Risen Lord* (Nashville: Abingdon, 1956), 44.

43. Ibid., 46.

44. Floyd V. Filson, *Three Crucial Decades: Studies in the Book of Acts* (Richmond, Va.: John Knox, 1963), 34.

45. H. J. Cadbury, "Acts and Eschatology," in *The Background of the New Testament and Its Eschatology*, ed. W. D. Davies and D. Daube (Cambridge: Cambridge Univ. Press, 1956), 313.

46. Rudolf Bultmann, "New Testament and Mythology," *Kerygma and Myth*, ed. Hans Werner Bartsch, trans. Reginald H. Fuller (London: SPCK, 1953), 2.

47. Ibid., 12.

48. Ibid., 29.

49. Ibid., 14–15.

50. Ibid., 32.

51. Rudolf Bultmann, *Theology of the New Testament*, trans. Kendrick Grobel (New York: Charles Scribner's Sons, 1951), 1.33.

52. Bultmann, *Kerygma and Myth*, 38.

53. Ibid., 39.

54. Ibid., 41.

55. Ernst Käsemann, *Essays on New Testament Themes*, Studies in Biblical Theology 41 (Naperville, Ill.: Allenson, 1964), 17.

56. Ibid., 21.

57. Ibid.

58. Ibid., 62.

59. Ibid., 100.

60. Ibid., 103–4.

61. Ibid., 106.

62. Edward Schweizer, "Two New Testament Creeds Compared," *Current Issues in New Testament Interpretation*, ed. William Klassen and Graydon F. Snyder (New York: Harper & Brothers, 1962), 170.

63. Ibid., 171.

64. Ibid., 172.

65. Ibid.

66. Ibid., 173.

67. Ibid., 174.

68. Ibid.

69. Ibid., 175.

70. C. F. D. Moule, *The Birth of the New Testament* (New York: Harper & Row, 1962), 165.

71. Ibid., 176.

72. Ibid., 177.

73. Ibid., 155–56.

74. Ibid., 156.

75. R. P. Martin, *Carmen Christi* (Cambridge: Cambridge Univ. Press, 1967), 304.

76. Ibid., 309.

77. Ibid., 301.

78. Ibid., 302.

79. Ibid., 311.

80. J. N. Sanders, *The Foundation of the Christian Faith* (New York: Philosophical Library, 1952), 114.

81. Filson, *Three Crucial Decades*, 40–41.

82. Ibid.; cf. Bultmann, *Theology of the New Testament*, 1.65; Hans Conzelmann, "The Address of Paul on the Areopagus," *Studies in Luke-Acts*, ed. Leander E. Keck and J. Louis Martyn (Nashville: Abingdon, 1966), 228.

83. See also Green, *Evangelism in the Early Church*, 31.

84. Hunter, *The Message of the New Testament*, 41.

85. Ivan L. Bennett, ed., *The Hymnal: Army and Navy* (Washington, D.C.: United States Government Printing Office, 1942), 28. William J. Abraham has gone so far as to argue that the creeds hold equal authority with Scripture because of their summary of the gospel. See his *The Logic of Evangelism* (Grand Rapids: Eerdmans, 1989), 145–52.

86. Bennett, *The Hymnal*, 28.

87. Ben Johnson has also argued that the gospel addresses the ultimate questions of life. See *Rethinking Evangelism* (Philadelphia: Westminster, 1987), 47–49.

Chapter 2

Creator God

The good news of salvation has a relationship to the idea of a Creator God in such a way that apart from this being, the idea of salvation makes no sense. The notion is rooted in the worldview expressed by Judaism, Christianity, and Islam and is meaningless to the worldviews of Buddhism, Hinduism, Tao, Shinto, animism, and the various tribal and nature religions of the world. That is, the proclamation of the Christ who came from the Father, died on the cross for sins, and rose from the dead presupposes a created cosmos over which the Creator has control.

The evangelization of Japan has met with little success. A number of factors may account for, or contribute to, this failure. One factor that deserves attention, however, involves the extent to which the proclamation of the gospel message in Japan has taken seriously the radically different worldviews of the messenger and the receiver of the message in Japan. While the West has never been "Christian" in the sense that all those living in the West have a genuine faith in Christ, it has held to a Christian worldview in many respects. In past centuries, even those who rejected Christ operated in a world they conceived of as created.

Since the beginning of the modern mission movement, evangelizing groups in the West have tended to communicate the gospel at home and abroad as an explanation of the doctrine of the atonement. More specifically, it is an explanation of how the vicarious substitutionary death of Christ brings justification. In this tradition, salvation equates with justification as the popular theological understanding, though theologians would acknowledge regeneration, sanctification, adoption, and glorification in the rubric of salvation.

Justification certainly lies at the heart of the gospel message, but it is not necessarily the door through which the gospel most easily travels in cultures that do not have the Christian worldview of

God as Creator. A religion that proclaims justification from sin has little appeal in a culture with no concept of sin. Apart from a Creator God, sin is a meaningless term.

While the experience of the *Mysterium tremendum et fascinans* may be universal, the understanding of that experience of "The Holy" has received varying interpretations around the world.[1] To communicate the gospel effectively, it helps to understand what the message receiver understands by the term "God."

On the day of Pentecost, Peter could assume a common worldview with his audience. Though gathered from the far reaches of the empire, the crowd in Jerusalem came to worship the Creator God. They had a common understanding of who God is and what he does. Everyone accepted the Law. While the Sadducees did not accept the Prophets, the Pharisees did, and their influence was probably far greater than the Sadducees among the dispersion Jews who gathered in synagogues to read and study the holy writings far away from Jerusalem. The fact that Jesus read from the prophet Isaiah at his inaugural sermon indicates a widespread use of the Prophets in the synagogues (Luke 4:16–21). Within his own culture, Peter could proceed with a straightforward declaration of the gospel in terms of the fulfillment of Scripture (Acts 2:16–21, 25–28, 34–35).

Paul, on the other hand, faced the same problem that has plagued efforts of communicating the gospel across worldviews in modern times. At Antioch of Pisidia, he recited the history of Israel and proclaimed the gospel in terms of the fulfillment of prophecy (Acts 13:16–48), just as Peter had done, for Paul had an audience composed of "Men of Israel ... Gentiles who worship God" (13:16), or "children of Abraham, and ... God-fearing Gentiles" (13:26).

When Paul and Barnabas went to Lystra, however, they had to alter the way they presented the gospel. They found themselves in a culture with a different worldview about the nature of deity. When Paul healed a crippled man, the citizens wanted to offer sacrifices to the apostles as the incarnation of Zeus and Hermes. In response to the crowd's understanding of spiritual reality, Paul and Barnabas presented the gospel in terms of the Creator God:

Men, why are you doing this? We too are only men, human like you. We are bringing you good news, telling you to turn

from these worthless things to the living God, who made
heaven and earth and sea and everything in them. In the past,
he let all nations go their own way. Yet he has not left himself
without testimony: He has shown kindness by giving you rain
from heaven and crops in their seasons; he provides you with
plenty of food and fills you hearts with joy. (Acts 14:15–17)

This stress on the Creator God seems to have characterized preaching of the gospel when the worldview of the audience seemed the primary obstacle to hearing the good news.

At Athens, Paul had a more sophisticated apologetic approach as he attempted to build a bridge from the various belief systems current in Athens at the time to the Creator God who will judge the world in justice through One he raised from the dead (Acts 17:16–31). Paul found himself in a culture where rival worldviews already argued for the minds of the populace. The old mythologies with their temples, idols, and style had a traditional following, but philosophies like Stoicism, Epicureanism, and Platonism offered alternative interpretations of reality. None of these rival views had room for a Creator. On the contrary, the prevailing philosophical view was that the material world was evil, the handiwork of a demon—the Demiurge.

BIBLICAL BACKGROUND

The Christian worldview that understands all reality as subject to the authority of a Creator is rooted in the Hebrew Scriptures—that is, the Law, the Prophets, and the Writings.

Old Testament

While the story of God's relationship to people forms the context of knowing God in particular, the story unfolds against a growing backdrop that reveals God as more than merely the family God of Abraham or the national patron deity of a minor Middle Eastern kingdom of brief duration. The one who called Abraham and created Israel was the one who created and now sustains the universe. This is a fundamental understanding of Christian faith apart from which the gospel makes no sense.

Creation psalms. Scholars disagree as to when in the story of salvation the people of Israel first understood their God as the Creator rather than as one of many gods. The debate tends to be carried out in a speculative framework that suggests conclusions that do not logically follow (e.g., if Israel did not understand God as the only God who created all things from nothing until the time of Isaiah, then the creation theme is the contribution of a creative thinker reflecting on their numinal experience rather than an act of revelation by God). Suffice it to say that the theme of creation forms an integrating element for *all* of Hebrew Scripture, not merely in terms of an initial act of God, but also in terms of the continuing implications of that act.

Throughout these texts, the various accounts of creation have a different tone from the mythologies about the origin of things that one finds in the old religions of the rival deities. The Bible pictures an effortless calling into being of things. While it speaks of creation in concrete pictures such as an "expanse" (Gen. 1:6–7) that separates the waters (more literally, a hammered-out brass bowl, like a turkey cover), this literal tone is augmented by the telling of creation in song and poetry rather than prose (e.g., Ps. 104). While Genesis receives the most attention as the account of creation, it is far from the only account.

In the creation account, God is distinguished from a mere nature god who acts out the continuing drama of the seasons and the cycles of planets. God has command over all that the Gentiles had deified. In their songs, the Hebrews distinguished their God, the God of creation, from the deified aspects of creation worshiped by the cultures living around them.

Lord of history. The psalms of creation carry the implication of creation forward from a prehistoric past to the implications for a Creator God in the present moment. Long after the beginning of creation, God continued to be active in his creation. In Psalm 33, after describing how "by the word of the LORD were the heavens made" (v. 6), the psalmist compares the majesty of creation with the futility of any earthly king's exercise of power. Israel believed that God not only looked down from heaven on all creation,

> But the eyes of the LORD are on those who fear him,
>   on those whose hope is in his unfailing love,

> to deliver them from death
>   and keep them alive in famine. (vv. 18–19)

By virtue of his role as Creator, God relates to the world and the universe as a king might to his kingdom: "The LORD has established his throne in heaven, and his kingdom rules over all" (Ps. 103:19). As King of creation, God exercises authority in all areas of life:

> He raises the poor from the dust
>   and lifts the needy from the ash heap:
> he seats them with princes,
>   with the princes of their people.
> He settles the barren woman in her home
>   as a happy mother of children. (113:7–9)

In terms of human history and God's involvement in the affairs of people, Israel could speak of him as "the King" (145:1).

In the Exodus experience, God had demonstrated his authority over the realm of nature in such a way as to put to shame the Egyptian mythologies of nature. In a typological separating of the waters at the Red Sea, where Israel experienced the authority of God as expressed in the creation psalms (Gen. 1:6; Ps. 33:7; 104:6–9; 148:4), Israel came to know God as more than the God of Abraham, Isaac, and Jacob. He was a king who could overthrow Pharaoh effortlessly.

The kingdom of God. At the conclusion of the great psalm of Moses and the Israelites following the destruction of the Egyptian army in the Red Sea, the implication of God's sovereignty of nature and the affairs of humanity is summed up with the declaration, "The LORD will reign for ever and ever" (Ex. 15:18). God was able to save Israel from Pharaoh because he had the power and authority to save Israel. In their Savior, Israel found the only worthy King, one who reigned by virtue of his creative power and sustaining authority over all things.

In relating to the Creator as King, Israel entered into a covenant relationship bound by the law of the King. Through the law, Israel came to appreciate the holiness of the Creator:

> Who may ascend the hill of the LORD?
> Who may stand in his holy place?

> He who has clean hands and a pure heart,
> who does not lift up his soul to an idol
> or swear by what is false. (Ps. 24:3–4)

The necessity of following the Lord exclusively without rivals became the cardinal assumption for the possibility of communion with the Creator. This assumption found first place in the Ten Commandments:

> I am the LORD your God, who brought you out of Egypt, out of the land of slavery.

> You shall have no other gods before me. (Ex. 20:2–3)

Though rooted in God's demonstrated control over all facets of creation from the miraculous birth of a child to aged parents to the plagues that befell Egypt, the idea of God as King takes on specific significance as Israel identified with God as sovereign over them. Israel looked to God as her King, the one who would protect their national integrity and identity as a people (Hab. 3:2–19).

Happiness depended on the active recognition in day-to-day life, however, that the God who created the nation had also created the cosmos (Deut. 32:1–43). God's law reflected his purposes for humankind within the created orders. Violation of the law represented the abandonment of both place and purpose within creation. Israel's experience of God in both rescue and punishment resulted in a heightened sense of the radical distinction between Creator and creation. Failure to honor this distinction leads to the failure of creation to fulfill its purpose and relationship to God.

In describing this distinction between the Creator and creation, the Bible uses such terms as holiness and glory to characterize God while using such terms as sin to characterize humanity.

New Testament

Creation continued as the worldview of the church after the coming of Christ. It forms the basis for the miraculous activity of Christ, not as a violation of the laws of nature, but as a continuation of the Creator's involvement with creation.

Christ and creation. The New Testament places salvation in continuity with the creative act of God. Salvation is a matter of re-creation by the Creator (2 Cor. 5:17). Salvation, in all its dimensions, is what one might come to expect of the Creator whose creative activity was not limited to a static moment in time, but who "sustains all things by his powerful word" (Heb. 1:3).

In emphasizing this continuity with re-creation, the New Testament stresses that Christ served as the agent of both expressions by the Creator. The prologue to the Gospel of John places Christ in the beginning with God as God. Nothing was made without him (John 1:3). John's Gospel places the message of salvation in the context of a worldview alien to the Hellenistic world for which he wrote. Using such categories as the Greek philosophical idea of the Logos, John laid the necessary groundwork to distinguish Jesus as the Son of God from one of the innumerable mythologies of the pluralistic Roman empire. The old gods had innumerable illegitimate offspring in the national and folk epics of the various regions of the empire. Before presenting any other gospel message, John carefully defined what he meant by "God" and what he meant by "Son of God" (1:1–18).

John is not alone among New Testament witnesses in defining the relationship between Christ as Savior and the reality of a created cosmos. In dealing with people from pagan backgrounds who had entered the church, Paul stressed the foundational importance of the Creator God and the relationship of the Savior to God:

> Yet for us there is but one God, the Father, from whom all things came and for whom we live; and there is but one Lord, Jesus Christ, through whom all things came and through whom we live.
> But not everyone knows this. (1 Cor. 8:6–7a)

What the Jerusalem believers would have known as their heritage, Paul had to make explicit as he encountered people who lived their lives according to a different worldview. In explaining the relationship of Christ to God Paul declared,

> He is the image of the invisible God, the firstborn over all creation. For by him all things were created: things in heaven and on earth, visible and invisible, whether thrones or powers or rulers or authorities; all things were created by him and for

him. He is before all things, and in him all things hold together.
(Col. 1:15–17)

The re-creation does not make coherent sense apart from a first creation. Paul stressed that the Creator is the one who changes people
into his own image (3:10).

Hebrews also stresses the role of Christ in creation, but for a
Jewish audience. Rather than explaining an alternative worldview,
Hebrews stresses that the gospel of Jesus Christ stands in perfect
continuity with the worldview taught by the prophets (Heb. 1:1–3).

Christ and the kingdom. Historically, the idea of the kingdom of
God had strong cultural ties to the people of Israel. Even at Jesus'
ascension, the apostles had difficulty distinguishing the kingdom of
God from the historical/cultural mindset in which the first-century
Jewish community held it (Acts 1:6). Kingdom terminology served
as a metaphor for a far greater reality. While the term had historical
meaning for Israel who had experienced God as King, if in no other
way than rebellion, the metaphor did not have the same meaning in
Greco-Roman culture.

When Jesus began his public preaching ministry following the
arrest of John the Baptist, he "went throughout Galilee, teaching in
their synagogues, preaching the good news of the kingdom" (Matt.
4:23). By leaving the text at this point, some expositors have made
the hermeneutical error of reducing the gospel to a proclamation of
the kingdom of God. This reduction is not necessarily erroneous,
except that its proponents tend to set the gospel of the kingdom
preached by Jesus in contrast to a gospel created by the early church,
and particularly Paul, which (so they claim) focused on Jesus rather
than on the kingdom. This line of thought generally reduces Christianity to an ethical system. Such a moralistic approach approxi-
mates nothing more than a neolegalism.

This bifurcation of the apostolic preaching from the preaching
of Jesus does not take seriously the cultural contexts of the ministries of either Jesus or Paul. The text in Matthew 4 goes on to say
that as Jesus was preaching the gospel of the kingdom, he was

> healing every disease and sickness among the people. News
> about him spread all over Syria, and people brought to him all
> who were ill with various diseases, those suffering severe pain,

the demon-possessed, the epileptics and the paralytics, and he
healed them. (Matt. 4:23b–24)

The kingdom is a metaphor for something greater, and it focuses on
the continuing authority and control that the Creator exercises over
his creation. In the healings and exorcisms, in the exercise of control over the elements, in the exercise of authority over death, the
gospel accounts depict the kingdom as a metaphor for the realm of
activity of the Creator. The good news is that the authority and
power of the Creator have no limits. The realm of the Creator is
from everlasting to everlasting. William J. Abraham and others have
argued that the gospel should be understood primarily as the proclamation of the kingdom.[2]

Purpose. The ancient cultures had a gloomy outlook concerning how the average person fit into the scheme of things. They lived
in fear of spiritual beings and languished in dread of their fate, set
in the stars, woven into the rope of life, or accounted in some other
mythical way. The children of Israel resolved the matter in antiquity.
Rather than being subject to the impersonal caprice of blind fate or
karma, the faithful of Israel saw themselves living in a world
ordered by a Creator who had personal concern for people and for
what became of them. Rather than relying on a self-existent destiny
or purpose that drew people through life, Israel trusted a Creator
who had a will for how his creation could perfectly function. Realizing one's purpose came only in relationship with the Creator.
Solomon expounded this theme in Ecclesiastes. Having found that
all the avenues of fulfillment in life led only to meaninglessness, he
declared:

Remember your Creator
in the days of your youth,
before the days of trouble come
and the years approach when you will say,
"I find no pleasure in them." (Eccl. 12:1)

Solomon ended his examination of the meaning and purpose of life
with this conclusion:

Now all has been heard;
here is the conclusion of the matter:

Fear God and keep his commandments,
    for this is the whole duty of man.
For God will bring every deed into judgment,
    including every hidden thing,
        whether it is good or evil. (Eccl. 12:13–14)

Within the will of the Creator, people may experience meaning, order, and purpose in an otherwise futile existence.

Paul sounds the theme of purpose in his letter to the Ephesians. In the worldview of the Ephesians, purpose and meaning were elusive dreams. In a city where the mystery religions, particularly the nature cult of the great mother Artemis, held sway, people were captive to the endless cycles of nature. Paul explained to the Christians of Asia Minor that before the creation of the world, the Creator willed that those in Christ would enjoy all the spiritual blessings at his disposal. Throughout Ephesians 1:3–14, Paul reiterates the idea of will, purpose, and plan (vv. 5, 9, 11), stressing that purpose comes as a benefit of salvation from the One who has ordered creation from before the beginning of creation.

Paul carries the theme forward as he describes how a sense of purpose extends beyond the initial experience of faith in Christ. Redemption does not come as the end of God's purpose for people, rather, it comes as the beginning of the unfolding of God's purpose. Purpose cannot be fully realized until one has experienced the re-creation of salvation that Christ brings about:

For we are God's workmanship, created in Christ Jesus to do good works, which God prepared in advance for us to do. (Eph. 2:10)

Moral demands. The moral demands of God emerge from the relationship of creation to the Creator. The early church appealed to this relationship in calling people to lead holy lives (1 Tim. 6:13–14; 1 Peter 4:19; 2 Peter 3:3–13). The disruption of the right relationship between creation and Creator results in a spiritually deformed, polluted, and depraved creation, which is a distorted picture of its intended purpose (Rom. 1:18–32).

Sovereignty of God. As Israel before her, the early church believed that God demonstrates his sovereignty through creation.

Furthermore, that sovereignty continues over all of creation (Rev. 10:6–7). God not only has a will and purpose for his creation, but he also involves himself in the affairs of creation so as to accomplish his will.

Paul stressed that the advance of the gospel itself, under most adverse circumstances, including his sufferings and those of others, occurred as a result of the "eternal purpose" of God (Eph. 3:11). The book of Acts contains a similar theme in several passages. In his Pentecostal sermon, Peter declared that all that happened to Christ occurred according to "God's set purpose and foreknowledge" (Acts 2:23). In the prayer of the church following the release of Peter and John from prison, believers expressed the conviction that the sufferings of Christ took place not because of the people who did the deed, but because of what God's "power and will had decided beforehand should happen" (4:28). Foundational to the gospel message is the worldview of a Creator God who orders his creation in a purposeful way toward a good end.

Biblical Implications

While the community of Israel and the early church held to the worldview founded on creation, discussions of creation in Scripture do not, for the most part, serve to explain the question of origins. On the contrary, such references occur almost exclusively to interpret contemporary life. Scripture speaks of creation to explain present existence rather than primordial origins. The reality of a Creator had profound implications for Israel and the early church in terms of present life and future destiny.

HISTORICAL/THEOLOGICAL DEVELOPMENT

The idea of a Creator became foundational to Christian faith as it had been for Hebrew faith. In the formulation of the creeds, this element of the gospel served to introduce the faith: "I believe in God the Father Almighty, Creator of heaven and earth. . . ." This element of the gospel served as the stackpole around which Augustine organized his theological system. The centrality of the Creator God in his thought emerged as a result of his conversion experience. In later centuries other theologians also organized their systems around the ideas of creation, but these other systems tended to remove theology further and further from the issues of conversion.

Augustine

The form of the *Confessions* reinforces Augustine's cardinal preoccupation throughout his theology, which emerged during the long journey of his conversion. He fixed his thoughts on the Creator and wrote the *Confessions* as a prayer of adoration and thanksgiving while confessing all that he was and all that God had done in saving him. Reflecting on the long conversion process, he confessed God's hand in his life at every turning, and he ascribed to God every good and excellent thing that had come to him. At the same time he praised the wisdom of God in every circumstance, for he concluded that God had "used the error of all who pressed me to learn to turn out to my advantage."[3]

Augustine lived in an age of cataclysmic change. Christianity continued to spread, but the old paganism persisted alongside the philosophical schools and the recent heresies. Augustine lived in a multicultural world without consensus, where competing worldviews warred with one another. In the midst of this diversity the old Roman political establishment crumbled in an accelerated fashion. Great migrations of people resulted in a succession of frontier battles between the dissipated Roman army and the waves of invaders, which culminated in the psychologically devastating sack of Rome itself by Alaric and his army of Visigoths in 410. In Africa, Augustine himself would die during the siege of Hippo by the Vandals in 430.

Augustine had an interest in religious, spiritual, or metaphysical matters that sought expression in Manichaeism during his school days. The followers of Mani, the founder of the movement, held to a fanciful and elaborate mythological understanding of reality centered in a dualism between Good and Evil, Light and Darkness. Mani mingled elements of Buddhism, Zoroastrianism, and Christianity. This syncretistic religion considered the material world the result of a primordial victory of Darkness over Light, which resulted in a mixture of the two. Thus, the Manichaeans devoted themselves to deliverance from the material world in order for the Light of their souls to be liberated from the bondage of the Darkness resulting from imprisonment in a body. They had a hierarchy of the Elect, who rigorously followed the ascetic rules of Mani, and the Hearers, who did not follow the same rigorous standards of behavior. Since procreation only prolonged the domination of the Light by Darkness, the Manichaeans rejected sexual intercourse. Since a bit of the Light remained captured in all living things, they ate only vegetables to avoid injuring the Light.[4]

Within the worldview of Manichaeism, Augustine could not receive the central tenets of the gospel. The cross had no attraction for him because, as a Manichaean, he believed the crucifixion had no objective reality but served merely as a symbol of human suffering.[5] He did not see how Christ could deliver him from sin if the cross were a mere "phantom."[6] From the perspective of Manichaeism, Augustine could not conceive of the Incarnation. For Christ to be born of Mary, he would "be defiled by the flesh."[7] Neither could he gain instruction from Scripture because the Manichaeans rejected the Old Testament. They reasoned that if God created humanity in his image, then the God of the Old Testament must be fleshly and therefore Darkness. Augustine viewed the Scriptures as corrupt and vile for their representation of God.[8] The worldview of Manichaeism, rooted in its conception of the divine, created a seemingly impenetrable wall that prevented Augustine from grasping the gospel:

> When I wanted to think of my God, I knew of no way of doing so except as a physical mass. Nor did I think anything existed which is not material. That was the principal and almost sole cause of my inevitable error.[9]

Because of the Manichaean doctrine of creation, Augustine believed "that it is not we who sin, but some alien nature which sins in us."[10]

As he pursued his education, however, Augustine suffered a conflict between his faith and science. In comparison with the rational explanation of eclipses and equinoxes put forward by the mathematical calculations of the philosophers, the myths of Mani seemed foolish to him.[11] As a budding intellectual, Augustine thought the teachings of Mani remarkably presumptuous in their efforts to explain all manner of phenomena from a position of ignorance. Troubled by the inconsistency between Manichaean teaching and philosophical inquiry, Augustine relied on a leading Manichaean bishop, Faustus, to resolve the difficulty, which he failed to do to Augustine's satisfaction. Instead, Faustus's superficial treatment of the issues rendered Manichaeism all the more unsatisfactory.[12] This intellectual failure of Manichaeism combined with an emotional failure Augustine had experienced at the death of a close friend. In the grief that engulfed him following this death, Augustine found no comfort in the deity of the Manichaeans:

> I should have lifted myself to you, Lord, to find a cure. When
> I thought of you, my mental image was not of anything solid
> and firm; it was not you but a vain phantom.[13]

During this period of religious and intellectual struggle, Augustine moved from Africa to Rome and thence to Milan in order to advance his career as a teacher and rhetorician. In Milan, he encountered the dynamic preaching of Ambrose. When Ambrose interpreted difficult Old Testament passages figuratively rather than in the literal fashion of the Manichaeans, his interpretations made sense to Augustine.[14] Still, he could not conceive of the God of the Old Testament, so strong had the Manichaean worldview been imprinted on his mind:

> If I had been able to conceive of spiritual substance, at once all
> their imagined inventions would have collapsed and my mind
> would have rejected them.[15]

Through Ambrose, Augustine began to understand that Christians do not believe that God had the form of a human body.

The categories of Platonic thought helped Augustine finally come to an understanding of the God who created all things. If evil did not exist as a separate force antithetical to God, then logically, he reasoned, God must have created evil. Augustine wanted to protect God from that charge. Through Platonic thought he realized that evil does not exist as a substance in its own right but as an absence of God. Since God is good and since he made all things good, "whatever things exist are good, and the evil into whose origins I was inquiring is not a substance, for if it were a substance, it would be good."[16]

Augustine now felt drawn to the beauty of God who had created all things good, yet he found himself "torn away" by the weight of his own sinfulness, which became apparent as he beheld his Creator.[17] He sought a way to ascend to embrace God, but he met with frustration until he embraced Jesus Christ as the mediator, the one who bridged the gulf between his wretched condition and the Creator.[18] Through reading the writings of the apostles, especially Paul, and through hearing the testimonies of various conversions, Augustine grew convinced intellectually of the truth of Christianity, but he despaired of the breakdown between his mind and his will to act. He found himself both willing and unwilling to become a Christian. While in this state of confusion, he visited a garden in Milan, where he experienced a vision of "Lady Continence," who showed him the young and old who had embraced God, not by their own strength or ability, but because God had made it possible:

> Cast yourself upon him, do not be afraid. He will not withdraw himself so that you fall. Make the leap without anxiety; he will catch you and heal you.[19]

He then heard a voice chanting from a nearby house, "Pick up and read, pick up and read."[20] Remembering the conversion of Antony, who heard the words of Matthew 19:21, "Go, sell your possessions and give to the poor, and you will have treasure in heaven. Then come, follow me," Augustine ran to where he had left a portion of Scripture he had been reading. Opening the book, his eyes fell on the text,

> Not in riots and drunken parties, not in eroticism and indecencies, not in strife and rivalry, but put on the Lord Jesus Christ and make no provision for the flesh in its lusts. (Rom. 13:13–14)[21]

Aquinas

Aquinas lived in a world largely constructed from the theology of Augustine. The medieval European worldview grew largely out of Augustine's description of the *City of God*. While Augustine argued that the *City of God* is not to be identified with an earthly system, the church endeavored to do so. On the rubble of Rome, the church laid the foundation for the city known as Christendom. The feudal order offered a hierarchy of responsibility and authority that gained its legitimacy from the Creator, who held domination over all things.

This world of order and stability, without rival worldviews, gave Aquinas and the Schoolmen of the high Middle Ages the freedom to pursue questions that did not torment the heart (as with Augustine) as much as they tickled the mind. Still, the intellectual questions of Aquinas and the others ultimately rested on the issues of worldview: What kind of world exists? With the presuppositions that God had created the world, Aquinas developed a theological system organized around what one might know within this orderly created universe and how one might know it. His teleological argument for the existence of God rests on the assumption of this orderliness, reflected and observable in creation.

Aquinas carried forward a new tradition of theological thought that had been advanced by Anselm. In his ontological argument for the existence of God, Anselm made a case for the God of creation as the basis for knowledge. The shift in emphasis from knowledge of God to knowledge made possible because of God helped pave the way for the revolution in scientific thought that came with the Renaissance. In contrast to the worldviews of Buddhism and Hinduism, the worldviews of Christianity, Islam, and Judaism encouraged knowledge about the created order, which was judged as good.

The church of the Middle Ages remained preoccupied with Augustine's priority in theology long after it ceased to be existentially concerned with the question Augustine asked. The natural theology of Aquinas elevated the place of human reason and the value of tradition. As a result, it was not prepared to deal with the questions of Luther, whose own struggle for faith drew him necessarily into a different direction from Augustine. Luther organized his theology around the element of the gospel, which became the bridge of faith for him. Unlike Augustine, who could not accept the deity of Christ and the significance of the cross until he comprehended the Creator, Luther believed it all but lacked faith until he came to rely on the authority of Scripture as God's Word to him.

Governed by the questions of a thousand years earlier, the church did not have a place for a scientific view that did not fit with the philosophical interpretation of the meaning of creation that had grown up during the scholastic period. The church, laboring to preserve the traditional Ptolemaic universe, fell into the same trap as the Manichaeans, who had teachings to explain what they did not understand. Thus, church and science grew apart from Galileo onward.

Calvin

Though they lived at the same time, Calvin and Luther inhabited different ages and asked different questions. Luther was a medieval monk while Calvin was a Renaissance scholar. In a sense Calvin lived in a world far more like that of Augustine. The old order had begun to unravel. Though the Western world still acknowledged a Creator, the revolution Aquinas had begun was now gaining momentum. Attention focused on the creation rather than the Creator as revolutions occurred in science, art, music, politics, and virtually every field of endeavor. The planet had even turned into a globe. Calvin did not have the same questions as Augustine, but in the disintegration of feudalism, scholasticism, and the well-ordered society that had been Christendom, the Creator God provided the solution to the questions Calvin asked.

Calvin's theological system, akin to that of Augustine, was based on the Creator God who orders the affairs of creation:

> My meaning is: we must be persuaded not only that as he once formed the world, so he sustains it by his boundless power, governs it by his wisdom, preserves it by his goodness, in particular, rules the human race with justice and judgement, bears with them in mercy, shields them by his protection; but also that not a particle of light, or wisdom, or justice, or power, or rectitude, or genuine truth, will anywhere be found, which does not flow from him, and of which he is not the cause; in this way we must learn to expect and ask all things from him, and thankfully ascribe to him whatever we receive.[22]

The sovereignty of the Creator became the central feature of the gospel message proclaimed by Reformed preachers in Europe and on the island of Britain during the cataclysmic changes of the sixteenth and seventeenth centuries. In the theological elaboration of this element of the gospel, the Reformed school of thought stressed "God's free grace in election and predestination" as the essence of the gospel.[23]

Deism

From a universe in which God orders every event that tran-
spires, by the early seventeenth century the Western church found
itself in a mechanistic universe as far as prevailing science understood reality. Though Copernicus, Galileo, Descartes, and Newton
all confessed the Creator, the mechanical universe that emerged
from the implications of their discoveries led to a new view of God.
Once again the West found itself in a period of radical change politically, economically, socially, and intellectually. In this ferment one
school of thought in the church attempted to respond to the new
worldview with *deistic theology*. This theological approach emerged
from the question of creation as much as Augustine's view had
emerged from the same issue, but the Deists went in a radically different direction. While Augustine was converted from a pagan view
of the world to one in which a Creator interacted intimately with
creation, the Deists converted Christian theology from a faith in an
involved Creator to a view of God compatible with the mechanical
scientific views of the day.

In Deism, a transcendent God is totally removed from the world
and does not intrude into the natural order. The natural and moral
laws comprise all of God that is present in the world. In such a world
there is no revelation, miracle, or interference from God. Paley characterized the world as a watch made by God, who wound it up to run
and then left.

Process Theology

One of the most recent theological systems to emerge from the
issue of creation is *process theology*. With the change from a scientific worldview of mechanism to a scientific worldview of evolution, a new school of thought sought to reconcile Christianity with
these prevailing trends. Influenced by non-Christian evolutionary
philosophers like Whitehead, the early contributors to what became
process theology included Archbishop William Temple of England
and Teilhard de Chardin of France.

Temple argued that the fact that Mind emerges at the end of the
evolutionary process suggests that Mind was present at the beginning. Temple advanced his theological position largely as an apologetic for the existence of God as

the only ultimate source of the whole World-process. All the more developed religions, which do not deny the reality of matter, have advanced this claim. It is the doctrine of Creation. It is not of direct importance to Religion to assert a date for the act of Creation, or even to assert that it is an act having any date at all; it may be a never-beginning and never-ending activity. But it is of vital importance to Religion to assert that the existence of the world is due to the Will of God.[24]

From this perspective, Temple argued that purpose runs through creation, for "when Mind expresses itself through process, its activity is called Purpose."[25]

THE CREATOR GOD AS GOOD NEWS

Over the last two thousand years for the church, and centuries earlier for Israel, the notion of the Creator God has come as good news, as a matter for contemplation, as an intellectual proposition for debate, or as a concept that needed modification. The last three cases tend to arise when the church fails to recognize the constantly contemporary implications of the existence of a Creator. While the truths related to this element of the gospel do not change, the extent to which they address the ultimate question a generation or group of people may be asking varies greatly from time to time and place to place.

While the goodness of a Creator may speak to every generation and culture, the message may be hindered by the way the church formulates the message. Rather than present the Creator as gospel, the church tends to present the Creator as doctrine. Instead of allowing the Creator to address the questions of life being asked at a particular time, the church tends to elaborate answers to questions of another generation or culture. While the truth of the Creator is universal, the questions people ask are not.

Worldview

The questions of many Westerners at the end of the twentieth century have more in common with Augustine than they have with William Temple at the beginning of the twentieth century. In this postmodern world people are increasingly eager to see the spiritual side of reality beyond a scientific face. But what kind of spiritual reality? Intellectual problems related to faith ultimately go back to the issue of what kind of spiritual reality lies behind the universe. The resurrection is an absurd notion with most worldviews, but it poses no problems in a world ordered by a Creator.

Augustine and C. S. Lewis represent those for whom the understanding of the Creator became the bridge of faith. For them, science and philosophy did not present obstacles to faith; rather, they became the arguments for a world in which faith seemed the only logical alternative. In a world created by God, the Creator makes all knowledge possible.

Ecology and Nature Religion

In the latter twentieth century, the crisis of the environment, produced largely from the human inability to control itself and its scientific breakthroughs, has resulted in a renewal of animism and other forms of nature religion in the West. After a hiatus of fifteen hundred years, the Great Mother cult has reemerged through the combination of ecological concern and feminist theology.[26] These matters relate directly to the issues of the Creator God. Rather than deity, the earth is a fragile creation susceptible to great injury.

Under the sovereignty of the Creator, the human race has a stewardship responsibility to God to care for and protect his handiwork. Indeed, "the whole creation has been groaning as in the pains of childbirth" (Rom. 8:22) in consequence of humanity's repudiation of its stewardship relationship to God. Apart from humanity's acceptance of its right relationship to the Creator with all of the moral implications that relationship brings, the rest of creation has no hope.

The credibility of the gospel message for someone concerned about the environment depends on a ministry of ecological concern by the church. If "the earth is the LORD's, and everything in it" (Ps. 24:1), those who claim to believe this assertion should act as stewards rather than as burglars or vandals. Environmentalists who have a sense of the sacredness of the earth often identify that sacredness as being an aspect of the essence of nature rather than as the result of the creation and present involvement of God. The Creator offers hope for the healing of the earth, but he also provides a basis in faith for understanding human responsibility before God for the stewardship of the earth. From an Asian perspective, Ken Gnanakan has argued that the relationship of Creator to creation is a major feature of the good news in the face of Hindu monism.[27]

Purpose

The existential philosophers from the time of Kierkegaard have argued that one of the great dreads of existence is the sense of meaninglessness that people suffer. This philosophical approach assumes a universal quest for purpose that may more appropriately be regarded as a feature of a Western mindset. Eastern religions do not, as a rule, offer any sense of purpose. The concept of Nirvana as the highest ideal suggests that the individual is utterly meaningless and without purpose. The concept of Karma argues for a blind, inevitable fatalism.

Existentialists speak of "the givenness of life," which at one level may seem a despairing way of describing the cynical sense that life is a trap. At a different level, however, givenness implies a giver and suggests that life is a gift. While the quest for purpose may be more culturally restricted than Western thinkers have traditionally thought, for those who do ponder the questions of meaning and purpose, the gospel gives an answer in the good news that a Creator exists who created with purpose.

Grace

Embedded in creation is the idea of grace. In creation God acts graciously, just as in all relationships with creatures God acts and deals graciously. Max Weber coined the phrase "Protestant work ethic" as a device for interpreting Western history since the Reformation. Ironically, the Protestant ethic of the Reformation was not one of work but of grace. The "work" ethic of the West is a vestige of the Old Northern paganism. Valhalla could only be reached by conquest. The gods were not friends, but adversaries.

The old nature gods of European paganism represented the hostility of nature as an enemy to be appeased or defied. The heroes were the ones who struggled and earned all that they had in every sphere of life. The gods could not be trusted, and they were as subject to fate as mortals. In comparison to the behavior of the gods, a European could justify any behavior as it contributed to self-interest.

The old paganism survives in the West, though divorced from the mythological origins. The presence of paganism in the West accounts for a great deal of the repudiation of the Christian faith by those who identify Christianity with Western culture.

The Creator demonstrates his graciousness through creation by sending the sun and the rain for those in right relationship to him and for those in unrighteous relationship to him (Matt. 5:45b). Rather than a hostile adversary, the Creator causes the world to be rejuvenated and restored, usually in spite of the efforts of the human race rather than because of them. The grace of God operates most visibly in the futility and failure of human effort.

Value

Creation introduces the idea of value as an objective public reality rather than as a merely arbitrary, private matter.[28] In the growing collapse of the Western cultures in which absolute values no longer have meaning, the Creator offers the point of stability, the perspective from which to consider if anything really matters. The cult of radical subjectivity and radical freedom present in American society and European society in the late twentieth century suggests the same chaotic situation that prevailed during the period of the Judges in Israel: "Everyone did as he saw fit" (Judg. 17:6b).

In a world without a Creator, one could legitimately say that no absolute values exist. If one examined many cultures phenomenologically, one might conclude that the diversity of values suggests that all values are relative. Behind all values, however, lies the absolute value that order is preferable to chaos. In creation, God first brought order out of chaos (Gen. 1:2–3). Without order, science would be impossible, for experimentation depends on probability and consistency in the behavior of the material universe. Likewise, spiritual chaos produces dysfunction in relationships that can range from interpersonal conflict at the micro level to warfare at the macro level. The Creator can bring order to a chaotic life.

Identity

One of the most important developmental crises of life revolves around the establishment of one's identity. Put simply, the question is "Who am I?" This question finds its answer in relation to the

Creator, though it is treated differently by other religions that do not worship a Creator. In Buddhism and Hinduism the answer to the question begins with the confession that all people are a part of the divine and that ultimately there is no distinction between anything. All is one.

Self-consciousness is generally understood to arise in the differentiation that comes when one is aware of another. To be aware of the other is to be aware of oneself. Ultimately, personal identity can only come through the same kind of experience with God. To be aware of God as the Other, totally different from oneself, gives individuals an awareness of who they really are. Isaiah understood himself as he understood the total otherness of God (Isa. 6:5). Apart from an understanding of one's creatureliness, people who crave identity tend to take steps to create identity. These exercises normally fall within the sphere of idolatry, by creating identity from fame, wealth, intellect, sexual prowess, or the various other means people have for calling attention to themselves. In knowing the Creator, however, people are free to be themselves without having to create a character deserving of attention.

NOTES

1. See Rudolph Otto, *The Idea of the Holy*, trans. John W. Harvey (New York: Oxford Univ. Press, 1979).

2. William J. Abraham, *The Logic of Evangelism* (Grand Rapids: Eerdmans, 1989), 17–39. Ben Johnson also stressed this dimension in *Rethinking Evangelism* (Philadelphia: Westminster, 1987), 115–26.

3. Augustine, *Confessions*, trans. Henry Chadwick (Oxford: Oxford Univ. Press, 1991), 15.

4. R. Michael Wilson, "Mani and Manichaeism," *The Encyclopedia of Philosophy* (New York: Macmillan, 1967), 5:149–50.

5. *Confessions*, 82, n. 14.

6. Ibid., 82.

7. Ibid., 86.

8. Ibid.

9. Ibid., 85.

10. Ibid., 84.

11. Ibid., 75.

12. Ibid., 79.

13. Ibid., 56.

14. Ibid., 88.

15. Ibid., 89.

16. Ibid., 126.

17. Ibid., 127.

18. Ibid., 128.

19. Ibid., 151.

20. Ibid., 152.

21. Translation from Augustine's *Confessions*.

22. John Calvin, *Institutes of the Christian Religion*, trans. Henry Beveridge (Grand Rapids: Eerdmans, 1957), 1:40–41.

23. Peter Heylyn, *Cyprianus Anglicus* (London, 1671), 180.

24. Archbishop William Temple, *Natural Man and God* (London: Macmillan, 1934), 37.

25. Ibid., 219.

26. See Tony Campolo, *How to Rescue the Earth Without Worshipping Nature* (Nashville: Nelson, 1992).

27. Ken Gnanakan, "Creator, New Creation, and Ecological Relationships," *Emerging Voices in Global Christian Theology* (Grand Rapids: Zondervan, 1994), 127–54.

28. See Lesslie Newbigin, *Foolishness to the Greeks* (Grand Rapids: Eerdmans, 1986).

Chapter 3

Scripture and Fulfillment

The character of holy writings depends on the spiritual reality one posits. All of the large world religions have holy writings, but these writings represent themselves in different ways. The Quran represents itself as the revealed word of God, delivered through the prophet Mohammed. The *Bhagavad Gita* of Hinduism is in the form of heroic epic poetry, which reflects allegorically the great cosmic struggle and represents the fruit of meditation that seeks illumination about the divine. The utterly transcendent deity desires nothing of people. *The Eightfold Path* of Buddha contains the teachings that proceed from the enlightenment that no god exists as a differentiated being.

Christians and Jews share the holy writings of Israel. These writings presuppose the Creator who revealed his will and purpose by inspiring prophets over a period of centuries. They often witness to a simultaneous act of revelation in nature and history, such as the revelation of the Law of Moses in the context of the Exodus. While the Quran claims to reveal the will of God, it also insists that God never reveals himself. In the writings of Israel, however, God revealed himself in intimate ways that express the desire for loving relationship with people.

The ministry of Jesus took place at a time when the study of the Scriptures had taken a central place in the life of the Jewish people. This concern held the Jewish people together after the temple sacrificial system and the priesthood came to an end with the destruction of Jerusalem in A.D. 70. As it was, the understanding of the nature and meaning of the Scriptures helped to define the ministry of Jesus and the gospel message.

BIBLICAL BACKGROUND

The issue of fulfillment appears throughout Matthew's Gospel as an underlying theme. In the Sermon on the Mount Jesus addresses the issue of the relationship of his ministry to the Scriptures:

> Do not think that I have come to abolish the Law or the Prophets: I have not come to abolish them but to fulfill them. I tell you the truth, until heaven and earth disappear, not the smallest letter, not the least stroke of a pen, will by any means disappear from the Law until everything is accomplished. (Matt. 5:17–18)

Jesus did not challenge the Jewish understanding of the nature of Scripture; rather, he challenged the contemporary interpretation of the meaning of the Law and the Prophets. He went further than a mere exercise in hermeneutics, however, for he claimed that he personally was the fulfillment of God's will and purpose as revealed in the Law and the Prophets.

In Luke's Gospel the same theme appears in the inaugural sermon of Jesus in Nazareth. After reading from the prophet Isaiah Jesus declared, "Today this scripture is fulfilled in your hearing" (Luke 4:21). Later, when John the Baptist sent two of his disciples to inquire of Jesus if he was "the one that was to come" (7:19), Jesus replied:

> Go back and report to John what you have seen and heard: The blind receive sight, the lame walk, those who have leprosy are cured, the deaf hear, the dead are raised, and the good news is preached to the poor. (Luke 7:22; cf. Matt. 11:5)

Again, his statement identifies himself as the One who came to fulfill the Scriptures. While the priestly party did not recognize the authority of the prophetic books, the Pharisees, who had a great following in the synagogues, regarded the Prophets as part of Scripture and looked for messianic fulfillment. John himself identified his own ministry as precursor to the appearance of the Messiah in the Gospels (John 1:19–23; cf. Matt. 3:1–3; Mark 1:2–4; Luke 3:1–6).

While the Synoptic Gospels each include the three predictions of Jesus' Passion, only Luke indicates, strictly speaking, that they were not predictions at all (see also Matt. 26:52–54). Instead, they were teachings that "everything that is written by the prophets about the Son of Man will be fulfilled" (Luke 18:31). Though the terminology of fulfillment appears only here, each of the Synoptics contains terminology in at least one of the predictions that places the announcements of the Passion in the framework of teaching (Matt. 16:21–23; Mark 8:31–33; 9:30–32; Luke 18:31–33; cf. John 18:31–32). The Gospels thus place the Passion predictions in the context of the teaching ministry of Jesus that challenged the contemporary notions of how the prophecies must be fulfilled.

Passion Teachings		
Matthew	Mark	Luke
1 16:21–23*	8:31–33*	9:22
2 17:22–23	9:30–32*	9:44–45
3 20:17–19	10:32–34	18:31–33*

*Passages that indicate teachings related to fulfillment of Scripture.

This connection proves all the more striking in light of Luke's postresurrection accounts of the teachings of Jesus. On the Emmaus road, Jesus declared:

> "How foolish you are, and how slow of heart to believe all that the prophets have spoken! Did not the Christ have to suffer these things and then enter his glory?" And beginning with Moses and all the Prophets, he explained to them what was said in all the Scriptures concerning himself. (Luke 24:25–27)

Luke also indicates that Jesus taught his disciples about his relation to the Scriptures:

> He said to them, "This is what I told you while I was still with you: Everything must be fulfilled that is written about me in the Law of Moses, the Prophets and the Psalms."
> Then he opened their minds so they could understand the Scriptures. (Luke 24:44–45)

Clearly, the fulfillment of Scripture in a way that the Jews of Jesus' time had not expected forms a major theme of the Gospel writers.

Oddly enough, the scholarly debate over whether Jesus actually taught about his coming suffering and death as a fulfillment of Scripture does not fall within the sphere of biblical study. The question relates to the issue of what kind of God exists and, therefore, what kinds of events are possible in this universe. One's presuppositions about the universe determine how one interprets Scripture. If a person does not believe in the kind of God who reveals the future and interacts with creation, then alternative explanations must be put forward for statements such as these about fulfillment on the lips of Jesus.

The idea of the fulfillment of Scripture appears in every book of the New Testament except James, and even James refers to the Law (James 4:11–12). In the evangelistic messages of Acts, the appeal to fulfillment of Scripture appears in every address except for that given by Paul at Lystra. Even the return of Christ for judgment mentioned by Paul in Athens is a fulfillment theme. Throughout the Gospels, the life and ministry of Jesus are presented in a context of fulfillment.

The Gospel writers took great pains to show that they did not proclaim a new faith or religion. On the contrary, their stress on fulfillment demonstrates their conviction that faith in Christ stood in direct continuity with all that God had been doing since creation. Jesus did not start a new religion; he fulfilled all of the hopes and aspirations of Israel.

Mark

Mark's Gospel begins with fulfillment, for the ministry of John the Baptist forms "the beginning of the gospel about Jesus Christ, the Son of God" (Mark 1:1). Mark places the ministry of John the Baptist as fulfilling Malachi 3:1 and Isaiah 40:3. The public ministry of Jesus begins with the proclamation that "the time has come. . . . The kingdom of God is near" (1:15). That is, the fulfillment of the promise of the kingdom has begun. The many teachings of Jesus about the kingdom stand within the context of the Jewish hope for fulfillment. The confession of Peter at Caesarea Philippi takes the form of conviction that the Christ/Messiah of prophecy has come (8:28–29). Mark also places the response of others to Jesus in the context of fulfillment. For example, the criticism of Jesus by the scribes and Pharisees is accounted as prophetic fulfillment:

He replied, "Isaiah was right when he prophesied about you hypocrites; as it is written:

"'These people honor me with their lips,
    but their hearts are far from me.
They worship me in vain;
    their teachings are but rules taught by men.'" (7:6–7)

In describing the response of the disciples to the arrest of Jesus, Mark records these words of Jesus:

"You will all fall away . . . for it is written:

"'I will strike the shepherd,
    and the sheep will be scattered.'" (14:27)

While Mark gives only a few citations of Scripture as being fulfilled, the very theme of the messianic secret that runs throughout his Gospel is a theme of fulfillment.

Luke

Luke likewise begins his Gospel with the theme of fulfillment: "Many have undertaken to draw up an account of the things that have been fulfilled among us" (Luke 1:1). At the presentation of Jesus following his birth, Luke refers to two prophetic figures, Simeon and Anna, who prophesy (Luke 2:21–38). Like Mark, Luke also indicates that the ministry of John the Baptist fulfilled the prophesy of Isaiah (3:4–6; cf. Isa. 40:3–5). Even the form that Jesus' temptation takes comes in the context of the Jewish community's acceptance of fulfillment:

"If you are the Son of God," [the devil] said, "throw yourself down from here. For it is written:

"'He will command his angels concerning you
    to guard you carefully;
they will lift you up in their hands,
    so that you will not strike your foot against a stone.'"
(Luke 4:9b–11)

As mentioned above, Luke stressed that Jesus placed his entire ministry and Passion in the context of fulfillment in the postresurrection teaching.

Matthew

While Matthew's Gospel makes many references to fulfillment, it particularly stresses fulfillment in the story of the birth of Jesus. Matthew's Gospel begins with a genealogy of Jesus, which establishes the continuity of Jesus with David and Abraham (Matt. 1:17). He explains the virgin birth as fulfillment of Isaiah 7:14 (Matt. 1:22–23). Scholars have debated whether the Hebrew *almah* should be translated literally as "young woman" or with its cultural context of "virgin." The debate is a mute one since Matthew uses the Septuagint for his text, and the Greek text settles the question of what Matthew says had happened. Even if Isaiah meant "young woman," Matthew declares that in fulfillment a virgin conceived.

To continue the theme of fulfillment surrounding the birth of Jesus, Matthew relates that the priests and teachers at the court of Herod believed that Messiah would be born in Bethlehem, as prophesied by Micah in Micah 5:2 (Matt. 2:3–6). The account of the flight to Egypt appears only in Matthew's Gospel as the fulfillment of Hosea 11:1 (Matt. 2:14–15). The slaughter of the baby boys in Bethlehem also is described as fulfillment of prophecy (Matt. 2:16–18; cf. Jer. 31:15). Finally, the settlement of the family of Jews in Nazareth after the death of Herod also fulfills a prophecy that "he will be called a Nazarene" (Matt. 2:23).[1]

Matthew likewise indicates that the ministry of Jesus fulfilled Scripture. He introduces the preaching, healing, and teaching ministries of Jesus with the testimony of Scripture (Matt. 4:12–17; cf. Isa. 9:1–2; Matt. 8:14–17; cf. Isa. 53:4; Matt. 13:34–35; cf. Ps. 78:2), which provided an external authority or verification for their legitimacy. Likewise, the establishment of the identity of Jesus as the servant of God (Matt. 13:11–17; cf. Isa. 42:1–4) and the failure of his generation to recognize him as the One who fulfilled the Scriptures (Matt. 13:11–17; cf. Isa. 6:9–10) occur within Matthew's Gospel as elements in the theme of fulfillment.

Finally, Matthew points to several events during the Passion week that fulfill Scripture. The Triumphal Entry is preceded by a brief account of the securing of a donkey for Jesus to ride. Matthew saw this episode foretold by the prophets (Matt. 21:1–5; cf. Zech. 9:9). The anecdotal account of how the priest used the money returned by Judas also appears as the fulfillment of Scripture, but in this case, Matthew must bring together several incidents from Jeremiah to see a pattern that finds fulfillment. Here the emphasis is not on prediction, but on fulfillment (Matt. 27:6–10; cf. Jer. 18:1–3; 32:6–15).

John

John's Gospel places the life and ministry of Jesus in the context of the popular expectation of someone great whom Moses and the prophets had foretold (John 1:45). This theme resonates with the similar tone found in Luke. John indicates that Jesus withdrew from the crowds because they began to say that he was the long-expected prophet (6:14–15). This resonates with the tone set by Mark concerning the messianic secret, an issue that concerns fulfillment.

In terms of fulfillment, however, John places his emphasis on the way in which the Passion fulfilled the Scriptures. He does this in two ways. He relates specific incidents in the Passion week to specific passages of Scripture that foreshadow the events. Among these are the unbelief of the crowds (John 12:38–41; cf. Isa. 53:1; also 6:10), the betrayal by Judas (John 13:18; cf. Ps. 41:9), the dividing of the clothes of Jesus by the guards (John 19:23–24; cf. Ps. 22:18), the cry of thirst from the cross (John 19:28–29; cf. Ps. 69:21), and the quick death of Jesus that avoided the necessity of his legs being broken (John 19:31–37; cf. Ex. 12:46; Zech. 12:10).

In addition to these overt references to fulfillment of particular Scriptures, John depicts the Passion as fulfilling the meaning of the sacrificial system. From the first declaration by John the Baptist that Jesus is "the Lamb of God" (John 1:29), this Gospel proceeds to demonstrate that by his death Jesus fulfilled the Law analogically (cf. Matt. 5:17). John describes the trial of Jesus before Pilate as taking place on "the day of Preparation of Passover Week" (John 19:14). In other words, Jesus was being prepared for crucifixion as the Passover lamb was being prepared for sacrifice. Even the text John uses in reference to the bones of Jesus not being broken is a text that refers to the Passover lamb. Thus, John's Gospel stresses that Jesus has fulfilled or completed the meaning of sacrifice.

Paul

Paul's conviction that Jesus is Lord, experienced at his conversion, required a new hermeneutic for him. He came to understand how the Law and the Prophets found fulfillment in Jesus. If his former hermeneutic had failed him with respect to the coming of the Messiah, it did not adequately deal with the rest of Scripture and its meaning either. Christ and his gospel therefore formed for Paul the hermeneutic for interpreting Scripture, and Scripture formed the undergirding authority for the truth of the gospel.

As one would expect from a Pharisee schooled at the feet of Gamaliel, Scripture provided the basis for Paul's thought and the substance for his theology. Luke hints at this reliance on Scripture in his description of Paul's methodology in Acts. At Antioch of Pisidia, Paul presented his message in the context of God's dealings with Israel from the time of their sojourn in Egypt (Acts 13:16–41), a style of preaching not unlike Stephen's (7:2–60) or the litany of Hebrews 11. Rather than defend his departure from the faith of Israel, Paul used Scripture to prove that in Jesus he followed the true faith of Israel.

Romans illustrates the place of fulfillment and Scripture in Paul's thought better than his other writings because with the church in Rome Paul did not have pastoral and discipling issues to address. The gospel for all people as the legitimate fulfillment of the Law and the Prophets may very well have been his intended theme for the letter. It begins and ends with it. Paul immediately authenticated his message as one God "promised beforehand through his prophets in the Holy Scriptures" (Rom. 1:2) and declared that this message was intended for "people from among all the Gentiles to the obedience that comes from faith" (1:5). Paul concluded similarly by declaring that the gospel was "now revealed and made known through the prophetic writings . . . so that all nations might believe and obey him" (16:26).

Paul sounds similar to Jesus in the Sermon on the Mount when he declares, "Do we, then, nullify the law by this faith? Not at all! Rather, we uphold the law" (Rom. 3:31). He states the essence of fulfillment as "Christ is the end of the law so that there may be righteousness for everyone who believes" (10:4). Because of Christ, Paul had to revise his understanding of the purpose of the law. The law brings self-understanding of sinfulness rather than righteousness: "For I would not have known what it was to covet if the law had not said, 'Do not covet'" (7:7). The idea that the Scriptures were given "to teach" (15:4) appears again in Galatians, where Paul describes the Law as a "custodian" or "schoolmaster" (Gal. 3:24 KJV). Beyond the Law and the Prophets, however, God had always intended to bestow righteousness through the goodness of Jesus: "But now a righteousness from God, apart from law, has been made known, to which the Law and the Prophets testify" (Rom. 3:21).

Romans, though written to Christians, might rightly be taken as a recapitulation of how Paul may have presented the gospel to non-believers. In describing his reason for writing the things he included in his letter, he stated,

> I have written you quite boldly on some points, *as if to remind you of them again*, because of the grace God gave me to be a minister of Christ Jesus to the Gentiles with the priestly duty of proclaiming the gospel of God, so that the Gentiles might become an offering acceptable to God, sanctified by the Holy Spirit. (Rom. 15:15–16, emphasis mine)

This reminder of the gospel is accompanied by approximately sixty-three quotations of Old Testament passages.[2] Beyond these quotations, Paul includes lengthy commentary on the law to explain the significance of Jesus. The gospel as Paul proclaimed it relied heavily on the relationship of Jesus to the Scriptures, both in continuity with Scripture and as the culmination of Scripture.

Paul wrote another brief reminder of the gospel to the Corinthians. In 1 Corinthians 15:1–8 he wrote to settle a doctrinal dispute concerning the resurrection. He appealed to the gospel for the answer, but he appealed to the Scriptures to authenticate the gospel:

> that Christ died for our sins *according to the Scriptures*, that he was buried, that he was raised on the third day *according to the Scriptures*. (1 Cor. 15:3b–4, emphasis mine)

This letter begins with an assertion of the power of the gospel, which Paul supports with an appeal to its fulfillment of the Scriptures (1:19, 31; 2:9, 16; 3:19–20). Rather than serving a purely doctrinal purpose as in Romans, however, his discussion of the gospel comes in the form of a pastoral appeal to urge unity in the church. Elsewhere in 1 Corinthians, Paul uses Scripture texts or allusions to support his exhortations to flee immorality (5:7, 13; 6:18; 10:7), to follow order in worship (11:7–10; 14:21), and to establish his rights as an apostle (9:9). Throughout, he writes from the perspective that the Law and the Prophets had a fuller meaning than is apparent from their original context. The writings were for later generations:

> These things happened to them as examples and were written down as warnings for us, on whom the fulfillment of the ages has come. (10:11; cf. 9:10; 10:6)

Peter

Paul's teachings on fulfillment find similar expression in the Petrine letters. In the conclusion of the recapitulation of the gospel at the beginning of 1 Peter, the role of fulfillment appears:

> Concerning this salvation, the prophets, who spoke of the grace that was to come to you, searched intently and with the greatest care, trying to find out the time and circumstances to which the Spirit of Christ in them was pointing when he predicted the sufferings of Christ and the glories that would follow. It was revealed to them that they were not serving themselves but you, when they spoke of the things that have now been told you by those who have preached the gospel to you by the Holy Spirit sent from heaven. Even angels long to look into these things. (1 Peter 1:10–12)

HISTORICAL/THEOLOGICAL DEVELOPMENT

Over the centuries, the relative importance of the apostolic understanding of fulfillment has varied widely, depending on the context in which the church ministered. The gospel teaching about fulfillment of the Scriptures related to the church's understanding of the Scriptures as revelation. The idea of fulfillment and the related idea of revelation also raised the issue of the authority of the holy writings.

The Patristic Period

The idea of fulfillment formed a major motif in the evangelization of the pagan world during the patristic period. As the gospel spread into the Hellenistic world, it met a people unacquainted with the Scriptures of Israel, for whom the worship of one God seemed a strange and intolerant notion.

The fulfillment of Scripture provided an intellectual dimension for demonstrating the truth of the claims of the gospel of Jesus Christ. In a world of competing philosophies and religions, revealed truth from God and the fulfillment of promises by God set the gospel apart. While Judaism enjoyed official recognition, Christianity was regarded as a seditious, immoral cult. Local and regional persecution afflicted the church throughout the second and third centuries prior to the great official persecution ordered by the emperor Diocletian. Popular rumor for several centuries persisted that Christians were atheists because they had no image of the God they worshiped. They were said to practice cannibalism because they ate the body and drank the blood of a sacrificial victim. They were also thought to practice incest because they were all said to be "brothers" and "sisters" to each other. In this climate the apologists arose to give a clear explanation of Christian practices and beliefs and to make a case for the truth of the gospel.

Justin Martyr. The fulfillment of the Scriptures provided the door for Justin's conversion to faith in Christ and went on to form the organizing theme of his work. Justin had pursued philosophy of various strands, including Stoicism and Platonism. While on a walk one day, he engaged in conversation with a man who shook his confidence in philosophy's ability to lead a person to God. The man then informed Justin:

> There existed, long before this time, certain men more ancient than all those who are esteemed philosophers, both righteous and beloved by God, who spoke by the Divine Spirit, and foretold events which would take place, and which are now taking place. They are called prophets.[3]

This conversation started Justin on an exploration of how Christ fulfilled the prophecies, which ultimately resulted in his conversion. He concluded that the Scriptures provided a superior philosophy and means to God.[4]

Justin's most well-known work is the *Dialogue with Trypho the Jew*, written probably not long before his martyrdom under Marcus Aurelius (c. A.D. 165). This work recounts a conversation between Justin and a Hellenistic Jew named Trypho thirty years earlier. Trypho and his friends were refugees from Palestine following the Bar Chochba uprising (132–135).

The *Dialogue* contains three main sections. In the first, Justin refutes Trypho's insistence on the observance of the Mosaic Law for salvation. Justin uses Scripture to demonstrate that throughout the history of Israel and before the giving of God's law to Moses, justification before God was a matter of the righteousness of the heart rather than of the observance of ceremonies. In the second section, Justin appeals to the Scriptures to demonstrate how the gospel message of the incarnation, the death, and the resurrection of Christ fulfilled prophecies. In the final section, he argues that those who have faith in Christ who fulfills the prophecies are the true Israel and the heirs of God's promises.

In his *First Apology* Justin also relied on the fulfillment of prophecy to defend the gospel. In chapters 31–53 he expounded the significance of prophecy fulfilled and explained the nature of prophecy through the "prophetic Spirit." In laying prophecy fulfilled as the foundation for the gospel, Justin corroborated the events and significance of the gospel by the ancient message of the prophets:

> In these books of the prophets, then, we find Jesus the Christ foretold as coming, born of a virgin, healing human sicknesses, raising the dead, being hated and unrecognized, being crucified, dying, rising again, ascending into heaven, and being called the Son of God.[5]

Thus, in his recapitulation of the *kerygma* Justin relied on Scripture for verification of the gospel.

Tertullian. Tertullian of Carthage appeared on the scene in the latter part of the second century as the founding force of Latin theology. While other apologists attempted to use the pagan philosophers in presenting their case, Tertullian took the offensive and granted nothing to philosophy or heathen religion. Believing as he did that the Old Testament provided the source for the prophecies that found fulfillment in Christ, he devoted himself "to define the correct principles of hermeneutics, and perpetually discussed biblical history."[6] That Tertullian wrote five books in his series *Against Marcion* underscores the significance he placed on the Old Testament and its relationship to the gospel. His third book particularly expresses his conviction that God would not have manifested himself in the world without giving some forewarning. The fourth book explores the significance of prophecy in the four Gospels:

> All start with the same principles of the faith, so far as relates to the one only God the Creator and His Christ, how that He was born of the virgin, and came to fulfill the law and the prophets.[7]

Feeling as he did, Tertullian depended on the Scriptures to prove the gospel of Christ, "by the evidence and antiquity of the divine books."[8] He reviled philosophers as enemies of truth who were seeking after personal glory.[9] In his *Apology* Tertullian asked, "But then what have philosopher and Christian in common?"[10] In *The Prescription Against Heretics* he wrote his well-known companion interrogatory: "What indeed has Athens to do with Jerusalem? What concord is there between the Academy and the church? What between heretics and Christians?"[11] Tertullian believed that heresies were instigated by philosophy. He repudiated any effort to synthesize Christianity with philosophical schools of thought, as would gradually happen in later centuries when Christianity became more respectable.

In the face of persecution, Tertullian also addressed the questions of Christian behavior from his understanding of Scripture in *De Corona Militis*. He prefigured a Reformation debate in his consideration of things of indifference (*res adiaphora*). Are Christians permitted to do what the Bible does not forbid? Or, are things not expressly permitted by the Bible forbidden for Christians? Here the question of the authority of Scripture and the place of tradition began to emerge as conflicting streams. In his time, Tertullian harmonized tradition and Scripture, largely because he was addressing a practical issue of facing martyrdom.

The centrality of Scripture and the concept of a revealed religion in the thought of Tertullian eventually became the pivotal factors in his embrace of Montanism, with its stress on ecstatic prophecy. Because God had revealed himself to the prophets and the apostles, Tertullian saw no reason why revelation would have ceased with the apostles.[12] Though he had defended the place of tradition in the church, he became separated from the Christianity of his day because of his refusal to accept the traditional understanding of the end of the apostolic age and the completion of Scripture.

Origen. Fulfillment of Scripture represented a primary integrating theme in Origen's apologetic work *Against Celsus* in the mid-third century, nearly one hundred years after Justin's *Dialogue*. Origen is best known as an interpreter of the Scriptures, devoting himself particularly to the understanding of the relationship between the Old Testament and the New Testament. The *Hexapla* represents his efforts at developing the discipline of critical Bible study. It contained in six parallel columns the Hebrew text of the Old Testament, a Greek transliteration of the Hebrew characters, and the four Greek translations of the Scriptures in use at the time.

Devoting most of his energies to biblical study and exegesis, the theme of fulfillment seemed a logical corollary to his work. Origen approached exegesis from the standpoint of typology, proceeding from the conviction that a text had a "literal or physical sense, a moral or psychical sense, and an intellectual or spiritual sense."[13] Origen had a strong interest in demonstrating the intellectual validity of Christianity in his answer to Celsus' attacks. He wrote not only to prove that Christianity was not a seditious group, but also that it had the right to take its place as the profoundest of philosophies.[14] The prophets, who Origen argued predated the Greek philosophers, lent a degree of intellectual respectability to Judaism, which Origen capitalized on while demonstrating prophecy's fulfillment in Christ.

Rather than presenting a systematic description of Christianity in *Against Celsus*, Origen answered Celsus' charges point by point. He also explained the legitimacy of suggesting that Christ fulfilled the pagan *Sibylline Oracles* as well as Old Testament prophecy.[15] That Origen referred to Christ as the "only-begotten Logos or Wisdom" illustrates how he linked prophecy and philosophical ideas.[16]

Apart from the inspiring Logos, prophecy could not happen. This apology reflects a thorough knowledge of philosophy and religious practices, which Origen critiqued by using the arguments that philosophical schools used against each other.

To Origen, Celsus had written "to criticize the assertion that the history of Christ Jesus was prophesied by the prophets among the Jews."[17] Rather than qualify the idea of fulfillment or take some other line of defense, Origen boldly asserted his intention to "take refuge for our defense in the prophecies about Christ."[18] For him, the study of Scripture was a great philosophical or intellectual endeavor when compared with the study of other systems:

> For in Christianity, if I make no vulgar boasting, there will be found to be no less profound study of the writings that are believed; we explain the obscure utterances of the prophets, and the parables in the gospels, and innumerable other events or laws which have a symbolical meaning.[19]

Origen firmly believed that the fulfillment of Scripture gave a dimension of credibility to Christianity that made it a strong competitor in the third-century world of ideas.

Eusebius. Eusebius wrote *The Proof of the Gospel* at a time when the church was beginning to enter a place of respectability in the empire (c. 315).[20] In his great apologetic work he employed a method designed to prove the truth of the gospel by appealing to the prophecies of the Old Testament.[21] He declared his intention at the beginning:

> I propose to show, by quotations from them, how they forestalled events that came to the light long ages after their time, the actual circumstances of the Savior's own presentment of the Gospel, and the things which in our own day are being fulfilled by the Holy Spirit before our very eyes.[22]

Only ten of the original twenty books in this work have survived, but they give ample evidence of the type of appeal Eusebius made to Roman society.

The books present the major themes of the gospel, and Ferrar follows Lightfoot in presuming that the lost books would have addressed the resurrection, ascension, gifts of the Holy Spirit, and the emergence of the church as fulfillment of the prophecies of the Old Testament.[23] Rather than a new religion, Eusebius was anxious to demonstrate that though salvation comes through faith, it does not come without "logical demonstration."[24] In this regard, prophecy and its fulfillment held a critical place:

> But I went on to say that our conversion was due not to emotional and unexamined impulse, but to judgement and sober reasoning, and that our devotion to the oracles of the Hebrews thus had the support of judgement and sound reason.[25]

Concluding observations. During the patristic period, a range of famous, and presumably unknown, Christians organized their presentation of the gospel around the theme of the fulfillment of Scripture. This theme provided an intellectual appeal, gave an objective basis for examining the claims of the gospel, and set Christianity apart from the mystery religions and philosophies as a "revealed" religion.

The Reformers and Scripture

A thousand years after Eusebius, Scripture once again came to prominence as the focus around which theology revolved. This is not to say that the church had ceased to believe in the Bible. The Scriptures had simply receded in importance with the growing traditions of the church. By the late Middle Ages, however, the credibility of the church had sunk to a low point as a result of a variety of abuses.

Wycliff. John Wycliff came to prominence after 1370, largely because of the publishing of views he had debated at Oxford. In his two tracts *On Divine Dominion* and *On Civil Domain* he argued that only those who enjoyed God's grace had the right to civil dominion and the possession of property, and that monasteries had no right to possess property.[26] Wycliff based his arguments challenging the traditions and structure of the church on Scripture, which he understood to be God's law. Scripture stands above the "Pope's law" and the "King's law," he maintained.[27] Winn argues that Wycliff had two favorite themes: "The paramount authority of Scripture and the wickedness of friars."[28]

Wycliff addressed a church that had grown accustomed to the sale of offices, the sale of indulgences, and the accumulation of church lands by the monasteries. The last of these presented an unusual problem. Each parish had property attached to it for the support of the priest, which he might farm or lease out for its income. Over time, the right to name the priest (the advowson) and to receive the income from the property (the glebe land) fell into the hands of religious orders, which had the vow of poverty as part of their rule. Increasingly the monasteries appointed the kind of people who would take the appointment for little pay, or they left the parish empty. In some cases a priest would accept multiple appointments in different parts of the country (plurality) and live himself in Oxford or London.[29] While Wycliff disapproved of the monks for their vast accumulation of wealth while theoretically under a vow of poverty, he most vigorously opposed them for failing in the primary responsibility of a priest, the preaching of God's word.[30]

The authority of the church was so discredited by the practice of simony, the sale of indulgences, the absence of a preaching clergy, and a dissipated monastic system that Wycliff offered a superior authority whereby people might know God and salvation through Christ. The need for a reliable authority became all the more heightened in 1378 when Christendom found itself in the embarrassing position of having two popes, each claiming infallibility. Instead of a pope, Wycliff insisted that Christ "is the heed of the Chirche; and He ordeynede a lawe to men, and confermede it with his lyf, for to reule holi Chirche, and teche how that men shulde lyve. . . ."[31]

While Wycliff's controversial teachings addressed the abuses and corruption of the church and its place in society (he even went so far as to reject transubstantiation), the basis for his teachings went back to the Bible as his authority. Wycliff respected the church fathers, especially Augustine, and used their arguments for support. But he did not place the tradition of the church on the same level of authority with Scripture.[32] Wycliff taught that "faith depends on the Scriptures" and that "to ignore the Scriptures is to ignore Christ."[33]

Because the Scriptures were God's law, Wycliff argued that nothing should be added to them as binding on the church. Tradition added by the church should be ignored as novelties that were "contrarie to Christ's ordenaunce,"[34] and nothing that the law of Christ does not touch on "shulde be dun or axid to do."[35] This stress on

Scripture as the starting point for faith and practice had long-term expression in Wycliff's effort to send out "poor preachers," called Lollards by his opponents, to bring the gospel to the people in the vernacular. His followers also translated the Bible into English. People needed a sure and certain guide to salvation in such an uncertain time, Wycliff felt, and he found that guide only in Scripture. He personally devoted himself to preaching, for "God hath ordained them to come to bliss by preaching and keeping of God's word."[36]

Hus. John Hus (1372/73–1415) also oriented his theological understanding around the idea of Scripture. He had begun his academic career with dreams of advancement and full participation in the ecclesiastical system as it operated in his day. He later remarked:

> When I was young in years and reason, I too belonged to the foolish sect. But when the Lord gave me the knowledge of Scripture, I discharged that kind of stupidity from my foolish mind.[37]

Spinka concludes that "it was the study of Scripture" that led to Hus's own conversion and subsequent concern over abuses in the church, which hindered others from knowing the gospel and coming to faith.

In his most important work, *De Ecclesia*, Hus declared the principal convictions of his ministry. He held that (1) the church consists of the predestined, wherever they might be, not the pope and cardinals, who may not be predestined; (2) Christ is the head of the church, not the pope; (3) the keys of the kingdom rest with the church, not the pope. Hus based these conclusions and his entire theological system on his conviction that the Scriptures given by God served as the guiding authority in matters of faith and practice.[38] For these convictions the Council of Constance (1415) condemned him to death by fire.

Though Hus depended on Scripture for his position on the issues he addressed, he relied on ancient expositors of the church for help in arriving at the correct interpretations. He found particular help from Augustine. To give the force of reality to his arguments, however, he made frequent reference to the checkered history of the church and the abuses of the papacy in particular.[39] He drew a clear line between the authority of Scripture and the authority of the fathers and the doctors of the church: "If any one venerate any other scriptures than these which the catholic church has received or has handed down to be held as authoritative, let him be anathema."[40]

The papal system had produced priests who used Scripture selectively, ignoring passages that created inconvenience by calling for "the imitation of Christ" and setting them aside "as not pertaining to salvation."[41] The clergy had assumed power belonging only to God, and Hus argued that by resisting the errors of the church a person did not "resist the ordinance of God but the abuse of power."[42] Hus and those in sympathy with him considered the abuses of the church "a plague, which is at variance with the Gospel," and they sought "to cure this infection by the Word of the Lord. . . ."[43] Hus himself viewed this plague of ecclesiastical abuse as the fulfillment of apostolic prophecy (Matt. 24:15; Mark 13:14; 2 Tim. 4:1–4; cf. Dan. 11:31–32).[44]

In the face of flagrant abuses and corruption in the church, obvious to all who saw the three rival popes, where might a person go for authoritative guidance in salvation and matters spiritual? Hus answered clearly in De Ecclesia:

> And for the reason that believing is an act of faith, that is, to put trust in—*fidere*—therefore know that to believe that which is necessary for a man to secure blessedness is to adhere firmly and without wavering to the truth spoken as by God. For this truth, because of its certitude, a man ought to expose his life to the danger of death. And, in this way, every Christian is expected to believe explicitly and implicitly all the truth which the Holy Spirit has put in Scripture, and in this way a man is not bound to believe the sayings of the saints which are apart from Scripture, nor should he believe papal bulls, except in so far as they speak out of Scripture, or in so far as what they say is founded in Scripture simply.[45]

Hus exposed his life to danger for his views about the authority of Scripture, and he was eventually burned at the stake as a heretic.

Luther. Luther did not realize until his debate with John Eck at Leipzig that he was continuing the line of thought advocated by Hus.[46] He had come to his convictions about the priority of Scripture in his pursuit of salvation, a pursuit that would lead him to an understanding of the doctrine of justification by faith.[47] His authoritative guide to faith came from Scripture, which he regarded not so much an article of faith as a guide to faith. He rejected the allegorical exegesis of the Middle Ages in favor of a grammatical-historical interpretation that focused on the centrality of Christ in Scripture.

Luther's view of the centrality of Scripture contained a tension between Scripture as authoritative and Scripture that depended on its witness to Christ for its authority.[48] The gospel message itself made Scripture authoritative for Luther and was the source of apostolic authority. For this reason James was an "epistle of straw" for Luther because it did not have the gospel as he understood it at its core.[49] People meet Christ through his Scriptures enlivened by his Spirit. The gospel, then, became the standard for Luther's ongoing critique of the church.

While the methodology of the scholastics placed philosophy functionally in authority over Scripture, Luther's stress on the priority of Scripture forced a rethinking of theological method and theological dogmatic. He spent most of his thirty-two years as a professor lecturing on the Old Testament.[50] He avoided system-building as he remained a biblical theologian. As a biblical theologian rather than a scholastic theologian, Luther rejected dependence on philosophy, particularly Aristotelian philosophy, in the interpretation of Scripture.[51] In this regard, Luther did not argue for the authority of Scripture. Rather, he argued from the authority of Scripture. Other matters were open to debate, but not this doctrine. The gospel held priority and authority over the church, not vice versa. The ministry of the Word, because of the priority of the Word, constituted the highest office in the church in Luther's theology.[52] Through the preaching of the gospel found in Scripture, faith arose in the hearts of those who heard.

Zwingli. While Luther set Scripture at the forefront of theological discussion in Germany, Ulrich Zwingli did the same in Switzerland. Zwingli came to his view of Scripture by way of Erasmian humanism, through which he had gained a profound appreciation for the Greek New Testament.[53] His movement from humanist to "protestant" reached a decisive point in 1516, when he resolved "to learn the doctrine of God direct from his own Word" rather than from the traditions of the church.[54]

Zwingli saw himself in a crusade to "rescue the Sacred Writings so wickedly tortured" by the preaching of the mendicant friars.[55] In his reply to the "Admonition of the Bishop of Constance," Zwingli challenged his opponents to debate him openly "and to show definitely by the authority of Scripture, where and in what I had done wrong!"[56] While Zwingli led the reformation of Zurich in a variety of directions, the driving issue in his reform of the church and its relationship to society rested on the principle of *sola scriptura* ("Scripture alone") as the basis for authority. This principle emerged from the pursuit of the ultimate question, "How might a person know the way to eternal happiness?"

Zwingli explained that since creation, people have sought happiness that lasts beyond the grave. While the philosophers offered too many divergent opinions to guide one to happiness, Zwingli complained of similar "confusion and vagueness" that come from the guidance of Christians who advise "human tradition" and "human notions" instead of the "mercy and promises of God."[57] As a result, Zwingli decided "to have trust in nothing and in no words so much as in those which proceeded out of the mouth of the Lord" as his guide to eternal happiness.[58] Zwingli believed that the Bible had supreme authority in the church because God had spoken it. Thus, he insisted that "to this treasure, namely, the certainty of God's word, must our hearts be guided."[59] With Scripture as the foundational integrating element for his theology, Zwingli used it as his "touchstone" for assessing all the teachings and practices of the church. This approach guided him and his followers to "eternal happiness" through "the freedom of the Gospel, for by that alone are we saved."[60]

Concluding observations. During the late Middle Ages, culminating in the Reformation, the church suffered from a credibility gap in spiritual authority. With the scandal of multiple popes, a schism between the Eastern and Western churches, the sale of indulgences, the neglect of preaching, and the corruption of morals within the priesthood, people sought a source of sure guidance in salvation. The Bible provided the authoritative guidance many sought as the medieval order and its institutions were collapsing. The problem of authority, which the Reformers solved by turning to Scripture, was the "fundamental issue of the Reformation," though it quickly moved on to other issues, once Scripture supplied it with a foundation.[61]

SCRIPTURE AND FULFILLMENT AS GOOD NEWS

With the rise of fundamentalism and evangelicalism, Scripture once again became the organizing principle of a theological perspective. Fundamentalism grew up as a movement within what were then called the evangelical denominations of Protestantism as a response to some views of the Bible emerging from higher critical study in the late nineteenth century. Besides the views of Scripture circulating in scholarly theological circles, fundamentalism also addressed broader cultural belief systems that began to arise as rivals to Scripture in the interpretation of reality. Darwinian evolution and Freudian psychology posed threats to the literal interpretation of the creation narratives and to the necessity of the existence of a Creator.

In terms of evangelism, Billy Graham brought his gospel messages from the perspective of the Bible as his organizing principle. While he preached Christ as the content of his message, he always used as his authority the phrase that runs through decades of his preaching: "The Bible says."

Fulfillment as the doorway for the gospel took on renewed importance through the efforts of Jews for Jesus in the latter half of the twentieth century. This organization, led by a converted Jew named Moishe Rosen, has as its primary purpose the evangelism of Jews. The theme sounded throughout their printed material presents Jesus as the fulfillment of the promises of God to the Jews.

While the church has held the Scriptures in reverence since the closing of the canon, the Bible has not always received the same emphasis. Its significance has taken on special meaning not only as the means to the good news, but also as an aspect of the good news. The idea of the existence of holy writings that reveal God, God's will, and the way to peace with God constitutes good news. Several major themes have emerged over the last two thousand years related to the Scriptures, which constitute good news.

Continuity

The early church took great comfort in the continuity of the gospel with the faith of Israel as demonstrated by the fulfillment of prophecy. For its adherents, Christianity had not appeared on the scene as one of a number of mystery religions in the first century. Rather, it stood as the culmination of the hope and faith of Israel. Jesus had not founded a new religion. He had completed an ancient religion that the church traced back through his genealogy to the patriarchs and, indeed, to the dawn of time.

Jesus Christ had a historical context to which the apostles bore witness, but he also had an eternal context to which the Law and the Prophets bore witness. This context placed Jesus in the same category as the Exodus; in Jesus God had acted. The appeal to Scripture pointed to the eternal context because fulfillment served to justify both the truth claim of Jesus as Messiah and the truth claim of the Bible as revelation from God. The fulfillment of Scripture in Christ demonstrated the truth that Jesus was the Messiah, and the fulfillment of Scripture in Christ demonstrated the truth that the Bible came from God and could be relied upon.

Faithfulness of God

Fulfillment also makes a strong statement about the faithfulness of God. The God of Abraham, Isaac, and Jacob revealed in the Torah is a God who makes and keeps promises. In writing to the Gentiles, who did not have the benefit of schooling in the Law, Paul tended to speak of the prophecies as the "promises." To a people who understood deity in terms of the caprices and treachery of the mythological pantheon, the idea of a faithful God who kept promises would have come as good news indeed. Fulfillment makes a strong statement about the character of God.[62]

The ancient conceptions of a god who cannot be trusted persist in our modern day with new mythologies to bolster them. The faithfulness of God in keeping promises argues against a view of deity or fate or karma that operates in a capricious or meaningless fashion. Fulfillment speaks of a personal God who cares about people and who takes care that his word means something. A God who keeps his word is a God whose Word is worth hearing.

Nature of God

Fulfillment of prophecy also speaks about the kind of God that exists. It speaks of a God who communicates with people, who takes the initiative in communication. Thus, Scripture comes as revelation rather than simply as human response to the experience of the Holy Other. While the experience of God may elicit a response that words cannot adequately utter, fulfillment speaks of a clear message communicated by God and presented through the means of a human servant who committed the message to writing.

From a backwards perspective, fulfillment makes the case for the kind of God who can communicate what will happen and who can then cause it to happen so that people will recognize fulfillment has occurred. Peter preached to a crowd who believed such things on the day of Pentecost. Such a belief system runs radically counter to the modern worldview. As the modern world gives way to the postmodern world, however, such a worldview and such a God are not necessarily irrational concepts. Fulfillment implies a personal God who cares enough about people to communicate with them and to maintain relationship with them.

Authority

In times of great social upheaval accompanied by the collapse of cultural norms and institutions, people have often sought a source of authority for ordering their lives. Scripture presents itself as a sure authoritative guide for people without one. The idea of fulfillment takes Scripture outside the realm of subjective or even culturally bound expressions of spiritual experience by pointing to a source outside itself for its own authority.

Scripture depends for its authority on the God who inspired its writings rather than on those who committed it to writing. Augustine considered the Bible "unworthy in comparison with the dignity of Cicero" until he understood that the Bible spoke to something far deeper than the superficial gratification of reader response.[63] This earlier comment of Augustine resembles certain late twentieth-century evaluations of the Bible by readers who view the Bible's value only in terms of its literary style.[64] Rather than being a piece of creative literary composition, however, the Bible presents itself as God's revelation confirmed by fulfillment of his promises from the patriarchal period through apostolic times. The authority of Scripture lies in the One who expresses himself through it, not in the humans by whose hands it was delivered. Thus, Luther's concern that the authority of Scripture lies in its presentation of the gospel parallels a twentieth-century concern for the authority of Scripture. Regardless of higher critical issues of authorship or redaction, the Bible's authority depends on God as revealer rather than on the church as receiver.

Fulfillment sets Scripture apart from other sacred writings as a source of authority and a guide to God. The appeal to tradition gives it no more authority than the appeal to tradition of other ancient texts by the faith groups that follow these texts. The reading of Scripture has proven to be the greatest door of faith to the people of Muslim and Buddhist backgrounds, while in preliterate societies, the repetition of the biblical story has a powerful impact.[65] The assertions of authority give no more authority to Scripture than such assertions give to other sacred texts. The authority for Scripture comes in the fulfillment of the promises of God attested by Scripture.[66]

Epistemology

The notion of fulfillment challenges the popular cultural notions of what can be known and how one can know. Fulfillment makes a case for revelation and the kind of God who reveals things that he has the power to bring to pass. Apart from such a reality, the gospel message does not have the same force outside the cultural context of habitual Christianity.

Scripture contains within it the recognition that anyone can make truth claims of spiritual experience that have authority for others. That is, anyone can say that they speak for God. Israel even had the institution of the professional prophet, who had a place within the cultural system to speak a word from God when a word in time served a political purpose (1 Kings 22:1–38; Amos 7:12–14). How could people know if the word spoken actually came from the Lord? After all, people believe what they want to believe. The mob follows the one who yells the loudest. Why should one religious zealot be followed rather than another? Following the tradition of Moses, however, someone was accepted as a speaker for God if their word came to pass (Deut. 18:18–22). Only what God had revealed could come to pass. Thus, Israel followed a form of verification in the assembling of the scrolls that formed Scripture. Fulfillment meant that God had spoken through a prophet, and whatever that prophet had to say from the Lord could be trusted. For Israel, it was an empirical way of proving that empiricism is not the only way of knowing. God speaks of the things that cannot be known otherwise.

NOTES

1. The origin of this prophesy remains a puzzle. In the first century, prophecy was not understood to mean only the specific books of the prophets.

2. The exact number may vary, depending on how one counts the Scripture fragments that Paul occasionally joins together.

3. Justin, *Dialogue*, 7.1.198.

4. Some scholars consider the episode a literary invention. See Erwin R. Goodenough, *The Theology of Justin Martyr* (Amsterdam: Philo Press, 1968), 58–63. Goodenough considers the conversation a literary conversation of the time to describe the movement from one school of thought to another in the form of an idealized conversation. For a more traditional view, see L. W. Barnard, *Justin Martyr: His Life and Thought* (Cambridge: Cambridge Univ. Press, 1967), 8–11. Barnard argues that the conversation "has the ring of truth" and that the eclectic philosophical training was typical of the day. Neither of these views, however, suggests the most compelling argument for literature of this type. One must look elsewhere than pagan literature for an example of the form Justin follows. By this time the Christian form of conversation testimony had been well established. The kind of detail and situation described fit the form of recounting significant passages in one's conversion.

5. Justin, *First Apology*, 31.

6. Timothy David Barnes, *Tertullian: A Historical and Literary Study* (Oxford: Clarendon, 1971), 91.

7. Tertullian, *Against Marcion*, 4.4.

8. Tertullian, *Apology, De Spectaculus*, trans. T. R. Glover and Minuscius Felix; *Octavius*, trans. Gerald H. Rendall (Loeb Classical Library; Cambridge, Mass: Harvard Univ. Press, 1966), 199.

9. Ibid., 201.

10. Ibid., 205.

11. Tertullian, *The Prescription Against Heretics*, 7.

12. Barnes, *Tertullian*, 131–32.

13. Justo L. Gonzalez, *A History of Christian Thought* (Nashville: Abingdon, 1970), 1.217.

14. Origen, *Contra Celsum*, trans. Henry Chadwick (Cambridge: Cambridge Univ. Press, 1953), ix.

15. Implications of this idea will be explored in chapter 9.

16. Origen, *Contra Celsum*, 458.

17. Ibid., 395.

18. Ibid.

19. Ibid., 12.

20. Eusebius, *The Proof of the Gospel*, ed. and trans. W. J. Ferrar (Grand Rapids: Baker, 1981; reprint of New York: Macmillan, 1920), xiii.

21. Ibid., 1.

22. Ibid., 2.

23. Ibid., xiv.

24. Ibid., 5.

25. Ibid., 7.

26. G. H. W. Parker, *The Morning Star* (Grand Rapids: Eerdmans, 1965), 21–26.

27. John Wycliff, *Select English Writings*, ed. Herbert E. Winn (Oxford: Oxford Univ. Press, 1929), xxviii.

28. Ibid., 118.

29. See George Maculey Trevelyan, *England in the Age of Wycliffe* (New York: Longmans, Green and Co., 1935), 111–41.

30. Ibid., xxvi.

31. Wycliff, "The Church and Her Members," *Select English Writings*, 132.

32. John Stacy, *John Wycliff and Reform* (Philadelphia: Westminster, 1964), 81, 94.

33. Ibid., 80.

34. Wycliff, "The Church and Her Members," 138.

35. Ibid., 136.

36. Stacy, *John Wycliff and Reform*, 99.

37. Matthew Spinka, *John Hus's Concept of the Church* (Princeton: Princeton Univ. Press, 1966), 10.

38. John Hus, *The Church*, trans. David S. Schaff (Westport, Ct.: Greenwood, 1976), xii–xxii.

39. Schaff argues that "Hus used history to prove the truth of Scripture" (see ibid., xxxvii).

40. Ibid., 132.

41. Ibid., 112.

42. Ibid., 114.

43. Ibid., 118.

44. Ibid., 241–42, 253.

45. Ibid., 71.

46. Timothy George, *Theology of the Reformers* (Nashville: Broadman Press, 1988), 80.

47. Timothy George argues that Luther's understanding of justification emerged from his growing reliance on Scripture (see ibid., 63–69). Rupert Davis, on the other hand, argues that Luther's reliance on Scripture emerged from the experience of justification (see his *The Problem of Authority in the Continental Reformers* [London: Epworth, 1946], 27).

48. Willem Jan Kooiman, *Luther and the Bible*, trans. John Schmidt (Philadelphia: Muhlenberg, 1961), 225–39.

49. George, *Theology of the Reformers*, 84.

50. Heinrich Bornkamm, *Luther and the Old Testament*, trans. Eric W. and Ruth C. Gritech (Philadelphia: Fortress, 1969), 7.

51. George, *Theology of the Reformers*, 57–58.

52. Ibid., 97. George observes that "the principle of *sola scriptura* was intended to safeguard the authority of Scripture from that servile dependence upon the church which in fact made Scripture inferior to the church," 81.

53. Ibid., 112. See also Kurt Aland, *Four Reformers: Luther, Melanchthon, Calvin, Zwingli*, trans. James L. Schaaf (Minneapolis: Augsburg Publishing House, 1979), 90–91.

54. George, *Theology of the Reformers*, 113; Aland, *Four Reformers*, 93.

55. Samuel Macauley Jackson, ed., *Ulrich Zwingli: Early Writings* (Durham, N.C.: Labyrinth, 1987; reprint of New York: G. P. Putnam's Sons, 1912), 201.

56. Ibid., 201.

57. Ibid., 203.

58. Ibid., 204.

59. Ibid., 205.

60. Ibid., 220.

61. Rupert E. Davies, *The Problem of Authority in the Continental Reformers: A Study in Luther, Zwingli, and Calvin* (London: Epworth, 1946), 11.

62. I am indebted to Liz Radic, who stressed this implication of fulfillment in a seminar presentation at Bethel Theological Seminary in the fall of 1993.

63. Augustine, *Confessions*, trans. Henry Chadwick (Oxford: Oxford Univ. Press, 1991), 40.

64. See Alan Cheuse, "Writing It Down for James: Some Thoughts on Reading Towards the Millennium" *Antioch Review* 51 (Fall, 1993): 495–96. "The organized modern religions hold no patent on expressing devotions to the universe. In fact, the pagan poets, the epic Homers of the oldest stories of the western Mediterranean, show a lot more imagination when it comes to creating great characters and overarching plots than the lyricists and lamenters of the Old and New Testaments. Some great poetry in the former, but nothing much in the latter unless you're spiritually bonded to the text. Apply the test of narrative coherence and the pagan epics win hands down. And if the response of the readers, the immersion into a story that delights and instructs in the deepest fashion we know, is any test of the presence of godliness, there's no doubt in my mind which stories shadow the mark of real deity."

65. I appreciate the insights of missiologists Herb Klem and Ronald Hill concerning recent conversion trends in predominantly Muslim and Buddhist countries. I am particularly indebted to Tint Lwin, a Ph.D. student at Southern Seminary, who helped me understand the significance of the authority of Scripture in describing his own conversion.

66. Interestingly enough, the arguments for the relativity of the Christian faith usually come in terms of the institutional structures, traditions, and violations of Scripture by Western society rather than by an examination of the claim to fulfillment. See John Hick and Paul F. Knitter, *The Myth of Christian Uniqueness* (Maryknoll, N.Y.: Orbis, 1987).

Chapter 4

Son of God/Son of David

The idea that Jesus Christ is both son of David according to the flesh and Son of God according to the Holy Spirit (Rom. 1:3–4) developed into the doctrines of the Incarnation, Christology, and, by extension, the Trinity. The Incarnation is the critical issue that separates Christianity from Judaism and Islam. The idea of the holy God taking on human flesh came as a blasphemous idea to first-century Judaism, and that verdict Islam has confirmed. This understanding of Jesus Christ as Son of God and son of David, divine and human, poses one of the greatest scandals of Christianity.

Modern scholarship has questioned whether Jesus ever represented himself as anything other than an itinerant rabbi calling people to repent. This line of thought ascribes the incarnational Christological teachings of the church as a creation of the apostles after the death of Jesus. Such an approach rests on a skeptical view of the reliability of the Gospel accounts of what Jesus actually taught, did, or represented himself to be. The response of the authorities to Jesus, however, suggests that they understood him to have blasphemed God by how he represented his relationship to God. The Sanhedrin condemned Jesus and handed him over to the Romans on a charge of blasphemy (Matt. 26:63–66; Mark 14:61–64; Luke 22:66–71). On earlier occasions the crowd had responded with hostility and tried to stone him because of his view of his relationship to God (John 8:58–59; 10:30–39). In other words, Jesus alarmed a great many people by the way he spoke of himself in relation to God, and he eventually suffered the consequences.[1]

With respect to other religions, however, the idea of deity taking human form does not seem strange. The *Bhagavad Gita* relates the story of the god Krishna, who took human form as a chariot driver for a warrior. But in Hinduism, though the gods have many avatars or manifestations, they do not partake of humanity, experiencing neither birth nor death.

Ancient Egypt regarded the pharaoh as a god dwelling in their midst. In modern times Japan has regarded the emperor as divine. The succession of monarchs over thousands of years represented the continuity of divine favor. The Romans had a much briefer experience of lunatic rulers who ascribed divinity to themselves. For the Egyptians and Japanese, the royal expression of divinity represented "god with us."

Among the mythologies of ancient Rome and Greece, as well as the mythologies of northern Europe, the gods frequently manifested themselves among humans, often for purposes of sexual entanglement. Zeus, Jupiter, and Wotan produced a troop of human offspring who animated the *Iliad*, the *Aeneid*, and the *Ring*. Mighty heroes though the offspring might have been, they did not share the nature and being of their sire. While the gods may have manifested themselves for the purpose of debauchery, they were never human. Christianity, by contrast, teaches that Jesus Christ shares the nature and being of God and that he was fully human.

Because of its affinity with the mythic accounts of divine visitation in human form, a number of scholars have taken the position that the Christian story of God's coming into the world through Jesus falls under the category of myth. Rudolph Bultmann championed the mythic nature of the stories about Jesus.[2] More recently a group of scholars explored this theme in a collaborative work, *The Myth of God Incarnate*.[3] While these schools of thought saw the affinity with myth as a reason for discounting any correlation to reality about the stories of the incarnation of Christ, an alternative view has come forward based on the same observations. J. R. R. Tolkien, the English philologist and scholar of Nordic mythology, argued in his famous evangelistic encounters with C. S. Lewis that the stories of Jesus and the Incarnation were most certainly myth, but they were the myth that actually happened. In the birth of Jesus the mythologies of the world's religions found fulfillment. This understanding proved to be a turning point in the long conversion of Lewis. As a student of classical mythology, Lewis later observed that the myths of divine visitation are a "real though unfocused gleam of divine truth falling on human imagination."[4]

The importance of the Incarnation might even be detected in religious traditions that do not incorporate mythologies of divine manifestation in human form. While the Buddhist tradition has no place for the manifestation of God since it affirms no self-conscious supreme being, it exalts the primary concept and logic of incarnation, if such a being existed. In the story of Gotama and how he became the Buddha, the necessary fact of his progress was the act of leaving his palace home and the security his royal father provided. In a sense, Buddha was a type of Christ and the Incarnation. Both entered a world of suffering. Only through entering an alien world and experiencing it could they be of help to others. In this sense, the incarnation of Jesus Christ fulfills the concerns of Buddhist thought.

Unlike the divine visitations of other religions, the doctrine of the Incarnation in Christianity makes a profound statement about the value of personhood and individual identity. This affirmation finds further confirmation in the resurrection of individual persons and the completing of their perfection by the Spirit. This notion contrasts sharply with belief systems such as Hinduism and Buddhism, where the loss of personhood represents the ideal.

The New Testament elaborates several ways in which the Incarnation represented good news for people. Jesus Christ as Son of God and son of David had implications for salvation that moved on several planes. Because of the inherent affirmation of the physical world by the Incarnation, however, the good news of Jesus Christ has implications for the physical as well as the spiritual well-being of people.

BIBLICAL BACKGROUND

Long before the church had developed doctrines of the Incarnation or Christology, the church proclaimed Jesus as Son of God and son of David. *Kerygma* and *didache* grew up together as the church both proclaimed that God had come in the flesh and struggled to explain what that assertion meant. For different audiences the apostles explained the significance of the Incarnation from different perspectives. That is, how they explained the person of Christ had more to do with their audience than with them. At issue was the question Jesus had raised at Caesarea Philippi: "Who do you say I am?" (Matt. 16:15). Matthew and Luke approached the issue in terms of the fulfillment of Scripture, describing the circumstances surrounding the birth of Jesus before elaborating the implications of his coming. John and Paul, on the other hand, ignored the circumstances of the birth of Jesus as they described the Incarnation theologically in terms of its meaning in life for people.

The Gospels

The Evangelists wrote the Gospels from the perspective of faith in the One who had risen from the dead. Any discussion of their notion of the Incarnation or Christology must proceed from the conclusion of the Gospels rather than from the beginning. After the resurrection, the followers of Jesus testified to him as "My Lord and my God!" (John 20:28). Modern scholarship has tended to neglect the significance of the experience of the resurrection in assessing the sense in which the Gospel writers understood the relationship between Jesus Christ and God. While the modern world concerns itself with the problem of how a human being could be divine, the first generation church had an entirely different problem. After the resurrection, they had to make a case for the humanity of Christ!

Bultmann and others have proceeded from the assumption that the birth narratives of Matthew and Luke were creations of the early church to establish the divine origin of Jesus.[5] Mark and John, however, present the divine relationship of Jesus and God without recourse to the account of his birth. Other writers of the New Testament present unambiguously high Christologies without mentioning the birth of Jesus. Rather than proving the divinity of Christ, the birth narratives function to demonstrate that the One who rose from the dead was fully and truly human in addition to his divine relationship.[6] Unlike the mythologies of the ancient world that pictured divine visitations in human form and the endless cycle of nature gods who died and rose with the seasons, Jesus Christ was fully human from birth to death in spite of his relationship to God which was made evident by the resurrection.

The Gospels proceed from the assumption that the Christ who arose is divine. They collect witnesses who name Jesus as Son of God. In the birth narratives, the angels announce the divine origin of the infant (Matt. 1:21; Luke 1:32). At the baptism (Matt. 3:17; Mark 1:11; Luke 3:22; cf. John 1:32–34) and at the Transfiguration (Matt 17:5; Mark 9:7; Luke 9:35), the Synoptic Gospels indicate that God bore witness to Jesus as the Son of God. In the temptation, Satan acknowledged his divine identity (Matt. 4:3, 6; Luke 4:3, 9). The demons who were subject to his authority declared his relationship to God (Mark 3:11; cf. 5:7). Even before the resurrection, those closest to him began to believe in his divine origin (Matt. 16:16; cf. Mark 8:29; Luke 9:20; John 11:27). This growing issue of his identity formed the central charge against him by the religious authorities (Mark 14:61–62). And even his death led one of his Roman executioners to wonder at his origin (Mark 15:39).

Though the Synoptics proceed from the assumption of the deity of Christ and give evidence to support their view, their accounts of Jesus focus on his human experiences and emotions as support for the idea of a true incarnation. John's Gospel, on the other hand, proceeds with a different purpose, writing to prove that Jesus is the Son of God (John 20:31).[7] In contrast to the lunatic emperors who claimed divinity, Jesus appears in John's Gospel as one free of the character flaws that typified the human-form gods of Asia Minor. Unlike the Synoptic writers, who nuanced their Gospels to show that Jesus Christ had really come in the flesh, John nuanced his Gospel to show qualitatively why the claims of the deity of Christ should be taken more seriously than the claims to deity by Caesar.

The Gospels describe Jesus as one who could heal all manner of illness, raise the dead, cast out demons, and perform a variety of "signs and wonders." The miracles appear as evidence of his divine origin and relationship to God, for through them Jesus exercised authority that could only be credited to God.[8] Besides healing, Jesus also forgave sin (Matt. 9:4–8; Mark 2:5; Luke 5:20–21). In connection with healing on the Sabbath, Jesus declared himself "Lord of the Sabbath" (Matt. 12:1–13; Mark 2:23–3:6; Luke 6:1–11). He indicated that these manifestations of power and authority formed the evidence that he was "the one who was to come" (Matt. 11:1–6; Luke 7:18–23; cf. 4:16–21). John's Gospel reports that at the Last Supper, Jesus pointed to his miracles as a demonstration of his relationship to the Father (John 14:8–11).

The Gospels also depict Jesus as someone subject to all the effects of human frailty. He wept, he hungered, he thirsted, he grew tired, he slept, he ate. His birth and death unmistakably place Jesus in the mass of humanity. By his baptism, Jesus identified with humanity. In his temptation, he was revealed as one who labored under the weight of humanity and had the true experience of temptation. Temptation came not only in the desert following his baptism (Matt. 4:1–11; Mark 1:12–13; Luke 4:1–13), but also following Peter's confession at Caesarea Philippi (Matt. 16:21–23; Mark 8:31–33) and in the Garden of Gethsemane (Matt. 26:36–42; Mark 14:32–40; Luke 22:39–44). In their accounts of temptation, the Gospels particularly portray the anguish of Jesus until the temptation passes. In all the cases, the temptation took the form of avoiding the path to the cross, the path to death. Thus, the essential temptation was not to have a true incarnation. By avoiding death, Jesus would not have experienced true humanity.

Christ's temptation must be seen in the context of his mission. Apart from it, the human/divine relationship of Christ has no meaning. The Gospels indicate that Jesus had a keen sense of mission. According to Matthew 4:17, he began his public preaching following his temptation in the desert with the message, "Repent, for the kingdom of heaven is near." The advent of the kingdom came in the ministry of Jesus (Matt. 4:23–24; Mark 3:7–12; Luke 4:18).[9] He went about his ministry as someone who had a crucial job to do, and everything depended on his completing that job (John 5:36; 9:4–5). He expressed that mission in a variety of ways in different circumstances:

- For the Son of Man came to seek and to save what was lost. (Luke 19:10)
- I have come that they may have life, and have it to the full. (John 10:10b)
- "The Spirit of the Lord is on me,
    because he has anointed me
    to preach good news to the poor.
  He has sent me to proclaim freedom for the prisoners
    and recovery of sight for the blind,
  to release the oppressed,
    to proclaim the year of the Lord's favor."
  (Luke 4:18–19)

- I have not come to call the righteous, but sinners to repentance. (Luke 5:32; cf. Matt. 9:13; Mark 2:17)

All four Gospels agree that the death of Jesus formed the culmination and completion of his mission, and they ascribe this interpretation of the mission to Jesus, especially in the Passion predictions (Matt. 16:21–28; 17:22–23; 20:18–19; Mark 8:31; 9:9, 31; 10:33–34; Luke 9:22, 44; 18:31–33; cf. John 3:14; 8:28; 10:11; 12:31–33). The anguish of Gethsemane suggests a mission that only Jesus could complete, for it was a cup only he could drink (Matt. 26:42; Mark 14:35–36; Luke 22:42–44). The divine mission was accomplished through a human life and death.

General Apostolic Writings

While the Gospels have a point of view about the divine/human relationship of Jesus, they primarily narrate his story. In the letters, on the other hand, little narration occurs. In these books, the early followers of Jesus explain the significance of the divine and the human coming together in Jesus. Several major themes that relate to the Incarnation recur in the New Testament literature.

Identification. Through Jesus, God identified with the human race. Paul described Christ as exchanging wealth for poverty for the sake of the human race (2 Cor. 8:9). Despite his divine form, Christ fully identified with the human race to the ultimate human experience of death (Phil. 2:5–8). The idea of God's taking on human frailty and experiencing true humanity has enormous implications for how God views people. By virtue of living the life of a human being all the way to death, Jesus Christ brings to the Godhead the experiential knowledge of the human race. Hebrews stresses that Christ "partook of the same nature" as people in order to face the death they face (Heb. 2:14–15). As a result of complete identification with the human race, Christ has a capacity for mercy and help to people that arises from sharing human suffering and temptation (2:16–18). Unlike the mythical avatars of the ancient religions, the followers of Jesus stressed that he had fully identified with the human race (1 John 5:6).

Reconciliation. By virtue of his full identification with the human race through Christ, God brought reconciliation with humanity.

Christianity presupposes an alienation of God and humanity that has its cause in human rejection of God. Even religions that profess a unity of all spirits address the issue of human alienation, though in terms that do not affirm physical existence. Paul taught that God took the initiative in reconciliation in Christ himself (2 Cor. 5:19). By implication, Paul stressed that the reconciliation of God and humanity forms the basis for reconciliation among people (Eph. 2:14–16). The fullness of God dwelt in Christ, and by virtue of this coexistence the alienation of the divine and human came to an end, Christ becoming the one through whom reconciliation is extended to all creation (Col. 1:19–22).

Example. While a theory of the atonement is associated with the example of Christ, the example of Christ might more properly be seen as a dimension of the Incarnation. The example of the divine emptying himself to take on the form of a servant in human likeness provided the early church with a basis for living their lives in humility, obedience, and service to others (Phil. 2:5–8). The life of Christ provided his followers with a concrete example of how to lead a life without sin or deceit. The Incarnation personified the will of God and provided people with a standard for living (1 Peter 2:21). By adopting Christ's attitude toward suffering, his followers had a basis for keeping destructive desires in perspective to the will of God (1 Peter 4:1–6). Conformity to the standard of Christ established by his teachings and his life provided his followers with a standard by which they could assess the genuineness of their profession of faith. The first followers of Jesus believed that faith in Christ should result in a life resembling the life of Christ (1 John 2:3–6).

Revelation of God. The early church believed that Jesus presented the clearest revelation of God. Hebrews begins with the assertion that Christ was a superior revelation to the prophets of Israel (Heb. 1:1–2). The signs and wonders that accompanied the ministry of Christ served as divine authentication of the ultimacy of his revelation (2:3–4). Whereas the transcendent power of God cannot be seen, Jesus could be seen. For the early church, Jesus represented God's self-disclosure (2:8b–10).

This concern for the concrete manifestation of God also formed the introduction to 1 John. In contrast with the esoteric understanding of the knowledge of God offered by Gnostic conceptions of the first century, the church's point of view stressed the importance of the physical manifestation of God. This manifestation provided the first Christians with an objective basis for knowing that God had actually done something about salvation (1 John 1:1–3). Jesus gave to his followers a personal and informed knowledge of God that proceeded from his intimate relationship and identification with the Father. The Johannine letters reflect the teaching found on the lips of Jesus in John's Gospel, that those who had seen the Son had seen the Father (John 14:9; cf. 8:55; 10:30, 38); thus, to deny the manifestation of Christ in the flesh is to deny God (2 John 7–9). Since Jesus came as the full revelation of God, those who reject Jesus have rejected the clearest possible vision of the heart and character of God the Father (1 John 2:22–23; 4:2–3a). Perhaps the ultimate expression of this revelation is the depth of love it represents, for to the early church the entry of the divine into human affairs represented a sacrifice of love:

This is how God showed his love among us: He sent his one and only Son into the world that we might live through him. (1 John 4:9; cf. John 3:16; Rom. 5:8)

Doing what no one else could do. The apostolic literature bears consistent testimony that because of the coming together of the divine and human, Christ could do what no one else could do for the salvation of the world. His uniqueness as Son of God and son of David provided the means for accomplishing salvation.

This theme finds major expression in the Pauline letters, which declare that by sending his Son in the flesh and condemning sin in the flesh, God has done "what the law . . . weakened by the sinful nature," could not do (Rom. 8:3). That is, because of the weakened state of people bound by sin, only God could fulfill the righteousness of the law (8:4; cf. Matt. 5:17). In Galatians 4:4 Paul stresses that because of Christ's identification with those born under the law, he was able to do for people what no one else could do. Only the unique relationship of Christ to God and humanity created the means for him to serve as the "mediator" in reconciliation, God having taken the initiative in Christ to recover his own people (1 Tim. 2:5–6).

Since the destruction of death and the powers of darkness could only be accomplished by God, God chose to deliver people from the bondage of fear and death by sharing the human experience and by conquering them through Christ's death (Heb. 2:14–15). Through sharing the human experience in every respect, Christ could, as a human being, make atonement on behalf of people. And because of his divine nature, he could make sufficient atonement (2:16–18). God made perfection a concrete reality rather than a theoretical ideal by demonstrating the obedience of faith in the face of suffering and adversity (5:7–8).

The apostles boldly asserted that Christ had always been God's intended means of salvation and redemption. Although God had dealt with people in a variety of ways (Heb. 1:1), he intended to deal with the problem of sin by coming and settling matters through Christ (1 Peter 1:20). No one else could do it. Only Christ could take away sin, because only Christ had no sin of his own (1 John 3:5). He came into the world as the only One who could destroy the devil and his works. God destroyed the enemy from within the human experience (3:8).

Expression of love. All of the above-mentioned themes relate to the concrete expression of love by God. In the New Testament, love is not so much an emotion as it is an action. Love is what one does in spite of the consequences, not because of the rewards. The apostles spoke of the coming of Christ as an expression of God's love. Ultimately, love saw expression most in the cross, but the cross had no eternal significance apart from God's presence in Christ. Thus, Paul wrote that the death of Christ demonstrates the love of God rather than the love of Jesus (Rom. 5:8). For John, the Son came as a gift from God because of his love (John 3:16). God sent the Son to die in order to express love for a world that did not return that love (1 John 4:9–10). Without the Incarnation, the cross becomes a cruel story of God's allowing Jesus to suffer for the world. A faulty understanding of the Incarnation creates a faulty understanding of the Fatherhood of God. Rather than a father who stands idly by while his children are in trouble, however, the Incarnation teaches that the Father delivers the child from trouble, because "God was *in* Christ" (2 Cor. 5:19, KJV).

HISTORICAL/THEOLOGICAL DEVELOPMENT

For a period of about 350 years, a series of challenges to the proclamation of Jesus as Son of God and son of David arose within the church. The controversies generally attacked this element of the gospel in terms of either the deity, the humanity, or the natures of Christ. In the early second century, for example, the Ebionites denied the genuineness of his deity, while in the early fourth century the Arians denied the completeness of his deity. In the second century the Docetists denied the genuineness of his humanity, while in the fourth century the Apollinarians denied the completeness of his humanity. In the fifth century the Nestorians denied the genuineness of a union of his two natures, while the Eutychians denied the completeness of his two natures (see Fig. 4-A).

These controversies have been treated extensively elsewhere and need not be repeated in detail here, but a brief description of the role played by the theme of Jesus Christ as Son of God and son of David will demonstrate how one element of the gospel could form the critical theological motif for the church for an entire era.

Irenaeus

Methodologically, Irenaeus proceeded in a fashion similar to his immediate predecessors, Justin Martyr and the apologists. He demonstrated the proof of the gospel through demonstrating its fulfillment of the ancient prophecies of Israel. In his *Proof of the Apostolic Preaching* he relied largely on Old Testament texts to demonstrate that Christ fulfilled the prophecies. His preoccupying theme, however, focused on how Jesus Christ as Son of God and seed of Abraham and David filled the gap between transcendent God and sinful humanity.[10]

Irenaeus oriented his exposition of the gospel around the Incarnation at a time when a Gnostic interpretation of Christianity posed a major problem. The Gnostics held that Christ could not have had a human body because of the essential evil of matter; therefore, Christ did not experience either human birth or death. Not having died, he could not have risen. This Docetic view posed a major threat to the gospel. Against it, Irenaeus stressed the necessity of God's coming in the flesh to bring salvation. Through his theology

ISSUES IN CHRISTOLOGY/INCARNATION

DEITY

Ebionites
(A.D. 107)
- Deny the Genuineness of His Deity
- Adoption

Arians
(Council of Nicea, A.D. 325)
- Deny the Completeness of His Deity
- The Son Has a Beginning

HUMANITY

Docetists
(A.D. 70–170)

- Deny the Genuineness of His Humanity
- Only Seemed to Be a Man

Apollinarians
(Council of Constantinople, A.D. 381)

- Deny the Completeness of His Humanity
- Half-Man and Half-God
- Flesh & Logos vs. Flesh & Mind

NATURES

Nestorians
(Council of Ephesus, A.D. 431)
- Divide His Person
- Two Separate Persons in Christ
- No Intrinsic Union

Eutychians
(Council of Chalcedon, A.D. 451)
- Confuse His Natures
- Only One Nature After Incarnation
- From Two Natures, but in One Nature

Monarchianism	—	God in a Human Body
Dynamic Monarchianism	—	Man Adopted by God
Sabellianism	—	One God in Three Temporary Manifestations
Patripassianism	—	Jesus Identified with the Father
Monophysitism	—	Only One Nature: Divine
Monotheletism	—	Two Natures, One Will

(FIGURE 4-A)

of recapitulation, Irenaeus explained that Christ summed up all of human history, undoing the Fall.[11] He reasoned:

> So he united man with God and brought about the communion of God and man, we being unable in any otherwise to have part in incorruptibility, had it not been for His coming to us. For incorruptibility, while invisible and imperceptible, would not help us; so He became visible, that we might be taken into full communication with incorruptibility.[12]

Apart from God's coming personally in the flesh, he could not engage death or triumph over it in the resurrection. Without the resurrection and the conquest of death, people would remain subject to death. Aulén has pointed out how this emphasis of Irenaeus on the Incarnation results in a wedding with the atonement, rather than the opposition that has occurred between the two doctrines in liberal Protestantism and Anglo-Catholicism.[13]

Athanasius and Nicea

Arius of Alexandria (250–336) did more, perhaps, to make the Incarnation a focal point of the gospel than any other theologian of the first Christian millennium. He made it an issue because of what he did *not* believe. To the orthodox believers, what he did not believe robbed the church of her Savior. When the great council met at Nicea to consider his assertions and the answers of Bishop Alexander, they met to answer the question, "Who can truly save us?"[14]

Though the Council of Nicea in 325 reached a conclusion and affirmed that the Son was "begotten, not made" and that he was "of one substance with the Father," it did not fully settle the matter for the church. The controversy continued to rage for decades after Nicea. Athanasius, who succeeded Alexander as Bishop of Alexandria in 328, championed the cause of the Nicene faith because of the necessity of a true incarnation of God for salvation.[15] Athanasius approached the issue of the relationship between the Father and the Son as a soteriological issue; it was a matter of salvation. If God has not come in Christ and Christ is only a divine creature, then God has remained aloof and Christ has not revealed God at all, much less redeemed humanity.

Even before the outbreak of the Arian heresy, Athanasius had stressed that the "Word of the Father," who had been "from the beginning," was "manifested to us in a human body for our salvation."[16] In his treatise "On the Incarnation of the Word," he laid out the reasons why the church believed in the unity of the Father and the Son while affirming both the true divinity and true humanity of Christ:

> For being Word of the Father, and above all, He alone of natural fitness was both able to recreate everything, and worthy to suffer on behalf of all and to be ambassador for all with the Father.[17]

The early work of Athanasius assumes this relationship between the Father and the Son and argues from that position.

With the new status of Christianity under the emperors Constantine and Constantius, however, the forces of polytheism ceased to exercise the same kind of pressure on Christianity from without. In this more relaxed climate, instead of proclaiming how the Son of God saved, the speculative theologians of the East turned to the philosophical question of the precise manner in which Jesus was the Son of God. When the Arian party grew in strength after Nicea, Athanasius devoted his energies to a defense of the Nicene understanding of the relationship between the Father and the Son. If Christ were only a creature, no matter how prominent, he could not have triumphed over sin and death,

> For if He were a creature, he would have been holden by death; but if He was not holden by death, according to the Scriptures, he is not a creature, but the Lord of the creatures, and the subject of this immortal feast.[18]

A number of conservative bishops from Asia who had supported the Nicene formulation at the Council of Nicea later opposed Athanasius at the instigation of the Arian party, who succeeded in confusing the issues with the earlier Sabellian controversy. Eusebius of Caesarea, the church historian, was among those who took an active role in opposing the orthodox position because they failed to recognize that the playing ground had changed and the issues of the age were different.

Post-Nicene Issues

Following the death of Athanasius, the cause of Nicene faith found its ablest defense in the Cappodocian fathers—Basil of Caesarea, Gregory of Nyssa (younger brother of Basil), and Gregory of Nazianzus—who zealously opposed Arianism and advocated the Nicene viewpoint until the new emperor Theodosius used imperial power and influence to establish firmly the conclusions of the Nicene Council. These were then confirmed by the Council of Constantinople in 381. With the quieting of Arianism, however, new questions about the sense in which Christ was both Son of God and son of David arose. Constantinople also condemned the views of Apollinaris, who taught that the human mind of Jesus had been replaced by the Logos.

Speculation continued to breed controversy into the next century. Nestorius, named patriarch of Constantinople in 428, argued that Christ consisted of two eternally distinguishable natures without an intrinsic union. This view called for intimate cooperation between the human and the divine, but it did not involve the divine taking on humanity. The Council of Ephesus condemned his views in 431.

A final major issue related to the Incarnation during this period came from the views of Eutyches, who held that Christ had only one nature after the Incarnation, the human and the divine being fused into a human-divine being. Leo, the bishop of Rome, led the assault on this position, which compromised a true incarnation. The Council of Chalcedon condemned the views of Eutyches in 451 and issued a creed that affirmed the orthodox view of the issues raised about the Incarnation during the preceding century.

Assessment of the First Five Hundred Years

The Incarnation/Christology debates rocked the church during the 140 years between the Edict of Toleration for Christians issued by Constantine in 311 and the Council of Chalcedon in 451. While the issue of salvation itself lay at the root of the controversies, their occurrence illustrates how the concerns of the church shifted from a concern to proclaim the message of the Son of God/son of David to those outside the church to a concern to reflect for those inside the church on the way in which Jesus Christ was Son of God/son of

David. Disputes of this sort had arisen earlier, prior to toleration by the state, but in a political context free from the earlier cultural hostility and persecution, the church engaged in public theological speculation in a way that its mission had not previously allowed. In the process, the Eastern church showed a growing preference for a speculative/mystical approach to theology that could tolerate ambiguity, while the Western church, following Origen, demonstrated a growing preference for a systematic approach to theology that left no room for uncertainty.

Black Church Theology

Safely imbedded in the creeds since the fifth century, the element of the gospel that focused attention on the human and the divine relationship in Jesus Christ ceased to be a preeminent issue for the church. Other crises and cultural situations called for concentration on other aspects of the gospel. For over a thousand years, the Incarnation remained a foundational assumption of the faith, but one that did not serve as the integrating motif of any particular group or movement—until slavery emerged as an institution in the European colonies of North America.

The Black Church affirmed the created order, but acknowledged creation's fallen state. Slavery posed the ultimate example of the fallen state. The slaves did not spiritualize away the harshness of forced labor or the cruelty of their chains of bondage. While affirming creation, they took the Incarnation as the dominant theme of their theology, for through Christ's coming into the world, God had taken concrete action to do something about the problem. The Black Church did not concern itself with the speculative metaphysics that preoccupied the Nicene and post-Nicene fathers. Instead, it called attention to the activity of God, who would engage the problem.

The Incarnation addresses the issues of oppression, poverty, misery, suffering, hunger, and all the social ills that result from the disruption of the created order by sin. It makes a powerful statement that God cares about the physical conditions of people. The ministry of Jesus in the relief of suffering and oppression demonstrates the character of God and his intentions for people. J. G. Davies has written, "If the West emphasized the cross and the Antiochenes the resurrection, the Alexandrians concentrated upon the incarnation."[19] The Black Church in America has demonstrated an interest in recent years to find its ancient theological heritage. In a sense, it has revived the ancient concern of the African church. William Pannell and others have lamented that none of the great Western theologians have dealt with the implications of the Incarnation that the Black Church has recognized.[20] It has been left to the Black Church to safeguard the gospel from Gnosticizing tendencies that do not take the Incarnation seriously.

Black Church theology is rooted in the slavery experience where through the Incarnation, Christ fulfilled the promise of a prophet like Moses to lead the slaves to freedom. Herbert Klem has argued that in most cultures, theology is sung before it becomes systematized.[21] In the songs of faith, the Black Church continued an ancient African tradition of proclamation through song. Such songs as "Go Down, Moses" found the significance of the Incarnation in the experience of real people whom God had set free in the past. This song repeats the story of the Exodus from Egypt, a concrete act of deliverance by God. Having established a basis for hope and expectation, the song then proclaims Jesus, who came to set people free. In contrast to conceptions of the kingdom of God that focus on the sovereignty of God as Creator or the rule of Christ as the exalted Lord, the Black Church's vision of the kingdom focuses on the coming of the King to reclaim his kingdom and all that rightfully belongs to him.

Because of the Incarnation, the Black Church has experienced God as personal and approachable. At Sinai, the people of Israel were afraid to approach God, so Moses became the intermediary between God and the people. Jesus was the prophet like Moses (Deut. 18:15, 18), who now intercedes as the go-between because he shows the face of God. Jesus is approachable by everyone, which he demonstrated by those whom he embraced in his earthly ministry. He can empathize and walk with us because he knows what it is like to walk this earth. God knows human frailty not simply from omniscience, but through the experience of Jesus. Because of the Incarnation, the Black Church has experienced God as one who cares. Thomas Dorsey expressed this perspective on the gospel in his hymn, "Precious Lord, Take My Hand."

Dwight Hopkins has observed of the Black Church in its slavery period:

> Slave theology consistently experienced God dwelling with those in bondage, personal and systematic. The black religious experience prevented any separation between the sacred and the secular, the church and the community. On the contrary, in the "Invisible Institution" black theology grew out of the community and the "church." As a result, *God* ruled with unquestioned omnipotence and realized release from total captivity. And *Jesus* assumed an intimate and kingly relationship with the poor black chattel. Slaves emphasized both the suffering human Jesus as well as Jesus' warrior ability to set the downtrodden free.[22]

This Jesus who has a human face but has the power to set the downtrodden free has continued to form the central integrating motif of the Black church in North America. If the evangelical white churches of North America look to Matthew 28:19–20 as the cardinal statement of what the church is to be, the Black Church looks to Luke 4:18–21.[23] This emphasis was reflected in the ministry of Martin Luther King. His preaching was permeated with the theme of the Christ who came to set people free.

At the end of the twentieth century, the integrating theme of the Black Church may be shifting, just as it did for the medieval European church. The black experience has its roots in the agrarian south, but now finds expression largely in the major urban areas. The Islamic faith has attracted millions of black adherents who had had some affiliation with the Black Church. The challenge of Christianity will be to present Jesus Christ from a perspective that addresses the new realities of the black urban America so that Jesus Christ is seen as good news.[24] A more recent approach calls for a look back to preslavery experiences of black people in Africa, combined with an awareness of black presence in the Scriptures. This approach seeks to bypass the European experience of Christianity and to return to the biblical record to inform the Black Church as it goes into the twenty-first century.

Social Reform Movements

Emerging from the piety of the first Great Awakening, evangelical Christians embarked on a variety of enterprises that took seriously an imitation of the earthly ministry of Jesus Christ. These enterprises affirmed the value and worth of people and sought to relieve suffering. Such ministries had an intimate relationship to the evangelistic concern of those involved. The pietistic question, "What would Jesus do?" fueled an enormous exertion of energy and financial expense in an effort to represent Christ as he had carried out his ministry. In this sense, those involved sought to be an incarnation of the incarnate Lord.

George Whitfield preached fervently for conversions in open-air meetings, but he also labored feverishly to raise money for his orphanages. William Wilberforce led the movement that resulted in the abolition of slavery in Great Britain. Evangelicals in Great Britain and in the United States became politically involved to bring about social change. In Great Britain the Reform Bill of 1832 resulted in a major realignment of political power as a huge group of the population received the franchise. In the United States, the evangelicals led the abolition movement and took the lead in fostering primary, secondary, and higher education. With the growth of the urban centers, the Salvation Army and other rescue missions established ministries that approached evangelism from the perspective of rescuing people from physical as well as spiritual danger.[25] During the same period the Roman Catholic churches in the cities embarked on far-reaching social welfare programs specifically designed for immigrant peoples for whom English was a second language.

Toward the end of the nineteenth century, the attention of socially concerned Christians shifted from demonstrating care for individuals to changing social structures and dealing with issues of justice and economics. This movement grew up in England under the leadership of Bishop Westcott, in Germany under Leonhard Ragaz and Hermann Kutter, and in the United States under Walter Rauschenbusch. The "social gospel" of Rauschenbusch drew strong fire from traditional evangelicals, who saw its emphasis on social structures as opposed to individuals as a subversion of the gospel message. This separation of perspectives created a dichotomy of ministries that left one group dealing almost exclusively with social issues and the other with spiritual issues.

Neo-orthodoxy moved in a different direction from the American social gospel trend after World War I, but from the perspective of the Incarnation. For people like Barth and Brunner, the Incarnation constitutes the ultimate revelation of God to people. Barth repudiated the natural revelation of Aquinas and rendered Scripture relative in comparison with the significance for salvation of the revelation of Christ.

INCARNATION AS GOOD NEWS

Almost a thousand years ago, Anselm of Canterbury wrote the book *Cur Deus Homo?* (*Why the God-Man?*) to explain the significance of the Incarnation for contemporary medieval society. Two thousand years after Bethlehem, what difference does it make that God entered the world as a man, and what sets off this coming of God from the pictures of God found in other religions?

A Savior

The announcement of the angel to the shepherds of the birth of a Savior sets the gospel of Jesus Christ apart from other world religions (Luke 2:11). These others offer teachers and prophets, but none offers a Savior who rescues people from difficulty from which they cannot save themselves. For people who have reached the end of their rope and find themselves hopelessly entangled in life, it is good news to know that God has taken the initiative to extricate us from our difficulty.

The Compassionate Face

The coming of God into the world reveals the compassionate face of God. While the understanding of God as Creator reveals his holiness and sovereignty, this idea alone can leave one with not only a healthy fear but also an unhealthy dread of God. By coming into the world in Jesus Christ, God revealed a compassionate face that one does not experience when only viewing the awesome beauty, power, and majesty of creation. While the monotheistic religions often picture a stern and judgmental God, the Eastern religions tend to picture an impersonal, remote, and disinterested divine essence. Through the Incarnation, God came out of hiding and showed the face of caring concern.

Identification

By entering into creation and experiencing it through the true humanity of Jesus Christ, God identified with the human race in a way that makes true sympathy and empathy possible for him. God translated theoretical omniscience into actual experience by learning what it feels like to be human and to deal with mortal life. Like the ancient adage of native American wisdom suggests, God took the ultimate step of understanding by "walking a mile in our moccasins." This identification reflects a specific concern for people.

Alienation and Reconciliation

Existentialists have identified alienation and loneliness as one of the three great dreads of human existence. By our very existence we as human beings are alienated from one another, from nature, and even from our own selves. The plight of human isolation ironically can occur most intensely in a crowd. By bringing together the divine and human in one person, God literally brought reconciliation between God and humanity in Jesus Christ. In the body of Christ, peace (wholeness) has occurred. Christ offers this same peace with God but also with ourselves and with others. Peace, whether personal or interpersonal, comes as a legacy of God's taking the initiative to make peace. For people who live broken, dysfunctional lives and who cannot maintain relationships, the gospel offers the good news that Jesus Christ brings the pieces back together and makes reconciliation possible.

Acceptance

While the Creator remains veiled in a holiness that mere mortals dare not approach, as the fetishes of tribal religion and the laws of monotheistic religion testify, the God who came in Jesus Christ calls on people to come to him. In his life and ministry, by his words and actions, Jesus called people of all classes and distinctions to come to him. He not only called, but he accepted people, regardless of the prejudices others might have. It is not uncommon in the African-American tradition to hear people speak of "my Jesus," reflecting their experience of the personal acceptance of the Savior into intimate relationship. Those who orient their faith around other elements of the gospel may regard this affirmation of faith as irreverent, but they have missed the amazing good news that Jesus calls those who come to him his "friends" (John 15:15).

Love

While most religions have holy writings that point to God or give instructions in living, none of these speak to the deep-seated human need to experience love. Love is not an assertion or an affirmation, or even a powerful emotion to be felt. Rather, love appears in the concrete actions of what one does. The Incarnation represents a logical consequence of God's love. The coming of God into the world portrays his love more vividly than any theological concept or any other action by God (except the cross, which could not have occurred without the incarnation), because of what it cost God to come into the world. Love that remains merely spoken but never acted upon does not constitute genuine love. The sophist demands a sign for the existence of God; yet when God appears, the sophist cannot accept it because an appearance of God cannot really be God. For the person who needs to experience self-giving, undemanding, unconditional love, the coming of Christ gives good news that love truly exists and is accessible.

Example

While the Scriptures present the expectations of God, they lack something that only God can offer: an example of how to live the expectation. As a teacher, Jesus not only spoke about God's will but demonstrated what it meant to live out one's life in a right relationship to God. Though he is the sovereign and almighty Ruler of the universe, God chose to enter the world and show it what life is really all about. Rather than being a demanding despot who commands without regard for people, the God who visits us in Christ portrays patient concern of one who teaches by walking alongside those who need to learn. He offers the yoke of two oxen working together. For the person who flees from authority yet leads a chaotic life, the coming of God in Jesus offers good news that in spite of his right to dignity, glory, and honor, God will embrace humility in order to help the one who needs to learn.

Physical Need

While the gospel in its entirety affirms the spiritual character of eternity and the reign of God beyond this mortal life, the coming of God into the world affirms the importance of physical existence. The ministry of Jesus emphasized the importance of caring for the physical needs of people. The Incarnation affirms the value God places on the physical world now, fallen and corrupt though it may be. Other monotheistic religions affirm creation and judgment, but they do not affirm the quality of physical life the way the ministry of Jesus does through healing and compassion. The polytheistic and nontheistic religions of the East deny the value of the physical realm, viewing the perception of physical reality as a curse. Care for the physical needs of a world at odds with itself, however, represents the good news that the kingdom of God is breaking in.

NOTES

1. On this issue, see especially Craig Blomberg, "Where Do We Start Studying Jesus?" *Jesus Under Fire: Modern Scholarship Reinvents the Historical Jesus*, ed. Michael J. Wilkins and J. P. Moreland (Grand Rapids: Zondervan, 1995), 17–50.

2. See Rudolph Bultmann, *History of the Synoptic Tradition*, rev. ed., trans. John Marsh (New York: Harper & Row Publishers, 1963), 253, 292, 306.

3. John Hick, ed., *The Myth of God Incarnate* (Philadelphia: Westminster, 1977).

4. C. S. Lewis, *Miracles* (London: Fontana, 1960), 138. In his spiritual autobiography, Lewis remarked, "If ever a myth had become fact, had been incarnated, it would be just like this. And nothing else in all literature was just like this. ... Here and here only in all time the myth must have become fact; the Word, flesh; God, Man. This is not 'a religion,' nor 'a

philosophy.' It is the summing up and actuality of them all." See C. S. Lewis, *Surprised by Joy* (New York: Harcourt, Brace and Co., 1956), 236.

Bernard Ramm has argued that novelists and literary figures like Lewis, Dorothy Sayers, T. S. Elliott, G. K. Chesterton, and Flannery O'Connor stand in a better position to assess the meaning of the Scriptures than technical experts who have lost all sense of wonder. See Bernard L. Ramm, *An Evangelical Christology: Ecumenic and Historic* (Nashville: Thomas Nelson, 1985), 52.

5. Bultmann, *History of the Synoptic Tradition*, 291–99.

6. See Millard J. Erickson, *The Word Became Flesh* (Grand Rapids: Baker, 1991), 21–24.

7. Ibid., 25.

8. G. R. Beasley-Murray, *Preaching the Gospel from the Gospels* (London: Epworth, 1965), 60–67.

9. Ibid., 62. "Throughout the Gospels, where the polemic atmosphere is not present, the miracles are narrated in the consciousness that they reveal the presence of the victorious Kingdom of God, quenching the powers of evil and coming to the aid of needy men."

10. Irenaeus, *Proof of the Apostolic Preaching*, trans. Joseph P. Smith (Westminster, Md.: Newman, 1952), 23–24.

11. Ibid., 68–74.

12. Ibid., 68.

13. Gustaf Aulén, *Christus Victor*, trans. A. G. Hebert (New York: Macmillan, 1969), 18.

14. Bernard L. Ramm, *An Evangelical Christology: Ecumenic and Historic* (Nashville: Thomas Nelson, 1985), 32.

15. Williston Walker sums up the motives of Athanasius in terms of his concern for salvation: "To him, the question at issue was one of salvation, and that he made men feel it to be so was the main source of his power." See *A History of the Christian Church*, 3d ed. (New York: Charles Scribner's Sons, 1970), 110. Archibald Robertson took up this same theme in his edition of the writings of Athanasius: "It was not as a theologian, but as a believing soul in need of a Saviour, that Athanasius approached the mystery of Christ." See A. Robertson, ed., *St. Athanasius: Select Works and Letters*, in *Nicene and Post-Nicene Fathers*, vol. 4, 2d series (Grand Rapids: Eerdmans, 1987; reprint of Edinburgh: T. & T. Clark,), xiv.

16. Athanasius, "On the Incarnation of the Word" (ibid., 36).

17. Ibid., 40.

18. Athanasius reiterated the importance of the Incarnation for salvation in his Easter letter of 339 ("Letter XI," ibid., 537).

19. J. G. Davies, *The Early Christian Church: A History of Its First Five Centuries* (Grand Rapids: Baker, 1980), 260.

20. William Pannell, *Evangelism From the Bottom Up* (Grand Rapids: Zondervan, 1992), 35–37.

21. Herbert V. Klem, *Oral Communication of the Scripture: Insights From African Oral Art* (Pasadena, Calif.: William Carey Library, 1982). While Klem's study focuses on Africa, it suggests that the Black Church in America has a rich theological heritage based on an oral tradition that remains vibrant rather than on a theological heritage, based on a written tradition, that tends to be kept only by the professionals.

22. Dwight N. Hopkins, "Slave Theology in the 'Invisible Institution,'" in *Cut Loose Your Stammering Tongue: Black Theology in the Slave Narratives*, ed. Dwight N. Hopkins and George C. H. Cummings (Maryknoll, N.Y.: Orbis Books, 1991), 2.

23. I am indebted to Archie Le Mone, executive director of the Home Mission Board for the Progressive National Baptist Convention, for this insight.

24. A number of young, university-trained black theologians began to emerge in the 1960s, who combined the older Black Church heritage with some of the emphases of liberation theology. See Jones H. Cone and Gayraud S. Wilmore, eds., *Black Theology: A Documentary History*, 2 vols., 2d ed. rev. (Maryknoll, N.Y.: Orbis Books, 1993).

25. See Timothy L. Smith, *Revivalism and Social Reform: American Protestantism on the Eve of the Civil War* (Gloucester, Mass.: Peter Smith, 1976), and Norris Magnuson, *Salvation in the Slums: Evangelical Social Work, 1865–1920* (Metuchen, N.J.: Scarecrow, 1977).

Chapter 5

Death for Sins

One week in the life of Jesus Christ has received dramatically disproportionate attention in the Gospels. Luke, forever concerned with details of the life of Jesus, devotes one-fifth of his Gospel to the final week of Jesus' life. Mark and Matthew devoted about one-third of their Gospels to the events of that week, and John gave almost half of his Gospel to the events surrounding the death of Jesus. Logically speaking, Jesus' death should have marked the end of any interest in him. The crucifixion effectively ended for three days the movement that had surrounded him. But on the third day, as the reports of the resurrection spread, that movement took on an entirely different character.

In the light of his resurrection, what did Jesus' death mean? Why did God let him die, only to raise him from the dead? In retrospect, his death became a greater surprise and mystery than his resurrection. The resurrection made sense in hindsight, for it declared Jesus "with power to be the Son of God" (Rom. 1:4). Since he was divine, then of course one would expect him to rise. More problematic, however, was the death. Why did the Son of God have to die?

BIBLICAL BACKGROUND

The four Gospels describe the death of Jesus in terms of the fulfillment of Scripture, as has been discussed in chapter 3. But while a significant group within first-century Judaism had a major concern for prophecies that would be fulfilled with the coming of the Messiah, suffering did not figure in that expectation. In other words, the suffering and death of Jesus came as a surprise to his disciples and formed a major obstacle to faith. In affirming the authenticity of Jesus as a prophet of God, Islam has denied the historicity of the crucifixion, insisting that Jesus ascended into heaven without experiencing death. The cross, a symbol for the suffering and death of Jesus, has posed a major scandal for Christianity.

The Gospels

The Gospels paint a picture of disciples who could not accept the idea of the suffering and death of Jesus, even when Jesus himself taught them about it. The Synoptic Gospels record three announcements from Jesus of his coming death:

Matt. 16:21–28	Mark 8:31–9:1	Luke 9:22–27
Matt. 17:22–23	Mark 9:30–32	Luke 9:43b–45
Matt. 20:17–19	Mark 10:32–34	Luke 18:31–33

These three predictions do not exhaust the teaching of Jesus on the subject. His teaching on the "sign of Jonah," for example, prefigures his death and resurrection (Matt. 12:39–40; Luke 11:29–30). The anointing at Bethany also announced the coming death (Matt. 26:10–13). In Luke's account of the teaching on the coming of the kingdom, Jesus indicated that first the Son of Man had to suffer (Luke 17:24–25). According to Mark, Jesus gave Peter, James, and John instruction about the prophetic basis for his pending suffering as they descended the Mount of Transfiguration (Mark 9:12–13).

Throughout such accounts, the theme of the necessity for suffering and death forms a common tone. This necessity finds its basis in the oracles of God. This was Jesus' own teaching about the prophecies, though it conflicted with the prevailing theology and hermeneutic of the day. As has been argued earlier, this teaching has its origin in Jesus, who reiterated it after the resurrection (Luke 24:25–27, 45–49). The theological norms of the day would have precluded an unsophisticated group like the disciples from developing such a theology.

The Gospel of John begins with a prophetic announcement by John the Baptist that foreshadows the rest of the book:

> The next day John was there again with two of his disciples. When he saw Jesus passing by, he said, "Look, the Lamb of God!" (John 1:35–36)

The imagery of the sacrificial lamb figures prominently in John's account. Writing for a Gentile audience, he includes a discourse about the meaning of Jesus' death that the other Evangelists do not. While the Jewish audience would have been concerned to know how that death could be consistent with the plan of God for Israel, the pagan audience wanted to know what it could tell them about the nature of God. Jesus made it plain in John 10:11, 14–15, 17–18 that the Good Shepherd lays down his life for his sheep. Dying on behalf of another represents the greatest expression of love (15:13). John explains the coming and dying of Jesus as God's expression of love toward the world (3:16). The vicarious death of Christ on behalf of others fulfills the sacrifices of the Law of Moses as Jesus' ministry culminates in his death at the initiative of the high priest during Passover week (18:14).

For the most part, however, the Gospels do not explain why it was necessary for Christ to suffer and die. They were written as narratives, and while twentieth-century scholarship has focused inordinate attention on the idiosyncrasies and theological issues of the writers, the Evangelists rarely depart from a straightforward account of what happened. The Gospels make clear that Jesus represented himself to be on a par with God and that his execution came as a result of his purported blasphemous declaration before the Sanhedrin:

> Again the high priest asked him, "Are you the Christ, the Son of the Blessed One?"
> "I am," said Jesus. "And you will see the Son of Man sitting at the right hand of the Mighty One and coming on the clouds of heaven." (Mark 14:61b–62; cf. Matt. 26:63–66; Luke 22:67–71; John 19:7; also John 5:18; 10:30–39)

Much has been written and preached through the years about how unjust Jesus' trial was. Some have charged that the Sanhedrin met at an extraordinary time under extraordinary circumstances, contrary to tradition. One must concede, however, that they had an extraordinary problem at a dangerous time, for the city of Jerusalem was filled with pilgrims for the observance of Passover. Though a group plotted Jesus' death, they did so for good cause: He represented himself to be divine. Even though false witnesses spoke at the trial, the Sanhedrin was not moved by their testimony. Not until Jesus himself spoke did they condemn him. They had no choice under the circumstances. He offered them the alternatives of believing in him or rejecting him.

While Jesus spoke of the *necessity* of his death in fulfillment of Scripture in many places, he gave the *meaning* of his death to the disciples during his Last Supper with them. With the imagery of Passover as the background, he explained it in terms of the fulfillment of the promise of a new covenant: "This cup is the new covenant in my blood, which is poured out for you" (Luke 22:20b; cf. Matt. 26:28; Mark 14:24). This dramatic declaration coinciding with the feast of the Passover placed the death of Jesus in correspondence with the killing of the first Passover lambs in Egypt, when death passed over the Israelites and when Israel was set free from physical bondage and slavery. Jesus was to the new covenant what the Passover lamb was to the old covenant, though the new covenant had a different character, as Jeremiah had foretold:

"The time is coming," declares the LORD,
"when I will make a new covenant
with the house of Israel
and with the house of Judah.
It will not be like the covenant
I made with their forefathers
when I took them by the hand
to lead them out of Egypt,
because they broke my covenant,
though I was a husband to them," declares the LORD.
"This is the covenant I will make with the house of Israel
after that time," declares the LORD.
"I will put my law in their minds
and write it on their hearts.
I will be their God,
and they will be my people.
No longer will a man teach his neighbor,
or a man his brother, saying 'Know the LORD,'
because they will all know me,
from the least of them to the greatest," declares
the LORD.

> "For I will forgive their wickedness
> and will remember their sins no more."
> (Jer. 31:31–34)

At the Last Supper, Jesus explained his death as the fulfillment of the Passover and the ancient covenant. His death instituted the new covenant, which went beyond the institutional/ceremonial matters related to the legal demands of the law. The new covenant offered both forgiveness of sin and cleansing of sin. The first related to the legal/volitional aspect of sin, the latter related to the ontological aspect of sin as an aspect of human nature.

Jesus indicated that his death served a vicarious function, for his blood was "poured out for many" (Matt. 26:28; Mark 14:24). Luke's language has an even more personal tone, for he speaks of the suffering of Jesus as blood "which is poured out for you" (Luke 22:20). Matthew includes the specific connection between the vicarious death and "the forgiveness of sins" (Matt. 26:28), while Luke includes this element as Jesus pronounces forgiveness from the cross itself as he dies (Luke 23:34). The pouring out of blood for sins draws on the symbolism of more than a thousand years of Jewish sacrificial practice. That practice proceeded from the fundamental disjunction between the holiness of God and the nature of humanity.

The problem of sin reflected in the sacrificial system went far beyond a view of sin as merely a legal problem. The mournful cry of Isaiah in his vision of coming into the presence of God reflects the human capacity to minimize the holiness of God until it is brought into the presence of God (Isa. 6:5). Not even Moses appreciated the impossibility of human coexistence with the holiness of God (Ex. 33:12–23). He was not allowed to behold God, for the radical disjunction between his nature and God's would result in his obliteration. In Isaiah's vision, cleansing of the pollution of sin came from the altar. In Zechariah's vision of the cleansing of Joshua the high priest, the ritualistic priestly robes appeared filthy, but God ordered them removed and replaced by clean garments. Zechariah then declared that the cleansing symbolized what God would do in the future through his servant, the Branch. The promise of the Lord was to "remove the sin of this land in a single day" (Zech. 3:9).

Israel received teaching about the unapproachability of God through the ceremonial laws governing sacrifice, the chief of which involved who could approach God to offer the sacrifice. Only the high priest, and he but once a year, was allowed to enter the Most Holy Place to sprinkle blood on the cover of the ark to make atonement for the sins of Israel. The curtain that barred entry to this place hung as a constant reminder of humanity. The Synoptic Gospels record without comment that when Jesus died, the curtain of the temple was torn from top to bottom (Matt. 27:51; Mark 15:38; Luke 23:45).

John, who wrote for a Gentile audience, omitted the new interpretation Jesus gave to the Passover meal at the Last Supper. He also omitted reference to the torn curtain of the temple. What the Synoptic writers could mention without comment for a largely Jewish audience, John could not include without major elaboration on the ceremonial practices of Judaism. The Gentiles would not have understood the significance of the new covenant nor the Jewish understanding of sacrifice. While all the ancient world practiced sacrifice, the Jewish people stood virtually alone in their understanding of the moral dimension in relationship to God. John dealt with these issues in his Gospel, but he did so from the perspective of the gift of the Holy Spirit, as we will discuss in a later chapter.

General Apostolic Writings

In their writings for the churches, the apostles related the significance of the death of Jesus to various themes identified in the Gospels. Not surprisingly, the letters address the issues of local situations, applying elements of the gospel to life situations and cultural contexts. The legal issue of forgiveness in terms of justification, for example, was an issue for the Romans. Since they did not have the Jewish traditions as a teacher, Paul elaborated the implications of Jesus' death for them. The ontological issue of purification concerned those Jewish Christians addressed in the book of Hebrews who, in the context of the Jewish world, would soon see the destruction of the temple and the elimination of the religion of Moses and its required sacrifices. Hebrews elaborates the implications of Jesus' death for these people.

When one examines the New Testament letters, the apostolic writers present a variety of implications of Jesus' death, which resulted in good news for humanity.

Purification. The need for purification was not understood as a part of ritual sacrifices in most of the Hellenistic world, but it was central to the Law of Moses. Virtually all of the ancient cultures practiced sacrifice as offerings to the gods to gain their favor or appease their anger. These sacrifices functioned more as transactions between mortals and immortals rather than as acknowledgment of sinfulness before a holy God. Those who worshiped Yahweh, however, believed that humanity had an aspect to it that needed the purification of a refiner's fire in order to be able to exist in the presence of holiness (Mal. 3:1–4; 4:1–3).

Hebrews takes up the theme of purification or cleansing as a benefit of the new covenant, which God instituted through the death of Jesus (Heb. 12:24). By his death, Jesus fulfilled all of the requirements for sacrifice under the old covenant "once for all," and by satisfying the Law, he supplanted it with the new covenant (7:27; 9:23–28). The old covenant made people aware of their unholiness (Rom. 7:7–25), but the new covenant makes people holy "through the sacrifice of the body of Jesus Christ once for all" (Heb. 10:10), "because by one sacrifice he has made perfect forever those who are being made holy" (10:14). Unlike the annual sacrifices to atone for the sins of Israel, which covered the sin but did not affect the hearts of people, Jesus died "to make the people holy through his own blood" (13:12).

This emphasis on blood has seemed strange and even barbaric in the West from the time of the Enlightenment, but this modern perspective fails to appreciate that it was the acceptance of the blood sacrifice of Jesus in ancient and medieval times that rendered the idea of blood sacrifice barbaric. Jesus died on the weekend of the great sacrificial festival of Passover at a time when sacrifice was the central event of Israel (Heb. 9:22). For two thousand years the church has perpetuated the blood sacrifice in the central act of worship when the faithful reenact the Last Supper in obedience to his command to remember (cf. 1 Cor. 11:24–25). The sufficiency of the sacrifice of Jesus Christ in superiority to the inadequacy of the animal sacrifices would have sounded a note of good news, indeed, for the church of

Jerusalem, which continued to worship in the temple until it was destroyed and the sacrifices ended (Heb. 10:12). The West has tended to view sacrificial customs of other cultures rather patronizingly as superstitious nonsense, adding the blood of Jesus with the lot, while failing to appreciate that animal sacrifice was abolished in the declining Roman empire because of the blood of Christ.

Purification deals with an entirely different issue than forgiveness or justification. The latter treat the legal dimension of transgressing the law, while purification deals with an aspect of sin that arises even where there is no knowledge of the law. Whether guilt in the West or shame in the East, purification treats an inward aspect of the heart that remains even if the legal matters are satisfied. The necessity of purification can be seen in the lives of people crippled by an inward sense of unworthiness or dirtiness. The death of Christ occurred to address this issue:

> How much more, then, will the blood of Christ, who through the eternal Spirit offered himself unblemished to God, cleanse our consciences from acts that lead to death, so that we may serve the living God! (Heb. 9:14)

By cleansing the conscience, Christ sets people free to live without regret.

Redemption. The idea of redemption connected with the death of Jesus occurs in at least ten New Testament books. At first, this broadly used concept seems strangely out of place in the Gentile world of Hellenistic culture where the churches would have read these letters. The terminology has its roots in the national beginnings of Israel, when God redeemed the people from slavery in Egypt. The idea of redemption from slavery and bondage, however, also spoke powerfully in a culture where the institution of slavery flourished.[1] By analogy, the apostles broadened the term to mean redemption from all forms of bondage, both physical and spiritual.

In ancient Israel, redemption was the process by which matters were restored to their right or original condition. In the Year of Jubilee, for example, a family had the right to redeem property that had passed out of the family's possession. The redeemer was the next of kin, who had the right of possession if he chose to redeem the property. He was expected to take action to rectify a distressful situation. In the book of Ruth, Boaz desired to marry Ruth, but the redeemer who had the responsibility of buying back her in-laws' property and fathering a child by her was another kinsman. When that kinsman chose not to exercise his right/responsibility, Boaz came to Ruth's rescue as her redeemer (Ruth 3:1–4:21).

Jeremiah exercised the responsibility of a redeemer when he bought his family's land, which had fallen into enemy hands, even though he knew he would never see it (Jer. 32:6–9). In the midst of his desperation, Job called out for a redeemer to justify him and declare his innocence before all of his accusers (Job 19:23–29). Redemption involved setting matters straight for those who were powerless to take action themselves, and it required the action to be taken within the family by the next of kin. Thus, the terminology of redemption infers the relationship God intends for those who experience redemption.

Within the terminology of redemption, the apostolic writings describe a broad range of implications. When a redeemer took action, he succeeded in bringing the kind of justification before accusation that Job had cried for (Rom. 3:24). The act of redemption itself demonstrated the forgiveness of all estrangement and the declaration that those in need of redemption were counted as part of God's family—children and not slaves (Gal. 4:4–5; Eph. 1:7; Col. 1:14). If redemption meant restoration to God, it also meant freedom from a variety of illegitimate masters to which people submit themselves. Just as Hosea redeemed his wife Gomer from slavery (Hos. 3:2) after she had prostituted herself, Jesus redeemed people from their experiences of bondage. He redeemed people from wickedness (Titus 2:14), from the empty way of life they followed (1 Peter 1:18), and from the curse of the law (Gal. 3:13). Through his redeeming work, God "has rescued us from the dominion of darkness and brought us into the kingdom of the Son he loves" (Col. 1:13; cf. Gal. 1:3–4). Jesus not only rescues us from the domination, but also from the consequences of that domination (1 Thess. 1:10b).

The Pauline, Petrine, and Johannine literature all speak of Jesus' purchasing those for whom he died (1 Cor. 7:23; 2 Peter 2:1; Rev. 5:9; 14:3b–4). This purchasing is even referred to as ransom on two occasions (1 Tim. 2:5–6; Heb. 9:15). The modern church has largely ignored the significance of redemption because of the notion of a purchase price. Since the Enlightenment, the two great rationalistic schools of theology in the West (liberalism and fundamentalism) have focused attention on the recipient of the purchase price, a matter totally ignored by Scripture. Logic dictates that the recipient of Jesus' blood as payment be either God or the devil. Fundamentalism is divided over which of these two received payment; liberalism rejects the doctrine outright as abhorrent.

The New Testament writers rely on the Old Testament concept of God's redemption rather than a more philosophical rationalistic view that would need to account for the recipient of a redemption price. The tradition of divine redemption was stated most clearly in the oracle of Isaiah:

> You were sold for nothing,
>   and without money you will be redeemed. (Isa. 52:3)

God does not have to buy what already belongs to him. Neither the pharaoh of Egypt nor the king of Assyria had a legitimate claim on Israel. God redeemed Israel from Egypt, but he paid Pharaoh with ten plagues and the waters of the Red Sea. The terminology of divine redemption in the Old Testament usually begins with God's "selling" his people into the hands of their enemies because they had abandoned him. In no case, however, did God receive any payment (Judg. 2:14; 3:8; 4:2; 10:7). Abraham acted as the redeemer when he rescued Lot from the alliance of Kedorlaomer (Gen. 14:1–16). Redemption occurred because Abraham did what was necessary to restore Lot, not because he paid a price to Kedorlaomer. The four New Testament texts that describe redemption in terms of the purchase by Christ through the shedding of his blood stress the costliness to Christ of being a redeemer.

Substitution. In the New Testament, the apostolic writers shift the imagery of redemption from the question of who received a ransom to the question of how the redemption took effect. Christ accomplished redemption as well as purification by a substitution of himself for those in need of salvation. The affirmation that Christ died in place of the rest of humanity may be found throughout the apostolic writings (1 Thess. 5:9–10; Heb. 2:9; 1 Peter 3:18; 1 John 3:16). Islam has criticized Christianity at this point because such a substitution would release people from any moral obligation in their behavior. In fact, Islam teaches that Christ did not die on the cross, but that he ascended into heaven without dying. The apostolic letters have an entirely different tone, however, than one that would decrease moral responsibility. Responsibility is actually created by virtue of the substitution.

The substitutionary death of Christ for sinners as described in the New Testament is not a one-sided substitution whereby Christ takes our death and we have no part to play. The substitution goes both ways. Christ takes our death only if we share his death. In turn, Christ gives us life only if we take his life. In this regard, the substitution operates like a double transposition. Faith in the saving death of Christ involves our entry into his death in order to die with him, while he enters into us to live through us. The idea is decidedly mystical rather than transactional in a legal sense.

While at least twenty passages in the Pauline, Petrine, and Johannine literature refer to this two-sided substitution, Paul's treatment of it in Romans is the most extensive. In chapter 6, he deals directly with the creation of moral responsibility based on the new relationship of being "alive to God in Christ Jesus":

> By no means! We died to sin; how can we live in it any longer? Or don't you know that all of us who were baptized into Christ Jesus were baptized into his death? We were therefore buried with him through baptism into death. . . .
>
> If we have been united with him in his death, we will certainly also be united with him in his resurrection. For we know that our old self was crucified with him so that the body of sin might be rendered powerless, that we should no longer be slaves to sin—because anyone who has died has been freed from sin. . . .
>
> In the same way, count yourselves dead to sin but alive to God in Christ Jesus. Therefore do not let sin reign in your mortal body so that you obey its evil desires. (Rom. 6:2–7, 11–12)

This line of thought culminates in 6:23, "For the wages of sin is death, but the gift of God is eternal life in Christ Jesus our Lord." In its context, this passage has a far richer meaning than a superficial one might imply. As 6:1–22 indicate, humanity does not stand exempt from death because of Christ's death. Rather, they are offered death with Christ. By dying in him on the cross they receive life in Christ. The operative concern is the double substitution whereby people find themselves "in Christ."

In Galatians and Colossians, Paul expounds the same theme of the death of Christ, applying it to those who mystically join him in death and thereby end their own existence apart from him. By crucifixion with Christ, those who are in Christ are no longer under the power of the world (Gal. 3:20–21; 6:14). This freedom brings profound implications for holy living, for our lives now belong to Christ (Col. 2:11–12, 20; 3:3).

This same theme also appears in 1 Peter. Christ bore our sins on the cross, to be sure. But he did so with the understanding that we should die to sin in the process. The double side of his death is that people should also "die to sins and live for righteousness" (1 Peter 2:24). The cross and suffering of Christ represent a positive dimension of salvation whereby people participate with him (1 Peter 4:13). In this sense, suffering is not a problem to be explained but a dimension of identification with Christ. This constant awareness of one's participation in Christ's death stands at the center of why the early church constantly reenacted the Lord's Supper (1 Cor. 10:16). Apart from dying with Christ, no one can live with Christ (2 Cor. 4:10; 13:4; 2 Tim 2:11). The moral and ethical implications of this double substitution may be summarized as "those who live should no longer live for themselves but for him who died for them and was raised again" (2 Cor. 5:15).

While the implications for moral responsibility are heightened on the human side by virtue of the substitutionary death of Jesus, his death reveals the character of God in a way that no other revelatory event has ever done. It reveals the love of God for humanity (Rom. 5:6–8; 8:31–32; 2 Cor. 5:14–15; Gal. 2:20–21; 1 John 3:16; 4:10; cf. John 3:16). This concept of Jesus' death reflecting God's love has recently received strong criticism as a barbaric idea.[2] Such criticism illustrates the intrinsic relationship between the elements of the gospel that tend to collapse if viewed in isolation. For God to "kill Jesus" does indeed seem an act of barbarism, but this way of viewing the cross ignores another element of the gospel that stresses the relationship between the Father and Son, "to wit, that God was in Christ reconciling the world unto himself" (2 Cor. 5:19, KJV). Apart from incarnational Christology, the cross is truly folly.

Further implications. While purification, redemption, and substitution represent the most frequently cited implications of Jesus' death for sins, they by no means exhaust the categories of what that death means in the New Testament. According to various passages, the death of Jesus:

- represents the final and complete atoning sacrifice that frees people from the fear of approaching Almighty God (Rom. 3:25; 1 Cor. 5:7; Heb. 2:17; 7:27; 9:23–28; 1 John 2:2; 4:10);
- brings justification from the legal demands of the law and forgiveness for transgression (Rom. 3:24; 4:25; 5:9; Col. 2:13–14; 1 John 2:12);
- represents a triumph over the hostile spiritual powers rather than a defeat by them (Col. 2:15; Heb. 2:14–15; Rev. 12:11);
- brings about reconciliation between God and humanity as Jesus makes peace on the cross (Rom. 5:10–11; 2 Cor. 5:18–21; Eph. 2:13, 15–16; Col. 1:20);
- releases the life blood of Jesus as the source of eternal life (Heb. 5:8–9; 13:20; Rev. 13:8; 22:14);
- clearly identifies the willing, obedient servant as the only worthy Savior and Lord (Rev. 5:6, 9, 12);
- serves as an example for life to all who follow him in faith (1 Cor. 8:11; Heb. 12:2; 1 Peter 2:21; 4:1; 1 John 3:16; 4:11).

Conclusion. None of the apostolic writers espoused a theory of the atonement. Rather, they all shared a profound awareness of the multidimensional implications of the death of Jesus for sins. The different aspects of what that death meant would have spoken more powerfully in some situations than in others. The apostles addressed the meaning of Jesus' death appropriately to various audiences with different issues relating to life and eternity.

HISTORICAL/THEOLOGICAL DEVELOPMENT

In the context of the early church's concern to demonstrate that Jesus Christ stood as the culmination point of all Scripture and that he represented the coming of God into the world, the assertion that

Christ had died for sins operated almost as a self-evident truth requiring little elaboration. While his death for sins continued as a central affirmation of the church throughout its early period, the New Testament believers did not develop its evangelistic message or theological orientation around that element of the gospel.

The Patristic Period

In his classic work on the atonement, Gustaf Aulén argues that the significance of the death of Jesus for the early church cannot be separated from the significance of the Incarnation. Christ conquered sin, the devil, death, and all spiritual realities in rebellion against God by entering into this world as a man and entering the domain of wickedness through death.[3] The primary emphasis in the atonement for the first one thousand years of church history was on the victory of Christ. It did not focus on the "legal" problem of sin as transgression against God so much as the power of sin's hold on people. It accented the dramatic work of God in Christ to break the power of sin. In the Hellenistic world, people lived in dread of "the rulers . . . the authorities . . . the powers of this dark world and . . . the spiritual forces of evil in the heavenly realms" (Eph. 6:12). Through his death, Jesus conquered all spiritual enemies, put them to shame, and thereby won the victory.[4]

Easter faith remained the central reality for the church during the centuries of intermittent persecution prior to Constantine's recognition of Christianity. Suffering and death were the necessary means of victory. The death could not lead to victory, however, apart from a true incarnation. Irenaeus argued,

> But what He did appear, that He also was: God recapitulated in Himself the ancient formation of man, that He might kill sin, deprive death of its power, and vivify man; and therefore His works are true.[5]

God captured the one who had captured the human race and held them under his power, while he "loosed from the bonds of condemnation" those who had been captives.[6]

Origen sounded a similar theme in describing the significance of Jesus' death. He took upon himself human darkness in order that he might destroy that darkness, and with it death.[7] While the patristic

writers saw the death of Jesus as part of the integrated work of salvation that involved his coming into the world, his death, and his
resurrection, that death had specific significance for the one who
hoped to experience salvation. Salvation meant participation in the
death of Jesus because

> each of those who have been crucified with Christ puts off
> from himself the principalities and the powers, and makes a
> show of them and triumphs over them in the cross; or rather,
> Christ does those things in them.[8]

Through being crucified with Christ, a believer died to the world
and experienced freedom from spiritual bondage.[9]

Aulén's study is not concerned so much to trace the history of
doctrine, however, as it is to identify those periods when a particular
element of the gospel in its doctrinal expression dominated the point
of view of the church. In that sense, the death of Christ was not the
focus of attention in the theological controversies of the early church.
If anything, it was the great cardinal fact of the Christian faith that
everyone accepted. Christ's death for the salvation of sinners
remained the obvious, if not self-explanatory, article of faith. But to
find that death as a *central orienting feature* of the church, we must
move to medieval Europe and the thought of Anselm of Canterbury.

Anselm and the Medieval Church

Anselm (d. 1109) explained the meaning of the death of Christ
in terms of the idea of penance, which had slowly emerged in the
church from the time of Cyprian. By this understanding, transgression required some act of satisfaction to make up for a wrong committed. An adequate act of penance would satisfy the party that had
been wronged. Anselm argued that the death of Christ satisfied God
for the wrong done to him by the human race. Whereas the patristic view had stressed that God as Christ took the initiative to free
humanity from sin, death, and darkness, Anselm pictured Christ as
man offering himself to satisfy God.[10]

In his book *Cur Deus Homo?* Anselm explored a question
designed to help believers give an answer to unbelievers:

> For what reason or by what necessity did God become man,
> and by His death, as we believe and acknowledge, restore life

to the world, although he could have accomplished this by means of another person, whether angelic or human, or simply by an act of His will?[11]

In answering this question, Anselm gave the medieval church a handbook for evangelizing skeptics.

Whereas the patristic view dealt primarily with the biblical issue of redemption, Anselm dealt primarily with forgiveness. For Anselm, forgiveness comes as the result of satisfaction received by God to atone for humanity's offense. Since people have offended God, a person must make satisfaction. Since all people are sinful, none can be found meritorious enough to make satisfaction; therefore, God becomes a human being in Jesus Christ in order to satisfy his own standard of righteousness. Through the exceeding righteousness of Christ, his death sufficiently satisfies all the legal demands against anyone, no matter how dreadful a person considers his or her own sin to be.[12]

Furthermore, according to Anselm, though God demands satisfaction for his offended honor, he did not demand the death of Jesus to satisfy his honor. If he had, then his death would have had no merit since Jesus was only doing what God required. Merit comes only in making an offering to God beyond what God already has a right to possess or expect. In other words, the death of Jesus brings satisfaction, not because God required it, but precisely because God did not require it: *"He was offered because it was His own will."*[13]

In his classic study of the atonement, Aulén criticizes Anselm's view because it "is closely related to the legalism characteristic of the medieval outlook."[14] He complains that the "dualistic outlook" of the patristic view has gone.[15] The emphasis on the Incarnation so prominent in the patristic view does not have the same tone in the Anselmic view, which focuses more on the problem of human sin than the hostile spiritual powers. In his complaint Aulén missed the point, as have those who have taken the side of Anselm against the patristic view for not taking sin seriously. The church fathers explained the significance of the death of Christ for the conversion of pagans in a heathen world populated by all manner of spirits and hostile powers. Anselm explained the significance of the death of Christ for the conversion of pagans in a Christianized world. He lived in the

Christendom that had been slowly growing for six hundred years, and the spiritual issues faced at his time were different from those of the Roman empire. In the ordered universe of feudal Europe, the legal dimension of sin met with common understanding.

Transubstantiation

The time in which Anselm wrote coincided with the development of the doctrine of transubstantiation, whereby the Western church came to believe that in the Eucharist, the bread and wine literally became the flesh and blood of Christ. The term and its philosophical formulation arose from the debates about the nature of the Eucharist in the eleventh century and developed during the twelfth century in the context of realist philosophy.[16] The Fourth Lateran Council (1215) finally declared transubstantiation to be the teaching of the church.[17] The Church of Rome revisited the doctrine from time to time, however, to nuance its meaning in times of major challenge; such as at the Council of Trent (1551) in the face of challenges to the doctrine by the Reformers.[18]

As sometimes happens in theological circles, theologians attempted to formulate the doctrine of transubstantiation long after the memory had faded of why the Western church began to think of the Eucharist in a way so different from the Eastern church.[19] While Augustine in North Africa (354–430) stood in the tradition of those who saw the Eucharist as symbolic, Gregory the Great (540–604) of Rome stressed the sacrificial nature of the Eucharist, not in terms of what happened on Calvary, but in terms of what happened on the altar as a result of the priest's words.[20] This pope's understanding of the Eucharist would have been important if only for his efforts in refining the liturgy of the mass. Because he energetically involved the Church of Rome in the evangelization of Britain and Germany, however, his position took on added import.

Augustine of Canterbury began his mission to England from Rome in 596, while Columba, Kentigern, and Ninian undertook the mission to present-day Scotland from their native Ireland.[21] Augustine used the old pagan temples of the Celts for churches as his mission spread from Canterbury. In the late seventh century, the Celtic religion was still strong enough to make a serious effort to retake Britain, though it failed. On the continent, Charlemagne used armed force to convert the Saxons of Germany; he then sent for Saxon missionaries from England to instruct them in the Christian faith. Alcuin (d. 804), the English advisor to Charlemagne in matters theological, followed Augustine's view that Christ is not sacrificed anew in the Eucharist, but he taught the true presence of Christ in the bread and wine.[22] In response to queries from the young Celtic churches founded during the Saxon conversion, Paschasius Radbert (c. 785–c. 860) taught that the body of Christ was present in the Eucharist as a result of the priest's words.[23] Ratramnus (d. 868), a younger monk in the monastery of Crobie where Paschasius resided, followed Augustine's view and challenged his elder. The debate they began, though never very public or polemical, continued for several centuries until settled by the Fourth Lateran Council.[24]

In other words, the emergence of the issue of transubstantiation cannot be understood apart from the evangelization of the Celtic peoples of Ireland, Britain, Germany, and Holland over a period of several centuries. This teaching did not arise as a result of theological speculation. Rather, it arose as the gospel encountered Celtic paganism, and it achieved formulation upon reflection in Celtic Christianity.

The Druid cult of the Celts involved extensive human sacrifice.[25] According to Julius Caesar, the Celts offered human sacrifices to appease the gods. People in danger traded the life of a victim for their own so that they might escape the danger. The Celts also believed that a victim could be offered as a sacrifice on behalf of the entire community to a god who wanted a life. The presence of pestilence or war indicated that a god wanted a life. The sacrifice might be a slave or captive, but it might also be a family member, preferably a firstborn child. The Romans suppressed human sacrifice in Gaul by A.D. 40, though it continued in Britain until A.D. 77.[26]

While the Celtic religion of Gaul continued in restricted form under Roman rule, it flourished in its pure form in unconquered Germany, Ireland, and Scotland. After the abandonment of Britain by the Romans, the Celtic Angles and Saxons brought their religion back to Britain as the Christian Britons retreated into Wales.[27] The adoption of Christianity came to some pagans (such as the Saxons) by force. To others like the Normans, it came as a matter of political concession. This mode of inclusion did not necessarily involve a change of theology and faith, though it may have involved a modification of behavior.[28] The church assimilated Celts, but had a difficult time changing their theology, particularly in terms of the cult of trees. In Gaul, Germanus (d. 448) and Martin of Tours (d. 397) were known for destroying Celtic shrines centuries after the Roman assimilation of Gaul. Rather than destroy shrines, however, the missionary policy of Augustine involved using the Celtic temples as churches.

With this background, the Celtic understanding of the ritual of human sacrifice has particular meaning against the development of transubstantiation. Apparently the Celts ate part of their sacrificial victim as a sacrament and drank its blood in certain sacrificial rituals in order to derive the benefit of the victim's life strength.[29] The most important rituals were connected with the sacred oak tree, which represented the divine source of life. A human who represented the divine spirit of vegetation and growth was slain so that his life might benefit all things. These human sacrifices were hung or impaled on the tree.[30]

As the Celtic peoples were being evangelized, the death of Christ spoke powerfully to their religious understanding of human sacrifice. In the observance of the Eucharist the life of the divine Christ who hung on a tree became available to those who ate his flesh and drank his blood. In the observance of his death, the Celts experienced the fulfillment of their own religious ideal.[31] This theological thinking forever changed the Roman Church's understanding of the meaning of the mass.

The correlation between the religion of the Celts and the emergence of the doctrine of transubstantiation during their evangelization appears striking. By the time of the official formulation of the doctrine of transubstantiation, however, philosophical considerations had long since eclipsed the evangelistic dynamic that the Celts found moving. From different perspectives, Anselm and the mass gave Europeans two different ways of understanding the meaning of the death of Christ: the first intellectual and the second experiential.

Closely related to the mass, a mysticism developed in the later medieval period that focused attention on identification with the suffering of Christ on the cross.[32] Meditation on the Passion of Christ was encouraged by the stations of the cross in church buildings. Not all mysticism focused on the death of Christ, but the form represented by Francis of Assisi and Catherine of Sienna did. These approaches to immediate experience with Christ had a stronger gospel orientation than some of the more philosophical and esoteric schools of mysticism, such as that founded by John Eckhart (c. 1260–c. 1327). Devotion to the sufferings of Christ offered a way of identifying with Christ, dying with him, and experiencing life in him.

Protestant Attention

Though the Reformers rejected the theology of the mass over five hundred years after the fading of Celtic religion, the lawyers Luther and Calvin followed the basic line of Anselm's understanding of the atonement with a significant departure. The medieval system of penance provides the structure for understanding the view of Anselm, a native Italian whose theology reflects "the Roman genius for law."[33] The Reformers' view with its focus on *sola scriptura* had its basis in the Old Testament sacrificial system, whereby transgression of the holy law required punishment.[34] The sacrificial system provided for a substitute to bear the punishment. While both expressions of substitution have a legal dimension, that of Anselm relates more to the Court of Equity, in which God's honor is satisfied by compensation, while that of the Reformers relates more to the Criminal Court, where transgression requires the satisfaction of a just penalty. Whereas under Anselm Christ offered his merit for sin, under the Reformers God imposed the punishment for every sin on Christ.[35] Later Protestant critics of this view complained that "the satisfaction theory of the Reformation ... which owed its existence to Anselm, was made the test of orthodoxy" until the late nineteenth century.[36]

A great deal of attention has been given to the alternative views of the meaning of the death of Christ. While the moral influence and example views have made for interesting theological reflection for those within the faith, they have not proved particularly compelling in eliciting faith in unbelievers. The views of Ritschl and Schleiermacher caused a stir in nineteenth-century academic circles, but in terms of a message of faith to which people responded, the debate in evangelical circles had greater merit. While the conversions that came with the Puritan movement of sixteenth- and seventeenth-century England, the pietistic movement of seventeenth- and eighteenth-century Germany, and the Great Awakenings of eighteenth- and early nineteenth-century England and America had a firm rooting in the penal substitutionary understanding of the death of Jesus, a shift came with mid-nineteenth-century American revivalism.

Charles Finney, perhaps the greatest of the nineteenth-century American revival preachers and a lawyer by training, spoke of Christ's death as satisfying "public justice."[37] This governmental view of the atonement was first advocated by Hugo Grotius (1583–1645), a lawyer who served in the States General of the United Netherlands and who was the father of international law. This view emerged in the context of the creation of the democratically based Dutch state and reemerged in the early days of American democracy. In this view, God does not punish sin for retribution, but for the upholding of moral government. Christ did not suffer as a substitute for sinners, but to demonstrate God's hatred of sin and to provide a deterrence from sin. His view of the death of Christ functioned like the death penalty, which in legal theory operates as a deterrent to murder.[38] Finney and his followers saw thousands of conversions on the American frontier where law and order were at a premium.[39] Finney's shift in describing the meaning of Jesus' death did not escape the notice of many congregational and Presbyterian clergy, who championed Calvin's understanding of penal substitution.

Dwight L. Moody, the methodological successor to Finney, lacked the theological precision of Finney or his Princeton-trained adversaries. While Finney preached like a lawyer pleading his case before a jury with logic and argument, Moody preached to the heart of his late Victorian audience by telling one sentimental story after another to make his point. He preached the reality of hell and the certainty of judgment, but when he spoke of the death of Jesus he spoke of love. Moody's emphasis on the love of God revealed through the cross resembles the moral influence view of Abelard (1072–1142). Moody also had a far-reaching evangelistic ministry that involved thousands of conversions and influenced the direction of evangelistic methods and messages in the United States.

Moody received his share of criticism as well from the defenders of Reformed orthodoxy. Princeton had been founded in 1812 by the Old School Presbyterians to preserve orthodox Reformed religion in the face of the Unitarianism that had taken hold at Harvard and Yale. Archibald Alexander, Charles Hodge, A. A. Hodge,

Benjamin Warfield, and J. Gresham Machen articulated "Princeton Theology" from 1812 until 1921, when the reorganization of Princeton resulted in the resignation of Machen to preserve orthodoxy at the newly established Westminster Seminary in Philadelphia.[40] Moody's expression of moral influence seemed tame to the Reformed camp, however, compared with the New Theology associated with Andover Seminary. An expression of nineteenth-century liberalism that found "new hope for human progress" in the scientific advances of the age, the New Theology under the banner of "progressive orthodoxy" shifted its concern from atonement to incarnation and offered "future probation" to those outside the fold of Christ.[41] The Andover controversy helped to place penal substitution once again at the center of evangelical theology. The evangelists who followed Moody returned to the Reformed doctrine and considered it one of "the fundamentals" of the faith.

The rift in evangelical Protestantism widened in the twentieth century as adversarial groups emerged around those who stood firmly for the fundamentals and those who held modern ideas. In the fundamentalist-modernist controversy, penal substitution joined the virgin birth, the deity of Christ, the bodily resurrection, and the return of Christ as the five fundamentals. While the other four were seen as crucial tenets of orthodoxy, penal substitution assumed the central position as the core of the gospel message. To a great extent evangelism became an explanation of how the penal substitutionary view of the atonement worked.

As a new stream of evangelicalism emerged after World War II, the two most popular plans for training American Christians to witness focused their attention on the penal substitutionary death of Christ. That is, both the "Four Spiritual Laws" tract developed by Bill Bright of Campus Crusade for Christ and the Evangelism Explosion model presentation developed by D. James Kennedy of Coral Ridge Presbyterian Church represent a commitment to the Reformation understanding of penal substitution. Billy Graham articulated the position of most evangelicals of the mid to third quarter of the twentieth century when he said that he could not take seriously a view of the atonement that neglects substitution because "then men could assume that God overlooked, winked at, or was indifferent to sin."[42]

THE DEATH OF JESUS AS GOOD NEWS

The death of Jesus on the cross remains the great historical fact surrounding Jesus.[43] So great is the significance of this event, though, that its occurrence is disputed by Islam, which affirms that Jesus ascended to heaven like Mohammed without dying. While the entire gospel has saving significance, the death of Christ forms the basis on which salvation occurs. The benefits and implications extend from the cross, yet they do so only because of the integral relationship between the death of Jesus and the other elements of the gospel.

Sigmund Freud's system of psychological analysis centers largely on the experience of guilt. By projecting his own experience of guilt on the universe, he viewed guilt as a universal driving force. He largely dealt with guilt through denial of the experience of neurotic guilt, which has no basis in fact. Yet not all people or cultures feel guilt in the same way as those who live in the West. The conscience has great capacity to deal with guilt in an unhealthy way. One dimension of the death of Christ relates to the satisfaction of matters for which one might feel guilty, but this dimension of the death of Jesus does not exhaust its meaning.

Redemption

As William Abraham has argued, evangelism has a certain logic because the gospel itself has a cohesive internal logic.[44] Apart from the relationship of Christ to creation, the concept of redemption does not make much sense. It makes great sense, however, for the Christ who acted for God in the creation of the cosmos. The idea of redemption assumes the corruption of creation. Ecologically, this corruption is seen in the environmental crisis. Anthropologically, it is seen in the crisis of all human endeavor—social, psychological, economic, spiritual, and physical. Theologically, this corruption results from the separation between God and creation. Without affirming the presence of God, philosophers as diverse as Hegel and Marx have commented on the origins of this experience of corruption, which they have accounted for in terms of separation from either nature or meaningful work. Large segments of the population experience the corruption of separation from something that they also describe as feeling "lost."

The gospel not only describes this situation, but also offers the solution for it in terms of redemption. The death of Christ reveals the costliness to God of redeeming his creation and restoring it to its proper relationship to him. While the Incarnation expresses the identification of God with humanity, only the death of Christ fully expresses what it meant for God to restore people from the curse of corruption that extends ultimately to the grave. Christ entered completely into the corruption for the love of the restored relationship to God. He died in order to bring humanity back from death to life with God. For people who live isolated and ruined lives and who can only look forward cynically to death, the redemption of Jesus Christ offers good news that people can find where they belong and experience life and eternity in a joyful way.

Relationship

The death of Christ expresses the depth of relationship that God desires to have with humanity. In ancient Israel, the redeemer was the next of kin who took it upon himself to set matters straight for the one who could not act on his or her own behalf. The redeemer bought back the family farm, restoring matters to the way they used to be. The redeemer married the relative's widow to ensure she was taken care of and had children to look after her in her old age. The redeemer endured self-sacrifice to make things right for those who were helpless to deal with circumstances on their own. In the sacrifice of Christ on the cross, he acted as a redeemer for those he counted as next of kin. Only this relational dimension of the voluntary death of Christ gives coherent meaning to why Christ endured the cross. For the relationally starved of earth who feel used, abused, and manipulated, the sacrifice of Christ on our behalf is good news that God cares in a profound and personal way for those who can do nothing for him in return.

Love

The cross of Christ represents the ultimate expression of God's love, for "God was in Christ, reconciling the world unto himself" (2 Cor. 5:19, KJV). Yet, it also represents the restoration of love in the cosmos. For love of humanity, Christ came to die. For love of God, Jesus laid down his life. The mystery of the Incarnation brought love to perfection on the cross, where the most selfless act of dying demonstrated God's love. For those who have lived with only sham imitations of love, the cross of Christ offers good news that God has already loved us and wants to love us more.

Substitution

The Redeemer died as a substitute for those he came to rescue. Such a substitution operates on virtually every level of moral development. Kohlberg has argued that people go through stages of moral development just as they go through stages of cognitive development.[45] While his study is flawed and probably only speaks about the experience of upper middle class white males in the United States, it does suggest the identification of attitudes toward morality. While this hypothesis remains unproven, my experience in different cultural settings suggests that entire cultures may operate on different levels of morality. When I was a prison chaplain, I observed that the general population of the inmates regarded something as wrong if they were punished for it. They were there to "pay their debt to society." Once the debt was paid, all was well. To be a snitch was the ultimate sin, because someone would kill you for it.

The rehabilitation process, however, operated on a moral basis of reward: Something was good if one was rewarded for it. Before I entered the ministry, I was heavily involved in politics. Professional politicians who have been accused of immorality have a different way of looking at moral decisions. Something is right if it works, brings benefits, or has a reward. It also corresponds to the morality of the corporate structure: "You scratch my back and I'll scratch yours."

Growing up in the South I learned that many people follow a moral structure based on what the neighbors would think. Something is right if everyone or a significant person approves; something is wrong if it is disapproved. One sees this same peer pressure operating in youth culture with its enforcement of sanctions on those youth who do not conform. I have seen people in Southern culture fall into moral collapse without any bearings when the neighbors no longer care about such things as extramarital affairs. Japanese culture historically operates like old Southern culture, though the penalty for violation of the community expectation is shame.

The law and order approach to morality operates in a number of cultures or subcultures, though it looks different. Islam and historic Judaism have an understanding of right and wrong, as does Confucianism. Whether based on law or tradition, people understand the boundaries because they are the law or the tradition. This approach can be seen in the legal profession with not only its laws but also its traditions. One of my law professors taught us that "the truth is nothing more than testimony which is believed." No subculture is more legalistic than young teenagers who declare, "If you did it for them, you have to do it for me."

The moral approach of the counterculture of the 1960s has entered the mainstream of Western life in Europe and the United States. Grossly stated it is this, "If it feels good, do it." In other forms it appears as "I would never knowingly hurt anyone." It is a morality that rejects rules and authority but looks for some universal principle or guide to give direction in its chaotic drift, which has led to destructive interpersonal decisions.

The death of Christ in his substitution speaks to each of these approaches to morality. At the punishment level of morality, Christ takes our punishment. At the reward level of morality, Christ offers us his life. At the peer pressure level of morality, Christ upholds the expectations of public morality. At the legal level of morality, Christ satisfies the demands of righteousness. At the universal principle level of morality, Christ serves as the example of sacrifice. At a higher level yet, the death of Christ demonstrates the righteousness of God that stands above human understanding of morality to do the appropriate thing in spite of the consequences. While all of these dimensions of the substitution of Christ for humanity are true, they do not completely express the significance of what one experiences at the personal level. It was not in conformity to a theory of the atonement that Christ died. Rather, he died for *me*. The substitution has a personal and intimate character.[46] In bringing about redemption, Christ substituted himself for us in a mystic relationship whereby we trade places. Those who feel the guilt of sin and the helplessness of their own ability to alter the conditions find good news that Christ has traded places with us.

New Beginning

By the substitution of Christ, people are offered a new beginning. By coming into the world, God identified with humanity, but by accepting the substitution of Christ, people identify with God. The old life dies with Christ on the cross. People who feel trapped by their past obtain the freedom in Christ to move on. The death of Christ takes sin and its consequences to the grave as the believer dies with him. For persons imprisoned by their past, that death offers good news that they can start over in life.

Purification

American society has largely lost the concept of purity except as it relates to ecology. What we have done to the environment, however, we have also done to ourselves. People experience pollution and defilement the same way that streams and the air experience it. When something corrupt that does not belong to a stream is added, the stream dies. It may continue to flow, but its purity has been defiled. People experience the same sort of pollution and defilement, both physically and spiritually. It manifests itself in a wide variety of ways from behavior to thought patterns. People can experience defilement at the hands of another, like the victim of rape who feels dirty, polluted, and violated. Unlike the stream, people also have the capacity for polluting themselves. In either case, Jesus Christ offers the good news that cleansing comes through his shed blood.

NOTES

1. See Leon Morris, *The Atonement* (Downers Grove, Ill.: InterVarsity Press, 1983), 106–10.

2. The Re-Imaging Conference in Minneapolis focused criticism on this element in the gospel.

3. Gustaf Aulén, *Christus Victor*, trans. A. G. Hebert (New York: Macmillan, 1969), 4–15. For a more recent study of the history of the doctrine of the atonement, see H. D. McDonald, *The Atonement of the Death of Christ* (Grand Rapids: Baker, 1985).

4. Aulén, *Christus Victor*, 43.

5. Irenaeus, *Against Heresies*, 3.18.7.

6. Ibid., 3.23.1.

7. Origen, *Commentary on the Gospel of John*, 2.21.

8. Origen, *Commentary on Matthew*, 12.25.

9. Origen, *Commentary on the Gospel of John*, 10.20.

10. Aulén, *Christus Victor*, 82–83.

11. Anselm, *Why God Became Man and the Virgin Conception and Original Sin*, trans. Joseph M. Collenon (Albany, N.Y.: Magi Books, 1969), 64.

12. Ibid., 139–41.

13. Ibid., 152; see also 136, 156, 158.

14. Aulén, *Christus Victor*, 92.

15. Ibid., 89.

16. Miri Rubin, *Corpus Christi* (Cambridge: Cambridge Univ. Press, 1991), 24.

17. Kenneth Scott Latourette, *A History of Christianity*, rev. ed. (New York: Harper & Row, 1975), 1:531.

18. Josef A. Jungmann, *The Mass*, trans. Julian Fernandes, ed. Mary Ellen Evans (Collegeville, Minn.: Liturgical Press, 1976), 85.

19. Ibid., 44–54.

20. Ibid., 56, 58.

21. Latourette, *History of Christianity*, 1:344, 346.

22. Jungmann, *The Mass*, 67.

23. Rubin, *Corpus Christi*, 14–15.

24. Ibid., 15–16; cf. Latourette, *History of Christianity*, 1:360–61.

25. Miranda Green, *The Gods of the Celts* (Gloucester, Mass.: Alan Sutton, 1986), 26–32. This book does not attempt to trace all of the cultural encounters of the gospel and other religious views, but the occurrence of human sacrifice plays a prominent role in the history of religion. See René Girard, *The Scapegoat* (Baltimore: Johns Hopkins Univ. Press, 1986). Human sacrifices figured prominently in both Aztec and Inca religions.

26. J. A. MacCulloch, *The Religion of the Ancient Celts* (Folcroft Library Edition, 1977; reprint of Edinburgh: T. & T. Clark, 1911), 233–37.

27. Ibid., 315.

28. Latourette, *History of Christianity*, 1:351–52.

29. MacCulloch, *Religion of the Ancient Celts*, 239–40.

30. Ibid., 198–200.

31. See also Jürgen Moltmann's discussion of the cross and pagan sacrifice in *The Crucified God* (New York: Harper & Row, 1974), 41–44.

32. Milton L. Rudnick, *Speaking the Gospel Through the Ages* (St. Louis: Concordia, 1984), 54–57.

33. George Cadwalader Foley, *Anselm's Theory of the Atonement* (New York: Longmans, Green, and Co., 1908), 104.

34. James Petigru Boyce, *Abstract of Systematic Theology* (Pompano Beach, Fla.: North Pompano Baptist Church; reprint of 1887 edition), 317.

35. Foley, *Anselm's Theory of the Atonement*, 223.

36. Ibid., 256.

37. Lewis A. Drummond, *Charles Grandison Finney and the Birth of Modern Evangelism* (London: Hodder and Stoughton, 1983), 226; Keith J. Hardman, *Charles Grandison Finney 1792–1875* (Grand Rapids: Baker, 1987), 385–87.

38. Millard J. Erickson, *Christian Theology* (Grand Rapids: Baker, 1985), 790–91.

39. See Ross Phares, *Bible in Pocket, Gun in Hand* (Lincoln: Univ. of Nebraska Press, 1964).

40. Daniel G. Reid, Robert D. Linder, Bruce L. Shelley, Harry S. Stout, eds., *Dictionary of Christianity in America* (Downers Grove, Ill.: InterVarsity, 1990), 941–42.

41. Walter A. Elwell, *Evangelical Dictionary of Theology* (Grand Rapids: Baker, 1984), 44–45; Boyce, *Abstract of Systematic Theology*, 298–309.

42. Billy Graham, *World Aflame* (New York: Pocket Books, 1966), 102.

43. For a recent recapitulation of the place of the cross as the central focus of evangelism, see Lewis A. Drummond, *The Word of the Cross*, (Nashville: Broadman, 1992).

44. William J. Abraham, *The Logic of Evangelism* (Grand Rapids: Eerdmans, 1989).

45. See Lawrence Kohlberg, *The Philosophy of Moral Development* (San Francisco: Harper & Row, 1981).

46. The personal experience of need for a substitute figures prominently in cultures around the world. I am indebted to Cher Moua, a Baptist pastor in St. Paul, Minnesota, for describing his conversion and explaining how Christ met the demands of his tribal religion's sacrificial system. I am also indebted to Michael Eldridge for describing the native American Sun Dance, which calls for participants to pierce their flesh as an appeal for pity and help from the Creator. The cross has figured prominently in the conversion of native Americans, who see the suffering of Christ as their substitute.

Chapter 6

Raised from the Dead

The religions of the ancient world did not find the idea of being raised from the dead an unusual one. In ancient Egypt, Osiris suffered at the hands of Seth, only to be brought back to life by his consort Isis. In Canaan, the death of Baal was rectified by his wife/mother, who raised him from the dead. The tales of ancient Greece include the adventures of heroes who traveled to Hades in order to bring back the dead, though not necessarily successfully, as in the case of Orpheus. Some of the native American religions include stories similar to those of the fertility religions of the ancient Near East, corresponding to the cycle of the seasons of the year as death came in winter followed by renewed life in spring.

BIBLICAL BACKGROUND

Despite the common occurrence of the raising of the dead in the religions of the ancient world, the Roman governor Festus responded in a startled way when he heard Paul declare that Jesus had risen from the dead: "You are out of your mind, Paul!" (Acts 26:24). The mythologies of rising from the dead all had nonhistorical qualities about them, from the hybrid animal-men to the nontemporal setting with its once-upon-a-time flavor. Paul, on the other hand, expected Festus to believe that a resurrection had actually happened to a real contemporary individual. It had not happened once upon a time, but the day after Passover, the year Caiaphas served as high priest, during the governorship of Pontius Pilate, and when Herod was tetrarch of Galilee. The death and resurrection of Jesus had not happened in a mythic or heavenly realm, but in the vicinity of Jerusalem, in the garden of Gethsemane, on the Mount of Olives, in the house of Annas, on the steps of the governor's residence, on a hill called Golgotha outside the city walls, and in a garden tomb.

The Gospels

The idea of resurrection formed an important part of the theology of the Pharisees within first-century Judaism. But this doctrine also divided Judaism, for the Sadducees did not believe in a resurrection. The Gospels reflect the extent to which the expectation of resurrection was a living part of contemporary thought in Palestine prior to the first Easter. The debate between the religious groups is reflected in the query Jesus received from a group of Sadducees, "who say there is no resurrection" (Mark 12:18; see also Matt. 22:23; Luke 20:27; cf. Acts 23:6; 24:15; 26:6–8). By his answer, Jesus clearly identified himself with the Pharisees and their understanding of the Psalms and the Prophets. He declared that the Sadducees were in error because they did not "know the Scriptures or the power of God" (Matt. 22:29).

Jesus taught that sexuality was a phenomenon of the present age, but that in the resurrection people would be asexual. Those who take part in the resurrection will not marry or be a part of marriage. Instead, people of the resurrection will be like the angels who do not procreate. Those found worthy to take part in the resurrection never die because they have become children of God (Luke 20:34–36).

At the mourning of Lazarus, Martha expressed the popular understanding of a future resurrection at the end of time. She expected her dead brother Lazarus to "rise again in the resurrection at the last day" (John 11:24). Even Herod expressed views on resurrection that demonstrate how theological understanding can pass to popular theology and finally to superstition. When he heard of some of the wonders related to the ministry of Jesus, Herod speculated that John the Baptist had been raised from the dead (Matt. 14:1–2; Mark 6:14–16; Luke 9:7–9).

In this climate, the Gospels record that Jesus raised the dead on several occasions. He raised to life the daughter of Jairus, a synagogue leader, (Matt. 9:18–26; Mark 5:35–43; Luke 8:40–56). On another occasion, he performed the same wonder by raising the dead son of a widow (Luke 7:11–17). Finally, Jesus raised Lazarus from the dead—after he had been in the tomb for four days (John 11:1–44). John indicates that the attention these acts aroused from the people served as a principal reason why the religious authorities wanted to stop Jesus (11:45–53). Bringing a dead person back to life, however, is a different idea from resurrection. Those brought back to life died again, whereas those who experience resurrection will never die. The act of raising the dead puts into perspective the significance of the announcements by Jesus of his own imminent resurrection. Such announcements do not appear in the Gospels until after Jesus demonstrated his power over death.

Resurrection Announcements

The Passion predictions in the Synoptic Gospels have received considerable scholarly attention. But the four Gospels actually contain more preresurrection announcements by Jesus than prepassion announcements. On at least ten occasions, Jesus announced that he would rise from the dead.

The sign of Jonah. Twice when his adversaries demanded a sign identifying who Jesus was, he offered them the sign of Jonah (Matt. 12:38–42; Luke 11:29–32; and Matt. 16:1–4; Mark 8:11–13). Jesus spoke typologically of his coming burial and resurrection, for that would be like Jonah, who spent three days in the belly of the great fish. While speaking cryptically, Jesus made it clear that the resurrection would comprise the definitive statement of his identity.

The Passion predictions. Strictly speaking, the three Passion predictions of the Synoptic Gospels are not exclusively about the Passion. While they all deal with the circumstances surrounding the death of Jesus, with the exception of Luke 9:44–45 they culminate in the resurrection ([1] Matt. 16:21–23; Mark 8:31; Luke 9:22; [2] Matt. 17:22–23; Mark 9:30–32; [3] Matt. 20:17–19; Mark 10:32–34; Luke 18:31–33). In these passages, the resurrection puts death and suffering as well as vanity into proper perspective (Matt. 16:22–28).

The rendezvous in Galilee. Matthew and Mark record a warning from Jesus that the disciples would all fall away, but in its context he announced a rendezvous with them in Galilee after the resurrection (Matt. 26:31–32; Mark 14:27–28). Matthew and Mark both cite the fulfillment of this announcement at the empty tomb when an angel reminded the women that Jesus would meet the disciples in Galilee after the resurrection (Matt. 28:7–10; Mark 16:7). John joins Matthew in describing what happened in Galilee after the resurrection (Matt. 28:16–20; John 21). While Luke does not mention the rendezvous announcement or that particular resurrection appearance, he does allude to an announcement of the resurrection when the disciples had been with Jesus in Galilee (Luke 24:6). This episode plays an important part in the impact of the resurrection on them, for it emphasizes how Jesus explained to the disciples things they could not comprehend until after they experienced them. The resurrection, in this sense, redefined reality for the disciples, who now remembered what Jesus had said. Everything that he had said now had to be taken seriously in a way that was not necessary prior to the resurrection.

Transfiguration and resurrection. Even though Peter, James, and John experienced the Transfiguration, they did not understand it. When the face of Jesus shone like the sun and Moses and Elijah appeared, Peter reacted by suggesting that they erect tents in honor of Jesus, Moses, and Elijah. In the midst of this event the disciples heard a voice from a bright cloud that enveloped them, declaring, "This is my Son, whom I love; with him I am well pleased. Listen to him!" (Matt. 17:5).

The Transfiguration demonstrated the significance of the teaching by Jesus that God "is not the God of the dead but of the living" (Matt. 22:32). Moses and Elijah had been dead for centuries, but they lived in the presence of the Son of God. In this context Jesus told the three companions not to tell anyone about the experience until after his resurrection (Matt. 17:9, Mark 9:9–10). At that time the implications of that event would extend to all like Moses and Elijah, who faced death. Furthermore, the private declaration of sonship that the disciples witnessed at the Transfiguration was superseded by a public declaration, for Jesus "was declared with power to be the Son of God by his resurrection from the dead" (Rom. 1:4).

The good shepherd. In John's Gospel, Jesus describes himself as the good shepherd who knows his sheep intimately and lays down his life for them (John 10:14–15). This announcement of the coming Passion also occurs in the context of a resurrection announcement. While laying down his life demonstrates his love, taking his life up again demonstrates his power and authority. The resurrection represents his ultimate demonstration of power and authority (10:17–18). Such a demonstration is echoed by Jesus in the resur-

rection account of Matthew, where Jesus declared that "all authority in heaven and on earth" had been given to him (Matt. 28:18).

Raising the temple. John's Gospel records another episode that
occurred in Jerusalem, in which a group demanded a sign of Jesus
to prove his authority. Jesus replied, "Destroy this temple, and I will
raise it again in three days" (John 2:19). Again, in cryptic, allegorical fashion, Jesus taught the significance of the resurrection in
advance in terms of its proof of his authority. By speaking allegorically, however, the significance of the teaching was not clear to the
disciples until after the resurrection (2:22).

After a little while. Finally, John's Gospel records an exchange
at the Last Supper that announced the resurrection: "In a little while
you will see me no more, and then after a little while you will see
me" (John 16:16). The disciples did not understand this cryptic
remark, but Jesus explained that when he was gone, they would
experience grief. When he appeared again, however, his appearance
would usher in an experience of complete and unending joy. The
experience of suffering is real, but the resurrection and its effect
would cause suffering to be forgotten (John 16:17–24; cf. Phil. 3:7–
11; Heb. 12:2). Even suffering turns to joy under the impact of the
resurrection.

Reaction to the announcements. The disciples have often been
castigated as insensitive to spiritual matters for their failure to grasp
who Jesus was while he was in their midst. Actually, they behaved
as perfectly rational people of any age or culture. They expressed no
less spiritual sensitivity than anyone would who heard someone suggest that he was going to rise from the dead. A resurrection at the
end of time was far enough away to be manageable. The resurrection of Jesus, however, was perfectly unreasonable until it happened.

The trial accounts in Matthew and Mark reflect the exchange
recorded in John about destroying and raising the temple (Matt.
26:60–62; Mark 14:58–59). The testimony of the two witnesses
reflects the basic misunderstanding that the disciples experienced.
Christ's statement was taken more as an insult to the temple than as
the blasphemy the court hoped to uncover. The people interpreted
Jesus' statement only to mean that he could actually destroy the temple and build another one in three days. At the crucifixion, this
episode was recalled again by the crowd as some cried, "You who

are going to destroy the temple and build it in three days, save yourself! Come down from the cross, if you are the Son of God!" (Matt. 27:40).

Finally, the authorities responded to the resurrection announcements of Jesus with caution. While they did not believe that he would rise from the dead, they had heard of the cryptic announcements and did not want any trouble coming from them. Matthew records the request of the chief priests and Pharisees that Pilate place a guard at the tomb to ensure that no one could steal the body of Jesus and then claim that he had risen (Matt. 27:62–66).

The Resurrection Accounts

While few events in ancient times had careful "dating" in the accounts written about them, all four of the Gospels specify that Jesus rose on the first day of the week following Passover. They also agree that the first people who went to the tomb at daybreak and found it empty were women. An angel announced the resurrection as the fulfillment of what Jesus had declared earlier. The women then ran to tell the disciples what had happened. Peter and John ran to the tomb to verify the report. In the meantime, Jesus appeared to Mary Magdalene and to other women. The reports began to spread among the disciples, and Jesus appeared to two others on the road to Emmaus before appearing to a gathering of the disciples that evening (Matt. 28:1–10; Mark 16:1–8; Luke 24:1–49; John 20:1–23). The fact that the longer ending of Mark and the Gospel of John support the account of Luke adds credibility to the record of the disciples' experience of the resurrection.

The agreement of the Gospels regarding the essential events of the first Easter is remarkable, considering the diverse recollection of details they record in both the story of the death of Christ and of his resurrection. While John's Gospel primarily tells stories that the Synoptic Gospels had not included, his account of the resurrection has a striking similarity to the basic occurrences found in the other Gospels. While the different writers agree about the events, John disagrees with the others over whether Mary Magdalene met the risen Jesus before or after Peter and John went to the tomb. The writers also reflect different impressions of exactly how many angelic beings appeared, though this issue reflects the thorny problem of knowing people from angels (Gen. 18:1–19:29; Dan. 3:24–25; Heb. 13:2) and of knowing exactly how many angels might be at a given location at a given time (Luke 2:9–15; cf. Num. 22:21–35). In similar fashion with the medieval debate over how many angels can dance on the head of a pin, twentieth-century Christian scholarship has focused attention on the inconsequential variations in the resurrection accounts rather than on the significance of the unanimous testimony of the Evangelists to the resurrection.

Implications

The resurrection firmly established the identity of Jesus as Lord for his disciples. Executed for identifying himself with God, the resurrection justified Jesus as innocent of blasphemy and created a basis for the disciples to understand finally his true identity (John 20:24–29). The resurrection also demonstrated the authority and power of Jesus over life and death. By extension, Jesus will share the resurrection with his followers (John 5:21, 28; 6:25–59).

General Apostolic Writings

The apostles pursued at least five major themes related to the resurrection that have significant implications for faith. They regarded the declaration of the resurrection as central to their faith and calling. Apart from the resurrection they had no faith, for faith had died for them with Jesus on Good Friday. Thus, it was crucial that their leadership be able to declare the resurrection with confidence from their own experience (Acts 1:22). Their preaching culminated in the announcement of the resurrection of Jesus (4:33; 17:18), and participation in salvation required that people believe God had raised Jesus from the dead (Rom. 10:9; 1 Cor. 15:1–11).

Vindication. The sermons in Acts have the resurrection at their core, though they nuance the implications of the resurrection in a variety of ways consistent with the teaching reflected in the letters. Regardless of the nuance the sermons follow, however, most make the point that God vindicated Christ by the resurrection and clearly established his authority (Acts 2:23–24, 32; 3:15; 4:10; 5:30; 10:39–40; 13:27–30). The same thought pattern appears in each of these sermons. Though they do not have a formulaic phrase, they all express the idea that people killed Jesus, but God raised him from the dead. Jesus was right after all. By raising him, God affirmed all of the teachings and claims of his Son. Thus, the resurrection has a variety of applications based on the ministry of Jesus.

Hope. If "faith is the substance of things hoped for, the evidence of things not seen" (Heb. 11:1, KJV), then faith in the resurrection supplies a substantial reason for hope and represents evidence of the transcendent realities that are not seen. The apostles certainly stressed the resurrection as a concrete basis for hope. In his Pentecostal sermon, Peter quoted from the book of Psalms to indicate that David had a hope based on the expectation of the resurrection (Acts 2:25–28). This theme appears also in 1 Peter, where believers are said to have a "living hope" as a result of the resurrection of Jesus (1 Peter 1:3). The resurrection of Jesus created a basis for faith and hope in God (1:21).

This theme of the resurrection also appears throughout Paul's sermons and writings. In his comments in Jerusalem and in Caesarea, Paul associated hope with the anticipation of the resurrection. He declared that he stood accused because of his "hope in the resurrection of the dead" (Acts 23:6; 24:21), the same hope that was a central tenant of faith for the Pharisees (24:14–15; cf. 23:6–8). Before Agrippa, Paul declared that the hope of Israel for the fulfillment of God's promises to the prophets for resurrection of the dead had been fulfilled in Christ (26:6–8, 22–23).

Paul's letters expand on the theme of hope that proceeds from the resurrection. Those who have faith in Christ have been called to live a life of hope because the same power that raised Jesus from the dead is at work in all who believe (Eph. 1:18–20). In the face of suffering, hardship, and adversity, the resurrection provides hope for those who trust God (2 Cor. 1:8–10; cf. 2 Tim. 2:8). Hope is not limited to this life, but it extends beyond the grave; otherwise it would not truly be hope (1 Cor. 15:12–19; 1 Thess. 1:9–10; 4:13–14). Without the resurrection, Paul reasoned that Christians had no hope and were to be pitied (1 Cor. 15:18).

Eternal life. Hope beyond the grave focuses on the gift of eternal life that comes through participation in the resurrection of Christ. The apostles proclaimed that the resurrection of the dead would occur for those in Jesus (Acts 4:2). The resurrection of Jesus served as the prelude to the resurrection of all who "belong" to Jesus (1 Cor.

15:20–23; cf. John 10:26–30; 17:2, 6, 24). Just as God raised Jesus from the dead, he will also raise those who have faith in Christ (Rom. 10:9–10; 2 Cor. 4:13–14). By the believer's relationship with Christ through faith, they share in his resurrection as God makes them alive with Christ (Eph. 2:4–9). The nature of this relationship finds description variously as "remaining in" Christ, as being "in Christ," as Christ being "in" us, as the Holy Spirit being in us, or as the Spirit of Christ being in us. This concept, though described in a variety of ways, is crucially important, for it explains how the resurrection of Jesus extends to those who have faith in him:

> But if Christ is in you, your body is dead because of sin, yet your spirit is alive because of righteousness. And if the Spirit of him who raised Jesus from the dead is living in you, he who raised Christ from the dead will also give life to your mortal bodies through his Spirit, who lives in you. (Rom. 8:10–11)

Baptism represented for the early church both participation in the death and resurrection of Jesus and incorporation into his Spirit (the discussion of the Spirit must wait for a later chapter). New believers went under the water as a corpse into the grave, but they came up out of the water as Christ emerged from the tomb, "having been buried with him in baptism and raised with him through your faith in the power of God, who raised him from the dead" (Col. 2:12; cf. Rom. 6:4–5). Unlike the mystery religions, which had initiation rites that were thought to save the new convert, Peter stressed that baptism served as a pledge of "good conscience" to God and that the resurrection it represented brought salvation (1 Peter 3:21).

Justification and righteousness. While the doctrine of justification is normally thought of in relation to the death of Christ, Paul also spoke of justification and its cognate idea, the forgiveness of sins, in relation to the resurrection. In Pisidian Antioch, Paul discussed the resurrection at length in terms of the fulfillment of promises made by God to King David (Acts 13:26–39). After elaborating the significance of the resurrection and the fulfillment of the prophecy that the "Holy One" would not see decay, Paul drew his overall conclusion:

> Therefore, my brothers, I want you to know that through Jesus the forgiveness of sins is proclaimed to you. Through him

everyone who believes is justified from everything you could
not be justified from by the law of Moses. (Acts 13:38–39)

This correlation between resurrection and justification also appears
in Romans 10:9–10, where belief in the resurrection leads to justification. Christ died for our sins, but he rose to justify those who
have faith in the God who raised him. God credits such people as
righteous (4:24–25).

Character of life. The resurrection has profound implications
about how a person lives his or her life. Because the resurrection
puts death and eternity in perspective, it also puts life in perspective.
If a person has faith that God has raised Jesus from the dead, then
it ought to have an impact on how he or she lives. Those who share
in the resurrection of Christ have been set free from slavery to sin,
but they have become slaves to righteousness (Rom. 6:13–14). God
has made the resurrection of Christ available to people in order that
they "might bear fruit to God" (7:4; cf. Gal. 5:16–23). Since by the
resurrection Christ has been made Lord of the living and the dead,
we ought to live our lives for him (Rom. 14:7–9). Because of the
resurrection, the bodies of those who have faith in Christ belong to
Christ; therefore, Christians ought to keep their bodies pure (1 Cor.
6:13–15). Accepting the resurrection of Christ creates an obligation
for how one lives. Paul suggested that the resurrection gives a motivation for moral behavior that human reasons lack (1 Cor. 15:29–
34). This motivation emerges from the love of Christ who died and
rose in order that people might have a new basis for living their lives
(2 Cor. 5:14–15).

HISTORICAL/THEOLOGICAL DEVELOPMENT

The resurrection has held a different place in the history of the
church than other elements of the gospel. It has never served as the
focal point of theology around which other elements of the gospel
revolved, though it does serve as the perspective of worship in the
Orthodox Church. Neither has it served as the center of controversy
in a major way. When it has been a part of controversy, its part has
tended to be secondary to another issue, as in the Gnostic controversy of the second century. Certainly an occasional theologian like
Oscar Cullmann has made it central, or others like Bultmann have

seen it as mythical, but for the whole church in a major epoch, these have been minor incidents, not to be compared with major theologies or movements.

The virtual absence of the resurrection as the integrating factor of a major movement, theological controversy, or school of theology seems surprising. It has been a part of all orthodox theological schools of thought, and Easter represents the central moment in the Christian year. Its absence from debate may actually heighten its significance for the many groups that make up Christianity. Since the Gnostic debates of the second century, the church has not had a significant dispute about the resurrection of Christ, and even the Gnostic dispute had more to do with creation and the role of matter in the divine scheme of things. Even the furor over Bultmann's demythologizing did not result in a significant shift to the resurrection as the organizing principle of evangelical theology. Evangelicals viewed the resurrection as only one of many issues related to one's view of Scripture.

The resurrection has remained the great article of faith that requires neither theories, interpretations, nor exposition. One either believes or disbelieves that Jesus came out of the tomb. As the one great undisputed article of faith, however, it has never played the central role of defining an epoch, school of thought, or movement.

The Patristic Period

While disputes with the Gnostics over the fact of the resurrection or the nature of the resurrection formed a minor theme for the church fathers, the emphasis of the debates lay on what would be the nature of the future resurrection of all the dead rather than on the resurrection of Christ. Even this generalization, however, requires some qualification. The early fathers laid their stress on the resurrection of Christ and the necessity of a "real" suffering, death, and resurrection for salvation.

Ignatius stressed that the suffering, death, and resurrection of Christ were fleshly and spiritual, but not Docetic. A real resurrection requires a real death, otherwise they would not result in salvation.[1] He insisted that Christ underwent real suffering while "heavenly, earthly, and subterranean beings looked on."[2] Refuting a Docetic understanding of the Incarnation, Ignatius declared that because of his true incarnation Christ experienced a true resurrection in which those who believe in him will share. Polycarp joined Ignatius in his attack of Docetism, arguing that resurrection and judgment are as crucial to the faith as are incarnation and passion.[3]

A treatise on the resurrection attributed to Justin refutes the views of those who argued that the flesh is the cause of sin and that Jesus only appeared to have a body of flesh.[4] This treatise appears to have been written to elicit faith in unbelievers, but not on the basis of the fulfillment of Scripture, as in the *Dialogue with Trypho*. Instead, *On the Resurrection* relies exclusively on philosophical argument from Plato, Epicurus, and the Stoics. In his *Second Apology*, however, Justin discussed resurrection in terms of the judgment of the wicked, a thoroughly biblical theme.[5] In *To Autolycus*, Theophilus of Antioch used arguments from the experience of the pagan world rather than from Scripture to demonstrate the reasonableness of the resurrection of the dead.[6]

In his treatise *On the Resurrection*, Athenagoras made a case for the reasonableness of the idea of resurrection without specific reference to Christ.[7] In his argument, however, resurrection proceeds from an understanding of God as Creator who has an ultimate plan for his creation, and from an understanding of a final judgment that will give a suitable end to life.[8] In this treatise, Athenagoras began by addressing "scholastic" arguments that raise the issue of a person who drowned and was eaten by a fish. If someone then caught the fish and ate it, what would happen in the resurrection when the same material particles had occupied a place in two different people at different times? To this challenge, Athenagoras developed a theory that excluded the possibility of human flesh ever being digested by another human to the extent that it would become an essential part of the flesh of another.[9]

References to the resurrection occur in the work of Irenaeus in the context of arguments with the Gnostics. The primary arguments relate to the creation of the physical world, the coming of Christ into the world in true physical, human fashion, and the implications of the resurrection of Christ for those who have faith in him. Irenaeus had a clear millenarian position, and the coming of the kingdom at the return of Christ composed the focal point of his discussion of resurrection in *Against Heresies*.[10] The resurrection of

Christ, however, is the assumption that makes all of the arguments necessary.

Tertullian's treatise *On the Resurrection of the Flesh* also discusses resurrection in relation to the Gnostic teaching of a Docetic Christ and the essential wickedness of the physical human body. Like Irenaeus, Tertullian stressed that the resurrection provides for the judgment of the total person before God.[11] In the debate with the Gnostics, who denied the goodness of creation, Tertullian affirmed that the Christian hope lies in the "resurrection of the dead," which means that the fallen body of flesh will rise because the fleshly body represents the aspect of people that dies, since the soul does not die.[12] He emphatically rejected the notion that the resurrection of believers refers to the experience in this life of putting on Christ in baptism.[13] The Gnostics tended to speak of resurrection as though it corresponded to the Christian experience of regeneration. Because they understood the human spirit to be a part of the divine, however, they could not speak of regeneration, which involved the Holy Spirit's coming. Instead, they spoke of the experience of God in this life as a resurrection or "restoration to the Pleroma," which for them meant a return to a preexistent state.[14] Whereas the Apologists had appealed to the Old Testament and its fulfillment for their authority, the Valentinians and other Gnostics appealed to the writings of the apostles, but with a mystical or esoteric interpretation.[15] While they may have affirmed resurrection, they meant something quite different, which might be confused for what a later generation would call "realized eschatology."

Origen's view of the future resurrection crossed the boundary of accepted orthodoxy because of his theory of spiritual bodies as opposed to material bodies. He derived his notion of spiritual bodies largely from his conception of the preexistent state of all rational beings. To Origen, God had given bodies as a punishment to the spirits who turned their wills away from him. Thus, material existence came as the result of the Fall. Having devoted his life to the exposition of Scripture, Origen could arrive at such a conclusion only because his allegorical method allowed him the freedom to accommodate his view of Scripture to his philosophical understanding. He viewed the coming resurrection as a restoration of the spiritual universe without particular concern for the material universe. In terms of how this understanding of body affected personhood, Origen held that the "body" has a variety of expressions for preserving the individual, matter being only one of these.[16] Origen advocated an "organic view" of resurrection, following Paul's metaphor in 1 Corinthians 15 of the seed, which allows something to change while remaining the same.[17]

In contrast to Origen's view, Caroline Walker Bynum has identified a Western tradition, emerging from Athenagoras and the early fathers, which viewed resurrection as essentially a reassemblage of the material parts of the body, without which people could only experience a partial or incomplete continuity beyond death.[18] Augustine followed Athenagoras, insisting that in the resurrection to come, the saints must have a resurrection like the resurrection of Christ. In affirming the resurrection of the flesh, however, Augustine also affirmed a transformation of the flesh, just as water may change to air while retaining the same material particles.[19] Augustine's understanding of resurrection followed his primary concern for creation and its redemption. The resurrection expresses the divine concern for the total person. The resurrection frees the body from the consequences of sin. It also preserves the uniqueness of a person, which makes them recognizable by preserving the body.[20]

Neoplatonists, Gnostics, and Manichaeans viewed the body as a vulgar prison that held the soul captive. The body caused immorality for the soul; thus, the soul longed to escape its prison to achieve reunion with the divine. To these thinkers, the idea of the resurrection of the body constituted punishment rather than salvation. The issue for Augustine and his adversaries was not the resurrection that came as a conclusion, but the initial primacy of the nature of humanity in relation to God. If people are a spark of God, then the body and resurrection constitute base ideas. If, on the other hand, people are created by God, then the body and resurrection are good.[21] In Augustine's thought, therefore, the resurrection takes on less significance in terms of metaphysical priority because of the worldview he strove to affirm. Resurrection assures the survival of the created person.

In the thirteenth century, several groups emerged that revisited the old Gnostic and Manichaean views of creation and resurrection. The Amauricians, a group in Paris, insisted that the indwelling of the

Holy Spirit was the resurrection.[22] The Cathari denied the resurrection because they denied the Incarnation and repudiated the physical world.[23] In 1215, the Fourth Lateran Council required the Cathari to agree that "all rise with their own individual bodies, that is, the bodies which they now wear."[24] At the same time, however, the idea of God's ability to reassemble the human body parts at the resurrection correlates with the growing practice of the mutilation of the bodies of dead saints to disperse the benefits of proximity to their bodies.[25]

Eastern Orthodoxy

One of the great generalizations of Christianity rests in the notion that the Western church emphasizes the crucifixion of Christ while the Eastern church emphasizes the resurrection. Both branches of the church emphasize both. Nonetheless, one may note certain nuances in how they emphasize these elements of the gospel they both affirm.

The Eastern church celebrates the Eucharist from the perspective of its fulfillment after the resurrection rather than its anticipation of the crucifixion. Thus, the Eastern church observes the meal with a mood of rejoicing over the victory rather than with a somber mood over the suffering—as would be reflected in a text like Acts 2:46, where the church "broke bread . . . with glad and generous hearts."[26] Unlike the Roman Catholic understanding of transubstantiation, whereby the elements of the supper become the body and blood of Christ as the priest speaks the words of the liturgy, the Orthodox believe that the presence of the resurrected Christ in the service causes the change in the elements.[27] For them, the Eucharist does not so much plead the sacrifice of the cross, as the Roman mass does. Instead, it opens the door of eternity beyond space and time where one communes with the resurrected Christ.[28]

The recurring motif of joy in Orthodox worship relates to the central reality of the resurrection for the church: "The light of the resurrection of Christ lights the church, and the joy of the resurrection, of the triumph over death, fills it."[29] Easter is the heart of Orthodoxy, which is characterized by joy over the resurrection that puts all other experience into perspective.[30] Thus, Orthodoxy as a whole is not a world-renouncing faith. With its stress on the light of the transfiguration and resurrection, it presents an optimistic faith.

The Orthodox continue to practice baptism by immersion, which represents the death of a sinner and his or her resurrection as a redeemed Christian.[31] It involves a spiritual birth whereby the "natural man," and the original sin that afflicts, dies through putting on Christ.[32]

Observations

The centrality of the resurrection can be seen in the decision of the church to move its principal day of worship from the Sabbath to the first day of the week, when Jesus rose from the dead.[33] While the church has steadfastly held to the resurrection of Christ as a basic assumption, her discussions of this doctrine have often actually been about creation, the Incarnation, the final judgment, or the coming of the Holy Spirit. Among current theologians, though, concern over the resurrection has received particular attention from Moltmann and Pannenberg. The resurrection of Christ has both present implications (as the Eastern church has stressed) and future implications (as the Western church has stressed). These implications include hope beyond this life and hope for living in this life based on the victory of Christ, the affirmation of creation, and the affirmation of the individual person.

THE RESURRECTION AS GOOD NEWS

The resurrection appeals to an entirely different set of spiritual concerns than the death of Jesus. Spiritual concerns do not necessarily mean otherworldly concerns. The spiritual issues that the resurrection answers speak both to the challenges of living and dying.

Hope

The resurrection offers a concrete basis for hope to people who have no reason for hope. Hopelessness has become a pervasive problem of late twentieth-century life, whether in the shanty towns of Mexico City, the slums of South Chicago, the dull block apartments of Moscow, or the exclusive neighborhoods of Orange County. People without hope have little reason to live, as the death rate among children and youth in inner-city gangs suggests. They live dangerously, and they treat one another with the same despair they have for their own future.

The woman who called my study ten minutes before the Christmas Sunday morning worship service to inquire if she could still go to heaven if she killed herself was not asking a question about the perseverance of the saints or about the extent of the efficacy of Christ's atonement. She wanted hope for living. The resurrection supplies that hope. If Christ could go through the darkness of death and the grave to emerge on the other side in a glorious new life, then he offers hope that on the other side of our immediate experience of darkness lies a new life that does not need to wait until heaven. For people who live in despair and depression, Christ's resurrection offers a concrete basis of hope for those who share in the power of his resurrection.

Victory

The resurrection powerfully demonstrates Christ's victory over all the adverse forces of the universe, from the prejudice that condemned him to the spiritual powers in opposition to him. Defeat and failure characterize many lives in the West as well as other parts of the world, but with the success culture of the West, failure can be an even greater source of agony. The resurrection speaks of the victory people may experience in spite of the circumstances of life, a victory that allows them to see the vanity of life from a different perspective. The resurrection victory provides a basis for moving out of the self-categorization of victim to the experience of victor with Christ. For people who live defeated lives, the resurrection of Jesus offers good news for living victoriously above the defeats of life. It does not deny the defeats any more than the resurrection denied the crucifixion, but it puts the most miserable defeat in perspective.

Freedom

The resurrection offers freedom from bondage. Ultimately this freedom extends to freedom from death and the grave. In the meantime, however, the resurrection offers freedom from the bondage of sin. For the person bound by physical or psychological addiction, the resurrection offers freedom from the bondage that controls one's life. Freedom from the slavery of sin, whether compulsion, obsession, or mere habit, is held out as an offer from Christ to those who share his resurrection. The shared resurrection presupposes the shared death wherein a person dies with Christ to sin. In contrast to suicide, however, which represents vain escapism without hope of anything better, death with Christ opens the door to the resurrection and freedom from what lies in the past. For those who languish in bondage to things they cannot overcome, the resurrection of Jesus offers the good news of freedom.

This freedom also extends to the spiritual realm. Cher Moua, a member of the Hmong ethnic group of Laos, describes how the resurrection freed him from the dread of an almost endless cycle of reincarnations that his tribal religion offered. Sharing in the resurrection of Jesus breaks that cycle and allows him spiritual freedom. This experience of freedom also has its implication for the significance of personhood.

Affirmation of Personhood

Resurrection stands in stark contrast to the idea of the immortality of a soul that will eventually remerge with the divine essence from which it has become disengaged, there to lose its individual existence like a drop of rain that falls in the ocean. Instead of a cycle of reincarnations required to allow this immortal soul to ascend to a higher spiritual plane, resurrection teaches that people have one life to live and have a personal identity created by God. Resurrection affirms each individual person and what they choose to make of their lives. Instead of souls that are a part of the divine immortal essence, people are creatures whom God preserves through resurrection. For the person who longs for personal acceptance and fulfillment, who longs for an experience in eternity characterized by meaningful relationship rather than unconscious oblivion, then the resurrection of Jesus Christ offers good news that God has created that kind of present and future.

Eternal Life

Earlier we observed that existentialism is concerned both with the dread of meaninglessness and with the dread of isolation. The existentialists mention a third dread related to human existence. To be aware of my existence is to be aware of my coming nonexistence. People everywhere dread death. Perhaps not *all* people dread death, but certainly most people do. The resurrection provides a basis for expecting life beyond the grave, and it gives some veiled under-standing of what that life may be like. The resurrection of Jesus pro-vides the grounds for belief in the general resurrection to come.

American culture has a pervasive dread of death and the aging that leads to death. Entire industries exist to help people deny their mortality. I once knew a man who was consumed with his regimen of physical fitness and nutrition. The crisis of his life came when he had a heart attack; it was not supposed to happen. Other people deny death by the clothes they wear, the cosmetics they apply, and the recreation they pursue. In an increasingly mobile society, children grow up not knowing old people. In such a society devoted to med-ical technology, old people who are dying are segregated from the rest of society in nursing homes. The society has structured itself not to deal with death, because it does not know how. For people who long to live but have no reason to expect anything but the grave, the resurrection of Jesus Christ offers good news that God has power to give life.

NOTES

1. Ignatius, *To the Smyrnaeans*, 7:2; 12:2. References to Ignatius and Polycarp come from *The Apostolic Fathers*, ed. Jack N. Sparks (Nashville: Thomas Nelson, 1978).

2. Ignatius, *To the Trallians*, 9:1–11:2.

3. Polycarp, *To the Philippians*, 7:1.

4. Justin Martyr, *On The Resurrection*, 1–2.

5. Joanne E. McWilliam Dewart, *Death and Resurrection* (Message of the Fathers of the Church 22; Wilmington, Del.: Michael Glazier, 1986), 69.

6. Ibid., 70.

7. Ibid., 73. Some dispute the authenticity of this treatise; see *Tertul-lian's Treatise on the Resurrection*, ed. Ernest Evans (London: SPCK, 1960), xxviii, n.1.

8. Athenagoras, *On The Resurrection*, chaps. 12–25.

9. Lynn Boliek, *The Resurrection of the Flesh* (Grand Rapids: Eerd-mans, 1962), 43–44.

10. Irenaeus, *Against Heresies*, 5.24–36; see also Dewart, *Death and Resurrection*, 97.

11. *Tertullian's Treatise on the Resurrection*, 39.

12. Ibid., 49–50.

13. Ibid., 51.

14. Malcolm Lee Peel, *The Epistle to Rheginos*: *A Valentinian Letter on the Resurrection* (Philadelphia: Westminster, 1969), 30.

15. Ibid., 17.

16. Boliek, *The Resurrection of the Flesh*, 60–66.

17. Caroline Walker Bynum, *The Resurrection of the Body in Western Christianity, 200–1336* (New York: Columbia Univ. Press, 1995), 159. Bynum argues persuasively that well into the late Middle Ages, Origen stands virtually alone in his view that dismissed the participation of the physical in the resurrection: "The idea of person, bequeathed by the Middle Ages to the modern world, was not a concept of soul escaping body or soul using body; it was a concept of self in which physicality was integrally bound to sensation, emotion, reasoning, identity—and therefore finally to whatever one means by salvation" (p. 11).

18. Ibid., 63. Within this tradition Bynum includes Irenaeus, Tertullian, Gregory of Nyssa, Augustine, Jerome, Cyril of Jerusalem, Methodius, Ephraim the Syriac, Macarius Magnes, Hilary of Poitiers, Honorius Augustodunensis, Hugh of St. Victor, Anselm of Laon, William of Champeaux, Hildegard of Bingen, Herrad of Hohenbourg, Bernard, William of St. Thierry, and Herman of Reun.

19. Boliek, *The Resurrection of the Flesh*, 69–73.

20. Henri Irenee Marrou, *The Resurrection and Saint Augustine's Theology of Values*, trans. Maria Consolata (Villanova, Pa.: Villanova, 1966), 16, 19–22, 26.

21. Ibid., 8–13.

22. Bynum, *The Resurrection of the Body*, 154.

23. Ibid., 215–16.

24. Ibid., 154–55.

25. Ibid., 201–3.

26. Ernest Benz, *The Eastern Orthodox Church: Its Thought and Life*, trans. Richard and Clara Winston (Chicago: Aldine, 1963), 22–23.

27. Sergius Bulgakov, *The Orthodox Church* (London: Century, 1935), 37.

28. Nicholas Zernov, *Eastern Christendom* (London: Weidenfeld and Nicholson, 1961), 244.

29. Bulgakov, *The Orthodox Church*, 9.
30. Ibid., 153–54.
31. Zernov, *Eastern Christendom*, 249.
32. Bulgakov, *The Orthodox Church*, 132.
33. J. G. Davies, *The Early Christian Church* (Grand Rapids: Baker, 1980), 104, 154.

Chapter 7

Exaltation

Because of the exaltation of Jesus after his resurrection appearances, the experience of the church with him has always been in the present tense. While the church affirms the apostolic faith of the witnesses who knew Jesus when he walked the earth, the Christian faith does not remain in the past concerning his identity and actions. As a result of his exaltation to the right hand of God, the Christian faith moves from the past to a present faith in who Jesus is and what he does. The debate between John MacArthur and Charles Ryrie over the nature of the gospel has hung on whether the exaltation of Christ represents a part of the gospel. MacArthur stresses faith in who Christ is whereas Ryrie stresses faith in what Christ did.[1]

Other religions affirm an ascension of people from the physical realm of earth to the spiritual realm of heaven. One of the holiest shrines of Islam is the Dome of the Rock in Jerusalem, site of the ancient temple of Israel. From that rock the faithful of Islam believe that the prophet Mohammed ascended into heaven, mounted on his horse. The prophet Elijah of Israel was taken up to heaven by a whirlwind (2 Kings 2:11). In these cases, and in the cases of the classic mythologies and tribal religions, the ones who ascend to heaven do so as a reward to themselves. But while the ascension of Jesus to heaven contains the element of reward for obedience, it goes beyond mere reward for him. His exaltation to the right hand of God comprises an essential element of the means of salvation to others. Furthermore, in the other stories of ascension, the characters do not die; their ascension provided a way to escape death. With Jesus, however, death comprised the necessary means to exaltation. Christianity does not deny death. Rather, it affirms a reality greater than death.

BIBLICAL BACKGROUND

Christ's exaltation to the right hand of the Father has a variety of implications that the New Testament addresses. These implications stem from his role after that exaltation. The Gospels allude to Christ's exaltation as something in the future, yet related to what he began in his earthly ministry. The rest of the New Testament views that earthly ministry of Jesus from the perspective of the present reality of his sitting at the right hand of Majesty.

The Gospels

The exaltation of Christ in the Gospels cannot be separated from the messianic expectations of the people of Israel, who were looking for a great king and deliverer. The Evangelists portray Jesus as a pivotal figure who redirects the understanding of his followers from the historically captive concept of the coming kingdom as a possession of Israel to a cosmically extended assertion of the reign of God. The Gospels begin with fulfillment of the promise to Israel with the birth of the King (Matt. 2:1–12; Luke 1:32–33), and they end with the establishment of that King's reign over all creation (Matt. 28:18). Throughout his ministry, Jesus demonstrates the reality of the kingdom of God, opens the door to life in the kingdom, and begins the campaign to extend the kingdom through his servants.

The kingdom. Alternatively referred to as "the kingdom of God" (Luke) and "the kingdom of heaven" (Matthew), the kingdom Jesus announced went far beyond the dream of territorial independence and self-determination cherished by the people of Israel. John had preached the nearness of the kingdom for which Israel longed (Matt. 3:1–2), but when Jesus preached the nearness of the kingdom it was accompanied by healings and exorcisms (Matt. 4:17, 23; 9:35; Mark 1:15; Luke 4:36; 5:17; 8:1–3). He demonstrated that the reign of God pertained to every realm of experience, physical and spiritual. In his presence, the kingdom of God had already come, for God's full authority was expressed by the authority Jesus exercised over such things as demons (Matt. 12:28; Luke 11:20) and diseases. Furthermore, Jesus exercised the authority of God in teaching (Luke 4:32) and in forgiving sin (Matt. 9:2–8; Mark 2:3–12; Luke 5:24; 7:49).

The powerful demonstrations of his authority inevitably caused his critics to ask by what authority he did the things he did. Did it come from God or Satan (Matt. 21:23–27; Mark 11:27–33; Luke 20:1–8; cf. Matt. 12:22–32; Mark 3:23–27; Luke 11:17–22)? Publicly, Jesus suggested the source of his authority by what he said about his own identity:

> While Jesus was teaching in the temple courts, he asked, "How is it that the teachers of the law say that the Christ is the son of David? David himself, speaking by the Holy Spirit, declared:
>
> "'The Lord said to my Lord:
>   "Sit at my right hand
> until I put your enemies
>   under your feet."'
>
> David himself calls him 'Lord.' How then can he be his son?" (Mark 12:35–37; cf. Matt. 22:41–46, Luke 20:41–44)

This quotation from Psalm 110:1 became for the early church the most frequently cited Scripture to describe the present majesty, power, and authority of Christ. Yet when Jesus raised the issue, it puzzled his hearers (cf. Acts 2:33–35; 1 Cor. 15:24–28; Heb. 1:3–4, 13; 10:13; 1 Peter 3:22; Rev. 4–5). That is, with their highly developed tradition of what the appearance of the kingdom must be like, the faithful Jews of first-century Palestine could not understand its coming in Jesus. That tradition was culturally related to the historical experience of Israel under the idealized King David. For Jesus to speak of the kingdom as being present within or in the midst of his audience made no sense to them (Matt. 24:37–39; Luke 17:20–21). Thus, Jesus used parables to describe the meaning of the kingdom.

To his disciples, however, and gradually to the wider audience, Jesus made clear that what Israel had hoped for would not come with his triumphal entry into Jerusalem, where the crowd hoped he would claim the throne of David and drive out the Romans. Instead, the expected reign of Jesus would begin when he returned to the Father. John's Gospel frequently cites private conversations in which Jesus spoke of returning to the Father from whence he had come (John 6:62; 7:33–36; 8:21; 16:5). Writing some years after the resurrection and exaltation of Jesus, John observed that "Jesus knew that the Father had put all things under his power, and that he had come from God and was returning to God" (13:3). In this vein, he recorded a portion of the prayer Jesus prayed before the guards came to arrest him: "And now, Father, glorify me in your presence with the glory I had with you before the world began" (17:5). The other Gospel writers agree that Jesus publicly announced his impending exaltation at his trial before the Sanhedrin where he declared, "In the future you will see the Son of Man sitting at the right hand of the Mighty One and coming on the clouds of heaven" (Matt. 26:64; cf. Mark 14:62; Luke 22:69). John adds that when Jesus appeared before Pilate he declared, "My kingdom is not of this world" (John 18:36).

Entering the kingdom. Jesus clearly made the point that not everyone would be a part of the kingdom. While God had authority over all things, the kingdom and the benefits of being a part of it did not belong to everyone. Loyalty meant everything. Jesus lamented that the rich have a difficult time entering the kingdom (Matt. 19:24; Mark 10:23; Luke 18:24). Divided loyalties create a tremendous barrier to being willing to enter the kingdom. Diversions distract people from entering even though they may have intended to (Matt. 8:19–22; Luke 9:57–62).

Jesus represented himself as the door or gate to the kingdom (John 10:7–10; cf. Matt. 7:21–23; Luke 13:22–30). By virtue of his exaltation, Jesus became the intermediary who opened the way of access between finite humanity and the holy God. He would go where no one could go, but he would open the way for others to follow (John 12:26; 14:2–6). Entrance into the kingdom, therefore, depended upon how one related to the exalted Lord. In one sobering passage, Jesus declared that some people would give lip service to him as Lord and do the sort of deeds in his name that he indicated should characterize the kingdom, yet he would turn them away with the judgment, "I never knew you" (Matt. 7:21–23). This passage comes shortly after his warnings about those who do good things but have wrong motives. The superficial approach to religion that fails to grasp Jesus Christ, for whatever motive, has failed to grasp the present experience of the kingdom and access to God.

Jesus said that he was the good shepherd. When the good shepherd calls, his sheep follow and they receive life. Furthermore, he declared, "no one can snatch them out of my hand" (John 10:28). Hearing and responding appropriately has an ancient warrant as the expression of faith in Scripture. Those who heard the words of Moses and placed blood on their door frames were saved from the curse that overcame Egypt (Ex. 11:1–12:30). People who had faith in God responded appropriately. Jesus said that people who respond appropriately to his words will live (Matt. 7:24–27; Luke 6:46–49; John 5:24; 8:51). He explained why this was so to his disciples at the Last Supper, when he said, "Whoever has my commands and obeys them ... loves me [and] ... will be loved by my Father" (John 14:21). Jesus described behavior as something that emerges from a relationship founded on love.

Entry into the kingdom means entry into a particular relationship with the One who is the kingdom. Jesus explained that "I am in my Father, and you are in me, and I am in you" (John 14:20). Those who enjoy intimate relationships with the Father through the Son have life. To the eleven remaining disciples, Jesus explained that the benefits of the kingdom come through one's experience with the exalted One who has lived through heaven and earth: "I am the vine; you are the branches. If a man remains in me and I in him, he will bear much fruit" (15:5). The benefits of salvation come through, from, and in the One exalted to the right hand of God.

Prayer. Those who have this kind of intimate relationship with the exalted Christ also have access through him to God in prayer. At first, the words of Jesus sound like a grand license to have one's wildest dreams fulfilled: "If you remain in me and my words remain in you, ask whatever you wish, and it will be given you" (John 15:7). Again he said, "My Father will give you whatever you ask in my name"(16:23), and "In that day you will ask in my name" (16:26). Rather than granting license to gratify every desire, however, Jesus invites his followers to abandon their prayers and enter into him. He invites his followers to let his words saturate them in such a way that they actually pray in his name rather than in their own name. "Knowing" Christ means everything for enjoying the benefits of the kingdom. He promised them that "in me you may have peace" (16:33). His final prayer for believers was that "in him" they might experience unity, love, and joy (17:13–26).

As the door to the kingdom, Jesus provides the means for believers to experience it in the present, before they die. The benefits of salvation are experienced "in him," which necessarily suggests a mystic relationship.

Extension of the kingdom. Having demonstrated his own authority over sickness, disease, and oppressive spiritual forces, Jesus then gave his disciples that authority to perform the same ministry in his name (Matt. 10:1; Mark 3:14; Luke 9:1–2). When he sent his disciples out on their mission, he charged them to preach a simple message: "The kingdom of heaven is near" (Matt. 10:7). He instructed them to perform the same healings and exorcisms that had accompanied his declaration of the same message. And when they returned from the mission, they marveled: "Lord, even the demons submit to us in your name" (Luke 10:17).

Jesus extended the kingdom through those who served him. He taught his followers that they would do even greater things than he had done in his ministry, "because I am going to the Father" (John 14:12). He entrusted his followers with authority to act in his absence and to extend his work (Luke 10:19). He left them with the "keys of the kingdom" (Matt. 16:19) and charged them to make disciples of all nations, based on his resurrected status: "All authority in heaven and on earth has been given to me" (28:18–19). The followers of Jesus, and all those who came to have faith in him, received a commission to act as servants or stewards of Jesus, their master, in his absence. The exaltation would create a new basis for relationship with him, who expected his followers to live as though he might return at any moment (Matt. 24:43–51; 25:1–13; Mark 13:33–37; Luke 12:35–48), yet who promised that even in his absence he would always be with them (Matt. 28:20).

Because of the uniqueness of the relationship between Jesus and his followers that he promised would transcend time, space, and physical separation, Jesus warned his disciples that they would find themselves facing persecution and death "on account of me" (Matt. 13:9–37; cf. Matt. 24:9–14; Luke 21:12–18). This expectation contrasts vividly with his warning that at his arrest the disciples would flee. After the exaltation, Jesus could offer to the disciples a quality of relationship that would put all other issues of life in perspective. Inclusion in the kingdom would not only affect how the followers of Jesus approached death, it would also affect how they approached life. The kingdom of God would become apparent in how the servants behaved toward one another and toward others in the absence of their Master (Matt. 25:14–30; Luke 19:11–27).

Observations. All of the Gospels deal with the theme of the exaltation of Christ. The Synoptic Gospels, oriented toward Jewish Christians, use the vocabulary of the historical tradition surrounding the kingdom of David. The Gospel of John, however, written for a Hellenistic audience unfamiliar with the traditions of Israel, strikes the same chords but stresses the relationship possible with God as a result of the exaltation.

General Apostolic Writings

While the Gospels have the benefit of hindsight in describing the good news of Jesus, they present the exaltation as an expectation. The rest of the New Testament, however, presents the exaltation as a present reality and experience of the church. The vocabulary of the apostles takes a shift from the Gospels. They say little about the kingdom in their letters, but they stress in various ways the nature of the present relationship between believers and their exalted Lord. Paul in particular shares the vocabulary of John's Gospel and the significance of being "in" Christ. The exaltation of Christ had tremendous implications for life and death to his early followers.

As Jesus had suggested, his followers did face death on account of him, Stephen being the first. This martyr also supplied the church with its first witness of the exaltation, for as he appeared before the Sanhedrin he declared, "I see heaven open and the Son of Man standing at the right hand of God" (Acts 7:56). An experience with the exalted Christ resulted in the conversion of Paul (9:3–6). The church also experienced a continuation of healings and exorcisms when done "in the name" of Jesus Christ (3:6, 16; 4:10, 30; 9:34; 16:18). The apostles appealed to the exaltation in at least 280 passages in their writings, excluding the Gospels and Revelation.[2] Several major themes appear in the writings: the present power and authority of Christ, access to God through Christ, faith in the Lord

Jesus Christ, relationship with Christ, the mediator of the benefits of salvation, Christ as a helper, revelation, the church, service for Christ, and Christian behavior.

Authority of Christ. In his Pentecostal sermon, Peter declared that the claim for which Jesus had been put to death had now occurred: Jesus had been exalted to the right hand of God and is both Lord and Christ (Acts 2:33–36). The knowledge that a benevolent being exercised authority over every other force in creation provided a compelling reason to give thoughtful consideration to the gospel. His followers claimed that he had power and authority over life, death, angels, demons, the present, the future, all spiritual forces that people of the first century understood to surround them and affect them, as well as the whole created, physical order (Rom. 8:38; Eph. 1:20–23; Phil. 2:9–11; 3:21; Col. 1:15–18; 2:10; Heb. 2:7–9; 1 Peter 3:22; Rev. 1:5; 6:1–17; 8:6–9:20).

By virtue of his relationship to the Father, Christ has the power to bring everything in submission to himself. The ambiguity over the identity of Christ that perplexed people in the Gospels before his death does not appear in the other apostolic writings, written in the experience of the exaltation. Paul, who had held the coats of those who stoned Stephen for bearing witness to the exaltation, boldly testified of "Christ, who is God over all" (Rom. 9:5). In Revelation, Christ the sacrificial Lamb shares the throne as well as the praise, honor, glory, and power of God (Rev. 4–5; cf. Heb. 1:3–4). All the forces of earth might oppose Christ, "but the Lamb will overcome them because he is the Lord of lords and Kings of kings" (Rev. 17:14). The early church, even in severe persecution, experienced the power and authority of Christ enough to believe that he would defeat his enemies (1 Cor. 15:24–28; Heb. 10:13). Christ has the power to save because he sits at the center of the throne of God (Rev. 7:17).

Access to God. Through his exaltation to the right hand of the Father, Jesus provided immediate access to God for his followers (Rom. 4:23–5:1; Eph. 2:8; 3:12; 1 Tim. 2:5; Heb. 4:14–16). This aspect of the gospel provided poignant meaning for those who thought of God as distant and unapproachable, as the Platonic view of God maintained. After the fall of Jerusalem and the destruction of the temple, marking an end of the religious rituals established by Moses with its priests and sacrifices, this element of the gospel also provided poignant meaning for those Jews who heard that they could have access to God through the priesthood of Christ.

Hebrews elaborates on how Christ continues eternally as a priest on behalf of those who have faith in him (Heb. 5:1–10; 6:20). Jesus Christ is a priest who meets human need, for he possesses the holiness and purity that everyone else lacks. Having given himself as a sacrifice to God in our place, he is now seated at the right hand of God to open access to God through him (7:26–28; 8:1–2; 9:11–28; 10:12–18). Those who have come to Jesus may now worship and praise God through him (12:24; 13:15).

The apostolic writings are ripe with the conviction that the followers of Jesus could enter into the presence of God and worship him through their mystic relationship with Jesus Christ, who had returned to the glory of the Father. They gave thanks to God "through" Jesus and "in" his name (Rom. 1:8; 7:25; Eph. 5:19; Col. 1:3; 3:17). They offered their prayers, blessings, and praises to God through Jesus (Rom. 16:25–27; 1 Peter 2:5; 4:11; Jude 25). Jesus made priests, soothsayers, necromancers, astrologists, oracles, and the like obsolete. Rather than relying on the occult or the cult to make contact with the powers and dominions of the universe, Christians can come into the presence of the Creator God through Jesus Christ our Lord, his Son, who lives eternally with him (Rom. 8:34; 1 John 2:1).

Relationship with Christ. The necessity for relationship with Christ in order for the exaltation to affect someone positively cannot be stressed enough. Some exorcists tried to invoke the name of Jesus to perform the same sort of wonders the apostles performed, but they lacked the proper relationship with Jesus Christ to be endowed with his power. They sought to use Jesus rather than to be used by Jesus (Acts 19:13–16). The fact that Jesus died, rose again, and was exalted did not in any way diminish for the early Christians their conviction that they could have a present relationship with him because those baptized into Christ have clothed themselves with Christ (Gal. 3:27). God, in fact, has called people into fellowship with his Son, Jesus Christ the Lord (1 Cor. 1:9). Fellowship with him opens the door to fellowship with the Father (1 John 1:3).

Knowing the Lord Jesus Christ puts everything else in life in perspective. Paul traded preferment, prestige, prominence, and power for a life of privation after he came face to face with the exalted Christ on the Damascus road. Everything that had mattered most seemed unimportant "compared to the surpassing greatness of knowing Christ Jesus my Lord" (Phil. 3:7–8). Thus, knowing Jesus Christ becomes the means of escaping the corruption of the world (2 Peter 2:20).

Benefits of salvation. The early church learned that the benefits of salvation came *through* and *in the name* of the Lord Jesus Christ as a present reality. Among the benefits that come through him are:

salvation from wrath	Rom. 5:9
reconciliation	Rom. 5:10
eternal life	Rom. 5:21
victory	Rom. 8:37; 1 Cor. 15:57
cleansing, sanctification, justification	1 Cor. 6:11
life and all else	1 Cor. 8:6
confidence	2 Cor. 3:4
strength	Phil. 4:13
grace and peace	2 Peter 1:2
forgiveness of sins	1 John 2:12
repentance	Acts 5:31

While the benefits of salvation come *through* the relationship with Christ, the experience of salvation occurs *in* the relationship with Christ. Salvation is not a commodity that early Christians accumulated and kept safely stashed. They experienced salvation in their relationship with Jesus Christ. He has eternal life, and those who live in him share his life (Rom. 6:23; 1 John 5:11–12). Christians experience grace to the extent that they are mindful of their relationship *in* Christ (1 Cor. 1:4; 1 Thess. 1:1; 2 Tim. 1:9; 2:1). Likewise, joy comes as a byproduct of the relationship believers find in Christ (Phil. 3:1; 4:4, 10). The experience of faith, love, and hope come in relationship with Christ (1 Thess. 1:3). Victory, freedom, and equality become real experiences in Christ (1 Cor. 11:11; 2 Cor. 2:14; Gal. 2:4; 3:28).

The exalted Christ is the one in whom the benefits of salvation are found as an added feature of knowing him (2 Tim. 2:10). God has blessed the followers of Christ with every spiritual blessing in Christ (Eph. 1:3). Standing at a distance from Christ by neglecting the relationship, however, deprives a person of the benefits that could be theirs. Such spiritual experiences as grace and peace meant a great deal to the early church that endured hardship and suffering, but those believers found a constant source of grace and peace in the Lord Jesus Christ (1 Cor. 1:3; Gal. 1:3; 6:18; Eph. 1:2; 6:23; Phil. 1:2; 4:23; 2 Thess. 1:2; 3:18; 1 Tim. 1:2; Titus 1:4, Philem. 3, 25; 1 Peter 5:14; 2 John 3). While "peace" had from antiquity served as a greeting and benediction in the ancient Near East, the church affirmed that it came only from God our Father and the Lord Jesus Christ.

The Lord as helper. In his vision of the exalted Lord, the martyred Stephen received the grace and the peace necessary to die (Acts 7:55–56). The Lord is a helper in desperate circumstances, even when he does not make the circumstances go away. Rather, he uses the circumstances to draw the believer closer to himself. While the early Christians sought deliverance from trouble, they found that Christ provides strength to endure troubles (Rom. 14:4; 1 Cor. 1:8; 1 Thess. 3:12–13; 2 Thess. 2:16–17; 3:3; 2 Tim. 4:17). They also found that Christ rescues people from the trials and attacks that might keep them from him (2 Tim. 1:12; 3:11; 4:18; 2 Peter 2:9). Because of his life in the flesh, the exalted Christ knows what it feels like to endure trials, and he is able to help (Heb. 2:17–18; 4:14–16).

Corporate relationship to Christ. As the exalted Lord, Christ draws his followers together into relationship with him and with one another. Metaphysically, he is the head of the body (Rom. 12:5; 1 Cor. 12:12–31; Eph. 3:6; 4:4–16; 5:22–24, 29–30; Col. 1:18), the foundation of the building (1 Cor. 3:11; Eph. 2:19–22; 1 Peter 2:4), and a king-priest over a royal priesthood (1 Peter 2:5, 9; Rev. 1:6; 5:10; 20:6). These different metaphors describe the corporate relationship of the followers of the Lord Jesus Christ as his church. Christians have a corporate relationship with and responsibility for each other by virtue of their relationship to the exalted Lord, the quality of which depends on the faithfulness of that relationship with Christ. The metaphors of body, building, and priesthood speak of the high value of unity that Christ expects of his followers. This quality was so important to those who first knew Christ that Paul declared that those who are divisive are not serving the Lord (Rom. 16:17–18; cf. 15:5).

The quality of community life in Christ depends on a constant awareness of his authority in the midst of the church. In the salutation of the apostolic letters to his churches, Paul reminded the faithful saints that the definitive reason for being a group rested in their experience of being "in" the Lord Jesus Christ (1 Cor. 1:2; Eph. 1:1; Phil. 1:1; Col. 1:2; 1 Thess. 1:1; 2 Thess. 1:1). As such, they were to "submit to one another out of reverence for Christ" (Eph. 5:21). When the apostles appealed to the churches in the matter of their relationship and unity, they appealed "in the name of our Lord Jesus Christ" (1 Cor. 1:10). While the churches were expected to exercise discipline over the behavior of members of the body, they were charged to do so in the spirit of carrying "each other's burdens" (1 Cor. 5:4–5; Gal. 6:2). Through his church, Christ offers a place of acceptance and belonging, free of favoritism or distinction, where everyone can have a place (Gal. 3:26–28; Eph. 6:6–9; Philem. 16; James 2:1). The extent to which a church corresponds to this expressed will of Christ depends on the extent to which the members recognize the present authority of Christ in their midst.

The apostles had a profound understanding that holy behavior or godly living did not come from the observation of rules or regulations. Rather, they constantly pointed to the living Lord and urged Christians to imitate Jesus Christ, who is exalted (Phil. 2:1–11). They encouraged believers to live life in a way that would please him, conscious that their life was hidden in Christ (Rom. 14:5–9; 1 Cor. 4:17; 6:13–17; 7:32–35; 2 Cor. 10:5; Eph. 2:10; Phil. 1:20–26; Col. 1:10; 2:6; 1 Thess. 4:1; 2 Tim. 2:21; 1 Peter 3:16; 2 Peter 1:8). Christian behavior should be governed by the reality that Christ has been exalted:

> Since, then, you have been raised with Christ, set your hearts on things above, where Christ is seated at the right hand of God. . . . And whatever you do, whether in word or deed, do it all in the name of the Lord Jesus. . . . (Col. 3:1, 17)

Extending the church. God chose to make known what Christ has accomplished through the church. Paul called this plan the "mystery, which for ages past was kept hidden in God" (Eph. 3:7–11). To lead in the oversight and extension of the church, Christ appointed leaders (Eph. 4:11; cf. Rom. 12:6–8). Paul and Peter both taught that Christians should recognize those in authority under the Lordship of Christ (1 Thess. 4:12; 1 Peter 2:13). The authority of the New Testament letters rests on the recognition by the early church that Christ had in fact designated apostles whom he sent to help accomplish his mission through the churches. Thus, the letters regularly begin with an acknowledgment that the authority for the letter rests in the commission of Christ. They wrote as apostles of Christ Jesus (Rom. 1:1; 1 Cor. 1:1; 9:1–2; 2 Cor. 1:1; Gal. 1:1; Eph. 1:1; Col. 1:1; 1 Thess. 2:6; 1 Tim. 1:1; 2 Tim. 1:1; Titus 1:1; 1 Peter 1:1; 2 Peter 1:1), who regarded themselves and other Christians as his servants or ministers and who carried out his instructions (Rom. 15:16; 1 Cor. 4:1; 2 Cor. 4:5; Phil. 1:1, 7; Col. 4:7, 12; 1 Tim. 1:12–14; 4:6; 2 Tim. 2:24; James 1:1; Jude 1; Rev. 1:1).

The apostles gave the church instructions they received through visions, under the inspiration of the Holy Spirit, and by angels (Acts 9:10–16; 10:1–16; 11:27–30; 12:6–10; 13:1–3; 16:6–10; 21:10–11; 22:17–21; 23:11; 26:12–19; 2 Cor. 12:1–7). These instructions came with the authority of the Lord Jesus by way of revelation (1 Thess. 4:2; Rev. 1:1). In the absence of a clear instruction from the Lord, however, the apostles offered their own opinion after stating that it did not have the authority of the Lord's command (1 Cor. 7:25). They also taught that the Lord would give insight and understanding with respect to his will for individual Christians (Eph. 1:17; 5:17; 2 Tim. 2:7). The Lord confirmed the message and authority of the apostles by enabling them to do miraculous signs and wonders (Acts 2:43; 3:1–10; 5:12–16; 6:8; 8:4–8; 9:17–18, 32–43; 13:9–12; 14:3, 8–10; 16:16–18; 19:11–12; 20:7–12; 28:1–10).

Faithfulness and suffering. The martyrs of the early church did not die for an idea or a philosophy. They died because the exalted Christ is Lord and more real to them than any suffering might be. Their faith rested not in the past but in the present, for they entrusted their lives to Christ. The gospel for them consisted in more than mere words about what Jesus had done to save them; the gospel introduced them to Jesus, who lives as Lord. That being the case, they stood firm for the person they knew rather than a religious ideal they espoused.

Esoteric theology had no staying power in the early church, and the apostles warned Christians against the sort of speculative theology that would lead people to "lose connection with the Head" (Col. 2:16–23). By standing firm in the Lord (cf. Eph. 6:12–14), people can face the troubles and hardships of life, for the exalted Christ is more than a religious affirmation. He gives peace, strength, and grace to those who remain in him. Faith for the early Christians was not "about" Jesus; it was "in" Jesus (2 Tim. 3:15; Philem. 5; 1 Peter 1:8–10; 1 John 2:24, 28).

Conclusions

The exaltation of Christ places the suffering and frustrations of humans in much larger perspective. In his life in the flesh, Jesus Christ experienced the dark side of life, but he persevered for the joy that lay before him in the exaltation (Heb. 12:2; cf. Phil. 2:6–11). By his supreme authority and power over all things visible and invisible, he can protect those within his kingdom from all the things that superstition and religion hurl at people to keep them in the bondage of fear. By his life, he makes it possible for people to experience the benefits of salvation even in the midst of turmoil. He creates a community of love and support through which he expresses himself by those sensitive to his presence. He brings people into the very presence of God even when they thought God was too distant, holy, and austere ever to know. He makes the kingdom of heaven more real than the kingdom of this world. He provides insight and understanding for living while providing strength to carry on in the difficult times of life. In Christ the early Christians found a Lord worth dying for.

HISTORICAL/THEOLOGICAL DEVELOPMENT

From the death of Jesus for declaring before the Sanhedrin that he would be exalted to the right hand of God to the death of Stephen while testifying of his vision of the exalted Jesus, the early church identified martyrdom with faithfulness to the living Lord Jesus.

Christians could face the death of martyrdom because they believed Christ reigned as King more than they feared torture and death. Martyrdom made possible a special relationship with Christ that included visions from him, grace to endure torture, peace, and immediate presence with him at death.

Martyrdom

Though local cases of martyrdom occurred in the first century, official persecution began under Trajan in 111 when he sent Pliny to Bithynia to establish order. The emperor's abolition of all clubs or societies, which he perceived as hotbeds of political foment, directly threatened the meeting of Christians, who did not enjoy official recognition as a legal religion. To prove they were not seditious, Christians were expected to offer incense to the emperor's idol and curse Christ. Symean, bishop of Jerusalem, and Ignatius, bishop of Antioch, died in this persecution.[3]

As an encouragement in times of persecution, the church began preserving accounts of the deaths of those who died for their devotion to Christ. *The Martyrdom of Ignatius* preserves the early attitude of the church that those who belong to "Christ the King of heaven" have nothing to fear from people or spirits.[4] Those who suffered as martyrs would come before the face of Christ and inherit their place in heaven by virtue of their confession of Christ unto death.[5] After the beasts devoured Ignatius in the public arena of Rome, his followers gathered what bones of him remained and carried them to Antioch, where his martyrdom was commemorated every year on December 20. Distraught over the death of Ignatius and fearful for themselves, the church at Antioch prayed for some assurance from the Lord. In response to their prayers, several members of the Antioch community reported visions of Ignatius in the presence of the Lord, praying for the church.[6] Thus, at an early date, Christians believed that the martyrs stood in a special relationship to Christ and that they continued to be concerned for those left behind.

Local persecutions erupted throughout the second century. Among the more notable martyrs, Polycarp died by fire about 155. In *The Martyrdom of Polycarp* the understanding appears that all martyrdoms occur by the will of God.[7] In this account of the death of Polycarp and his companions, the martyrs did not cry out under severe lashing, showing that "the most noble martyrs of Christ in that hour under torture were absent from the flesh, or rather, that the Lord was at hand and was conversing with them."[8] The exalted Christ embraced the martyrs in their suffering, and they exchanged an hour's torture for eternal life.[9]

Visions played a major role in the martyrdom of the early Christians. Three days before his arrest, Polycarp reported a vision in which his pillow was burning up. He interpreted this experience to mean that he was being called upon to die by fire.[10] Also connected with the martyrdom of Polycarp was a voice from heaven overheard by other Christians as the moment of death approached, which said, "Be strong, Polycarp, and play the man."[11] These revelations from the exalted Christ formed the context of Polycarp's response to the proconsul when called upon to take the oath to Caesar as Lord and to curse Christ:

> I have served him eighty-six years and in no way has he dealt unjustly with me; so how can I blaspheme my king who saved me?[12]

The church held the martyrs in special honor "because of their incomparable loyalty to their own King and Teacher."[13] The church collected the bones of Polycarp after his burning and celebrated his martyrdom each year at the repository of his bones as a means of strengthening those who would be martyred in the future.[14]

Justin Martyr died in Rome under Marcus Aurelius in 163 after Crescens the Cynic denounced him. Apparently professional jealousy played a part in the charges since Justin had defeated Crescens in public debate about the Christian faith.[15] In his testimony before the prefect, Justin affirmed both his faith in the Creator, the Lord Jesus Christ, whose appearance the prophets had foretold, and the certain expectation that those who die for faith in him will ascend to heaven and be saved at his universal judgment seat.[16]

A number of Christians died in Lyons and Vienne in 177 during the festival of the three Gauls as an offering to Rome and the emperors. A dozen Christians were beheaded in Carthage in 180 during the reign of Commodus. The governor of Cappadocia instituted a fierce persecution during the same period after his wife became a Christian. As the number of martyrs increased, the practice spread of commemorating the faithfulness of those who died for Christ on the anniversary of their death. These ceremonies and the growing body of literature describing the martyrdoms brought a heightened sense of the importance of faithfulness to Christ the Lord.

The third century began ferociously for the church, with provincial persecutions in Egypt and North Africa during the reign of Septimus Severus in 202. Origen's father was a victim of this persecution in Alexandria while Perpetua and her friends died in Carthage. *The Martyrdom of Perpetua and Felicitas* describes the visions these martyrs received to prepare them for their ordeal.[17] This account also describes how the martyrs escaped the pain of their martyrdom because of their presence with Christ.[18]

In the face of growing persecutions, Tertullian wrote two treatises designed to encourage Christians not to flee martyrdom. He commended the ascetic life because it prepares the body for the hardship of suffering.[19] Rather than fear death, Christians should face death by martyrdom as the means to divine reward and heavenly glory.[20] Tertullian taught that persecutions were not merely allowed by God, but were actually the will and purpose of God:

> For what is the issue of persecution, what other result comes of it, but the approving and rejecting of faith, in regard to which the Lord will certainly sift His people? Persecution, by means of which one is declared either approved or rejected, is just the judgment of the Lord.[21]

Through persecution Christ proves those who belong to him. Rather than experiencing fear of renouncing Christ when brought before the authorities, Christians should face martyrdom boldly, knowing that they would receive power to render a faithful witness.[22] Christ, therefore, rejects those who refuse to suffer persecution for his name's sake, for refusal of persecution is refusal to believe or follow the Lord.[23] Willingness to share the sufferings of Christ comes from faith in the Lord himself, "who will stand by us to aid us in suffering as well as to be our mouth when we are put to the question."[24]

Local persecutions continued under Maximianus (235–238) and Philip the Arabian (244–249), but the great universal persecution began in 250 at the command of the Emperor Decius. Bishop Fabian of Rome and Alexander of Jerusalem were martyred, but some bishops like Cyprian of Carthage went into hiding. Origen was imprisoned but later released. Another group, represented by Bishop Eudaemon of Smyrna, renounced Christ. This persecution was renewed under Gallus and Valerian. Sixtus II of Rome and Cyprian died in 258 along with many others who remained faithful to their confession of Christ. This persecution ended under the reign of Gallienus, who granted Christianity official status as *religio licita* in 261.[25]

Following the Decian Persecution, Gregory Thaumaturgus stressed the faithfulness of the martyrs in his evangelization of the pagans. The remains of the martyrs were brought to the services in their honor and the commemorations took on a festival atmosphere. According to Gregory of Nyssa, the former Gregory permitted them to enjoy themselves at the commemoration of the holy martyrs, to take their ease, and to amuse themselves, since life would become more serious and earnest naturally in process of time, as the Christian faith came to assume more control of it.[26]

The Decian persecution raised an enormous disciplinary problem for the church concerning those who had not kept the faith under persecution. Cyprian, bishop of Carthage, before his own martyrdom followed a policy of letting the severity of the penance fit the nature of the lapse. Fortunatus held that no discipline at all should be exercised. Novatian, a presbyter of Rome, on the other hand, took the position that no one who failed under persecution could be readmitted to fellowship. The dispute resulted in the election of two rival bishops to succeed Cyprian: Fortunatus and Maximus, a follower of Novatian.[27]

Persecution returned in 298 when Galerius purged his armies of all Christian officers. He then pressured Emperor Diocletian to renew the persecution of the church, though local officials had broad discretion in how to punish those who violated the prohibition of Christian worship. This persecution produced another controversy similar to the Novatian one regarding the status of bishops or lesser clergy who had handed over sacred books to the authorities. The controversy erupted in 312 when Felix of Aptunga, a bishop who had handed over books, consecrated Caecilian as bishop of Carthage. The strict disciplinarians consecrated Majorinus in opposition and upon his death, Donatus to succeed him. The Donatists argued that since Felix had lapsed during persecution, none of the sacraments he administered had validity. Thus, the consecration of Caecilian had no validity. The consensus view of the church held that the sacraments had validity in and of themselves, but the Donatists persisted in rejecting the validity of sacraments administered by those clergy who had failed to bear faithful witness to Christ under persecution.[28]

Martyrdom and discipline represent two different kinds of issues implied by the status of Christ as exalted Lord. As king he deserves total loyalty, and as priest he enables total loyalty. As head of the body, however, he upholds the church and disciplines it. With the end of persecution and the official recognition that came with the reign of Constantine, martyrdom for Christ became a fading memory, but the problems of the administration of the body of Christ became a major preoccupation as the division between an Eastern Church and a Western Church became more apparent.

What did survive as a legacy of the persecutions was a veneration of special holy people who were regarded as holding special status with Christ. The tombs or places of martyrdom held special significance as places of grace, especially on the saint's holy day of martyrdom. Thus, the original intent of encouraging the church to endure suffering ended. What had shown the nearness of the exalted Lord now created an impression of the distance of the Lord, which the martyrs could mediate.

The willingness to face martyrdom because of love for Christ did not end, however, in the fourth century. Christians throughout the centuries from Japan and China to Russia and Germany to South Africa and Brazil have accepted martyrdom for Christ. This willingness emerges from what Dietrich Bonhoeffer called the quest "for Jesus Christ himself," and it is driven by the concern for "what Jesus Christ himself wants of us."[29] Bonhoeffer's thoughts on martyrdom reflect the thesis of this book: that at different times and places, different elements of the gospel have a stronger appeal to people. In place of the traditional Lutheran concern for forgiveness, during the rise of Hitler, Bonhoeffer found powerful attraction to "the kingly rule of Christ."[30] Rather than repudiating grace, Bonhoeffer insisted that one only experiences grace when one gives up all to follow Christ. This view did not constitute a "works" solution for

Bonhoeffer because he believed that *"only he who believes is obedient, and only he who is obedient believes."*[31] In this sense, grace comes most to the martyr in their hour of trouble, because they truly believe in Christ who stands beside them.[32]

As Mediator Christ calls people to follow him, and he cuts them off from everything else. All else in heaven and earth can only be experienced properly in and through him.[33] Because of his mediation, however, relationships with others become a true possibility as well as genuine prayer to God. By this act of mediation, Christ creates the church, his body, through which people experience salvation. Bonhoeffer does not mean that they experience salvation by virtue of joining an organization; rather, he stresses that salvation is the corporate experience of those "taken up in the Body of Jesus."[34] In this regard the church is not an institution, but a person, the real presence of Christ.[35]

As Lord of his own body, Christ also offers to some a unique privilege to share the sufferings of the cross:

> But there is a far greater form of suffering than this, one which bears an ineffable promise. For while it is true that only the suffering of Christ himself can atone for sin, and that his suffering and triumph took place "for us," yet to some, who are not ashamed of their fellowship in his body, he vouchsafes the immeasurable grace and privilege of suffering "for him," as he did for them.[36]

Dietrich Bonhoeffer himself met a martyr's death on April 9, 1945.

Monasticism

Monasticism developed in the closing period of the persecutions of the early church. Asceticism had its place within the churches before monasticism developed, but as a movement apart from the life of the congregation, monasticism had its great impetus toward the end of the third century on the eve of the last great persecution of Diocletian. Anthony (b. 251) of Egypt inspired many to follow the life of a hermit monk as the monk succeeded the martyr as the model of obedience and devotion to the Lord.[37]

Several of the fathers prepared the way for monasticism to succeed martyrdom as a way of totally following Christ. Clement had seen martyrdom as a special calling for a few and not the model for Christian perfection. The broad model consisted in a willingness to die for Christ made manifest in how one lived.[38] Christians may bear witness to Christ by living for him as well as by dying for him. Those not called to die may still achieve martyrdom by the excellence of their daily lives, whereby they conform themselves to the teachings of Christ. To this concept, Origen added the notion that one pursued perfection in the imitation of Christ through asceticism and not just through suffering unto death.[39] Tertullian, Cyprian, and Commodian also provided undergirding to the developing ideal of "spiritual martyrdom" through living for Christ.[40]

Spiritual martyrdom required both the desire of martyrdom and the experience of some form of suffering that the martyr bore patiently out of love for God through the example of Christ. This suffering might take the form of an ascetic practice, such as was recommended by Athanasius, Pachomius, Macarius, and Diodochus of Photice; adoption of a lifestyle such as virginity, as recommended by Methodius of Philippi, Jerome, Basil, and Ambrose; or the experience of some form of externally inflicted malice, such as envy, hatred, or ill will.[41] The Irish saints of the fifth, sixth, and seventh centuries included "white martyrs" (those who renounced the secular world), "green martyrs" (those who practiced penance and self-mortification), but no "red martyrs" (those who died for Christ).[42]

The monks of the southern Egyptian desert who followed the example of Anthony led in the conversion of pagan Egypt, often through the demonstration of the miraculous. Accounts of the miraculous often coincided with those figures who devoted their lives as an offering to their Lord, whether among the pagans of south Egypt, Ireland, Gaul, or Germany. Evangelism in these encounters frequently occurred as a clash between Christ and the demonic forces feared by the local people.[43] The miracles surrounding the Desert Fathers fell into four categories: prophetic knowledge, healing, dreams and visions, and nature miracles. Their breadth indicates Christ's power and deity in all realms.[44] The prophetic knowledge and the dreams and visions have a striking similarity to the experience of the martyrs. The victory over the demonic came in confessing the Lordship of Christ: "I have Christ as my King, whom I adore without ceasing; you are not my king."[45] Many converts came to faith through the example and ministry of these ascetic monks who bore witness to Christ by offering their lives and by manifesting Christ's power.

The approach to monasticism offered by Pachomius (d. 346) proceeded from an understanding that the physical body and the human spirit cannot be divided from one another. Thus, the ascetic practices he advocated did not represent a dualism that sees the body as evil. Rather, his approach respected the dynamic relationship between body and spirit.[46] Pachomius's conversion was strongly influenced by his observation of the character of love among Christians, and his development of communal monasticism reflects a concern for the community of salvation. Pachomius experienced visions and voices that led to his embrace of asceticism and the establishment of a monastic community that would serve as God's instrument of salvation for others.[47] Leaving the hermit model of Anthony, Pachomius established a Christian village that exercised discipline as the members supported and helped one another offer themselves to Christ. This approach to monasticism quickly spread to Palestine, Mesopotamia, and Cappadocia and Pontus, where it interested Basil.

Basil the Great (c. 330–379) and Gregory of Nazianzus (c. 330– c. 390) decided to follow the ascetic life of retirement about 350. Together they developed two *Rules* to regulate monastic life. *The Rule of Basil* serves as the foundation for the monastic life of the Eastern Church to this day. Martin of Tours probably established the first monastery in Gaul about 360. A monastic community developed around Jerome in Bethlehem about 390. Augustine intended to follow the monastic life, and he established a monastery in Hippo, though duty compelled him to accept the ministry of bishop.

While the ascetic life of the monks seemed to stress the outward form of human activity, the experience of the monks placed stress on the grace of Christ. He alone supplied the grace to follow a life that crucified itself daily. This experience of grace corresponded to a martyr's experience of grace in the hour of trial.[48] Monasticism had an equally strong attraction for women. Female asceticism had a long history in the church before the monastic movement began. Virgins consecrated to God wore a veil, just like married women, as a mark of their relationship to Christ. The virgins had already established communities when Anthony entrusted his sister to one such house about 280.[49] Mary, the sister of Pachomius, established a convent near his monastery at Tabennisi about 330. Paula founded three convents near Bethlehem about 389 with the support of Jerome, and Melania founded a convent on the Mount of Olives about the same time.[50]

By the time of Cassian (d. 433) monasteries began to show the earliest signs of reorientation from the obedient community of spiritual martyrs to the contemplative community of learning that some monasteries assumed in later centuries. The monks under Martin of Tours did no labor except for the copying of books. By the sixth century it had become customary for monasteries to be founded by wealthy patrons, who endowed them with land and money, leaving the monks and nuns free to follow a contemplative life. As a result of the new relationship, large numbers of pagan laborers on the monastic farms of Gaul converted to Christianity or paid a fine if they did not.[51]

Rome used the monks to evangelize the Celtic north. To modern-day Ireland, Holland, Britain, and Germany the monks went as witnesses for Christ. The monks of the Eastern Church likewise carried the gospel into the Slavic lands beyond the Danube. In Ireland the saints were those who had led in the evangelization of the island. Because of the wonders they performed, they were judged to have a special relationship with God, by which they could intercede for their allies. The later monks promoted the shrines of the saints, which they administered as holy places for pilgrimages, building on the old Celtic belief in sacred places.

Stories of the miraculous abound in the accounts of the monks who brought the gospel into lands where the religious worldview led people to give their allegiance to the most powerful god.[52] After the initial work of evangelizing, however, the monasteries became centers of learning as monastic schools developed to educate the new monks from Celtic society.[53] From the sixth century on, the kings, bishops, lords, and popes in the West made decisions about monastic life, for the monastery and convent had become important institutions of the society they had been founded to escape.[54] *The Rule of St. Benedict* became the standard for monasticism in the West during this period.

Benedict (c. 480–c. 547) began his monastic career as a hermit, but the miraculous stories circulating about him drew a group of followers, for whom he developed his *Rule*.[55] It contains a guide to discipline within the community, but it seems to have had an intentional goal of providing a consistent ecclesiastical government rather than allowing for the earlier monastic vision of freely imitating Christ.[56] Thus, Benedict's *Rule* formed a covenant for the community following Christ and a basis for monastic government under Christ the King. In this sense it differs markedly from the rules of Basil, Pachomius, or Cassian, which were used in the Eastern Church and which dealt almost exclusively with the ascetic and moral virtues.[57]

Unfortunately, the monasteries during the Carolingian period became a base for royal power, and the abbots became de facto royal office-holders. From this time on, the history of monasticism in the West is the story of a series of reforming movements that called the religious orders back to their original ideal of following Christ and of being useful for the "winning of souls."[58] Whether the Cluniac reforms of the eighth century or the emergence of the mendicant orders in the thirteenth century, the ideal of giving one's life completely to Christ has continued to emerge in different fashions from ancient times to the twentieth-century streets of Calcutta and the ministry of Mother Teresa.

Church Government

The recognition of Christ as head of the church has resulted in a variety of expressions of church government. In the thousand years following the peace that Constantine brought to Christianity, the church developed a highly sophisticated organizational structure. The Eastern church and the Western church developed along different lines, largely because of the different political and social realities they faced. With the collapse of the Western empire, the bishop of Rome took on responsibilities normally exercised by a secular ruler. The Eastern church, on the other hand, lived with the constant intervention of the emperor for a thousand years. While the bishop of Rome had enjoyed priority of honor among the five patriarchites (Jerusalem, Antioch, Alexandria, Rome, and Constantinople), he enjoyed priority of power as well in the West. The universal patriarch of Constantinople has never held such a position among the national Orthodox churches.

At its worst moments, the hierarchy of the church represented ambition, corruption, and political intrigue. At its best moments, however, the hierarchy of the church, East and West, sought to honor the Lord and advance his kingdom. The missionaries sent out by the pope and the patriarch evangelized western and eastern Europe. In most cathedrals, the ever-present reminder of Christ the Lord, *Christus Pantokrator*, gazed down in fresco from the ceiling in case an overly ambitious prelate should forget whose church it was.

The kingly rule of Christ in the church erupted as a major issue in the West during the Protestant Reformation. In the English Reformation in particular, the issue of his rule in the church led to a variety of splinterings. The Puritan argument could be rendered with the assertion that if one will not have Christ as King, one cannot have him as Savior.

The concept of the kingly rule of Christ took two major directions among the Puritans. One concept, which stressed the rule of Christ in the hearts of believers, encouraged individual conversion, whereby a person came personally under the rule of Christ. The other concept, which stressed the rule of Christ in the church, led to controversy over worship and discipline. Those who went into separation tended to stress the latter concept, while men like Richard Sibbes stressed the former. The two emphases did not serve mutually to exclude one another, for both traditions had a place for each other in their concept of the kingly rule of Christ, but each one had a major emphasis that tended to encourage either evangelism or controversy. The practical manifestation of these emphases came in the forms of church discipline proposed by men like Cartwright and casuistry (self-examination) proposed by men like Perkins.

Perhaps the primary complicating factor of the controversies of the Puritans lay in their understanding of Scripture.[59] The Puritans disagreed with the authorities in one fundamental matter: While the authorities took the general Lutheran position that things might be allowed in the church that Scripture does not specifically prohibit, the Puritans took the Calvinist position that only those things commanded by Scripture may be allowed in the church. For those who saw the gospel as the proclamation of the kingdom, letting Christ be king in the church as well as priest meant adherence to all the commands of God. This stream of thought tended to level all Scripture as of equal import. As well as differing on the authority of Scripture, the Puritans lacked an accepted hermeneutic for interpreting it even among themselves. The disintegration of Puritanism came when they could not agree among themselves about what government and ceremonies Christ had commanded in his Word.

The Puritans viewed the Scriptures as a divine blueprint and rule for all time. Walter Travers, a Presbyterian Puritan associated with Cartwright, presented the reasoning that characterized the Puritan attitude toward the Scriptures in *A Full and Plain Declaration of Ecclesiastical Discipline*, which he wrote while in Geneva in 1574. Travers's arguments rested heavily on the Old Testament and the example of Moses and the Law of Israel. The structure of Jewish worship in the Law of Moses was rigidly and absolutely laid down.[60] Nothing could be added or taken away. God, the King of Israel, gave the Law fully and completely, and Moses, the faithful prophet, delivered the commandments to Israel, whereby she was disciplined.

Travers then turned to Christ, who embodied the offices of king and prophet in his establishment of the church. He reasoned that Christ must have done at least as much as Moses in giving a rule of government for the church. Travers considered it unreasonable to think that God would take less care with the church than he took with Israel.[61] Furthermore, if Christ is a prophet like Moses, then he must have done at least as much as Moses or else he would prove to be an inferior prophet. Unwilling to let Christ be inferior in any way to Moses, Travers argued that Christ "fully and perfectly declared unto us whatsoever was needful for the government of the Church."[62] Based on the premises that Travers allowed, he could only conclude that Christ left a perfect rule and discipline "which is common and general to all the Church and perpetual for all times."[63]

The Puritan understanding and interpretation of Scripture had a direct bearing on their attitude toward church government, discipline, worship, and every other issue over which they came into conflict with the authorities of the Church of England. In *An Admonition to the Parliament*, attributed to Thomas Wilcox, which was published together with *A View of Popishe Abuses Yet Remaining in the Englishe Church*, attributed to John Field, the Puritan complaints are clearly outlined. Throughout the pamphlet the criticism leveled at the Church of England is its failure to conform to Christ's model of a church. True religion consisted in doing only what Christ commanded. Herein lies the fundamental cleavage between the Puritans and the Elizabethan Settlement with respect to church government.[64]

> They hould and maintaine thet the word of God contained in the writings of the Prophets and Apostles, is of absolute perfection, given by Christ the head of the Churche, to bee unto the same, the sole Canon and rule of all matters of Religion, and the worship and service of God whatsoever. And that whatsoever done in the same service and worship cannot bee instified by the said word, is unlawfull.[65]

The controversy over discipline had an effect on the terms in which Puritans preached the gospel. Two major streams developed: one that stressed outward form and another that stressed inner piety. The Puritans reasoned that while preaching was the means of salvation, salvation involved more than mere assent to doctrine. They sought after conversion. For the Calvinist Puritans, election implied the setting apart for salvation, and predestination implied the eschatological realization of salvation, but salvation and the assurance of salvation emerged in the process of conversion. Since salvation involved more than a static moment of time, the Puritans had to be concerned with more than the preaching of the gospel. Since salvation manifests itself in the process of conversion, the Puritans also sought to encourage spiritual growth through discipline.

Cartwright protested the distinction Archbishop Whitgift drew between matters of faith necessary to salvation and those things of indifference introduced into the church:

> But you say that in matters of faith and necessary to salvation it holdeth: which things you oppose after and set against matters of ceremonies, orders, discipline, and government; as though matters of discipline and kind of government were not necessary to salvation and of faith.[66]

He continued by arguing that church government, excommunication, censures, other matters of discipline, and the sacraments and other ceremonies are all matters of faith and necessary to salvation. This conviction led to a stream of thought within Puritanism that considered church government, or submission to the kingly rule of Christ, as a fundamental element of the gospel.[67] The stress on the kingdom as the essence of the gospel reappeared with devastating consequences for the Puritans and their evangelistic fervency in the 1630s. This stress was a prime motivation for separation and tended to divert men from the work of preaching for conversion to the work of erecting the true church.

As presbyterianism was coming to an end as a form of church government in the late 1580s, William Perkins was developing a form of discipline that concentrated on the individual believer and the pastoral care by the pastor.[68] Perkins's construction of a Puritan casuistry provided a framework of personal discipline for those who sought to live a godly life. Godly living had a profound relationship to salvation for the Puritans, who believed that the assurance of salvation grew out of one's godly life. His approach to discipline reflects a concept of the gospel rooted in the hyper-Calvinist interpretation of Reformed theology. His evangelistic approach consisted in offering cases whereby people might determine if they were elect or reprobate.

Puritans from the time of Cartwright and earlier had complained about those who professed Christ as prophet and priest but refused to submit to him as king. Thomas Goodwin came to think of the gospel as the preaching of the kingdom—first, with his persuasion that as king Christ commanded the pattern of worship and government for the church, and second, with his conviction of the imminent consummation of Christ's kingdom.[69] In the political and ecclesiastical confusion of the 1630s, Goodwin and his followers withdrew to Holland to await the establishment of Christ's kingdom on earth, safe and secure with the knowledge that in their congregations, "the Lord God omnipotent reigneth."[70]

The concept of the kingdom affected the evangelistic fervency of the Puritans in two ways. Those who stressed the kingly rule of Christ in the church went into controversy over discipline and worship, and as a result they often separated. Those who stressed the kingly rule of Christ in the heart devoted themselves to evangelism, the only hope they saw for the reformation of the church. For the most part,

Puritans avoided controversy over ceremonies and government during the reign of James I (though ceremonies figured prominently in the Millenary Petition). Instead, they devoted themselves to training preachers and establishing lectureships. Not until renewed pressure from the authorities did the Puritans begin to shift their emphasis back again to the outward forms of obedience to the commands of Christ in the church.

These are merely representative ways of how the issue of ecclesiology emerges from the acknowledgment of the authority of Christ. Unfortunately, as we have seen, the issue can easily lead to heated debate over how Christ intends the church to organize and live out its life.

THE EXALTATION AS GOOD NEWS

Exaltation appears to be one of the emerging themes of late twentieth-century Christian life in several parts of the world. In Korea, prayer holds the dominate integrating theme in the context of a church that is growing rapidly in a Buddhist culture. In India, the expression of power in the church in the form of healings and exorcisms popularly known as "signs and wonders" has resulted in significant growth of churches in areas dominated by tribal religion. In the United States, contemporary worship services that emphasize the Lordship of the exalted Christ have resulted in dramatic growth of churches that try to reach baby boomers and busters. All of these dimensions of the exaltation address significant spiritual issues of the groups for whom the exaltation represents good news.

Prayer

Prayer represents one of the most remarkable privileges that Christians enjoy. Through Jesus Christ, in whom a Christian lives, conversation may take place with Almighty God. Part of the religious nature of humans in all parts of the world is the quest to have some contact and interaction with the spiritual world. Depending on how people conceive of deity, these experiences can take different forms. Whether through the spinning of prayer wheels, assuming a particular posture, the recitation of fixed prayers, approaching intermediary spirits, or the emptying of one's thoughts, people desire some meaningful contact with the transcendent. The use of tarot cards, horoscopes, tea leaves, casting sticks, peyote, channeling, and ouija boards also represent an attempt to hear from the spirit world. Rather than deal with other spirits who may be friendly, hostile, or manipulative, Christians may converse with the Creator in the mystic experience of prayer. For the person who longs for meaningful spiritual experience, the exaltation of Jesus offers good news that people may have access to God in this life.

Signs and Wonders

In the premodern world people live with an awareness of spiritual realities that go beyond sensory experience. In the postmodern world people have rediscovered that science can observe the observable but that it does not speak about all possible reality. Premodern tribal peoples and postmodern technological societies have an interest in the "spirit world," though these different groups have different understandings of what this means.[71] It is not surprising to observe that the United States, with its amazing interest in the occult, varieties of New Age thought, and experimentation with spiritual religion, shares with underdeveloped cultures a growing expression of "power evangelism." Power evangelism occurs when people respond to Christ with faith on the basis of his exercise of authority over disease or demons through Christians who minister in his name. For people beset by fears of spirits or indecision over which spirit to worship, the exaltation of Jesus offers good news that he has authority and power over all physical and spiritual realities.

Worthiness

Perhaps the greatest songs of worship in all Scripture are the songs of praise in Revelation that glorify the exalted Christ who reigns forever and ever, the Lamb who is worthy. One of the characteristics of younger American society is its rejection of authority, yet those being converted in the context of their own cultural mediums predominantly sing songs about the exalted Lord. These people have found someone worthy to submit to as their authority. The rejection of authority by this generation is perhaps more a search for a worthy authority, which they find only in Christ, who is Lord of all. For people who have spent their lives disappointed by authority, the exaltation of Jesus offers good news that there is someone who is worthy to receive glory, honor, and power.

Tradition

Religion is often seen in terms of observable structures, such as ceremonies, organization, official beliefs, and traditions. Sometimes people come to faith through these formal expressions of the Lordship of Christ over his church because of his mystic presence in the body. When this happens, it is usually unintentional on the part of the church. This phenomenon is not unusual through worship experienced in the Anglican communion and the Orthodox church. If the Lord inhabits the praise of his people, then one should not be surprised to find that his habitation has an impact on people who come into the worship of true believers. Not even my own biases and prejudices about ecclesiology and worship will allow me to ignore the number of my friends who have come to faith out of atheism through the Anglican service. For people who have shut themselves to logical argument, the exaltation of Jesus who guides his church in worship offers good news of transcendent reality to people who are not even aware that they are searching.

Personal Relationship

On the other hand, many more people in late twentieth-century Western society have rejected institutional religion outright. Living in a complex, organized society, they have no interest in yet another complex structure over which they have no control. For many, the church represents the obstacle to spiritual truth. They are looking for something "that works for them." What they are asking for, in fact, is a return to something personal in an impersonal society. The message about the Lordship of Jesus Christ does not offer an organization, but a person. In spite of all the teachings of the church, it does not offer knowledge or information, but relationship with Christ. In him one becomes part of a community rather than a member of an organization. Personal relationship with Christ becomes incarnate through his body, the church. For those who long for personal religious experience, the exaltation of Jesus offers good news that it is available in him.

Martyrdom

After two thousand years, people still suffer persecution for their faith in Christ. At the end of Communist domination of Russia and its persecution of believers, many members of Russian society now ask why atheism failed and why Christians remained true to their faith in Christ in spite of persecution. Sharing in the sufferings of Christ creates an unnerving feeling after the fact for many casual observers. Russian society now has a remarkable openness to the gospel of Christ because of the testimony of those with whom he was present powerfully during the great persecution. For people who can only think of self-preservation in the face of adversity, the exaltation of Jesus offers good news that God offers more through relationship with Christ than the world can ever take away.

NOTES

1. See John F. MacArthur, Jr., *The Gospel According to Jesus* (Grand Rapids: Zondervan, 1988), and Charles C. Ryrie, *So Great Salvation* (Wheaton, Ill.: Victor, 1989).

2. Revelation represents one long, extended elaboration of the work of the exalted Christ, leading up to his second coming.

3. J. G. Davies, *The Early Christian Church* (Grand Rapids: Baker, 1980), 77.

4. *The Martyrdom of Ignatius*, chap. 2.

5. Ibid., chaps. 4–5.

6. Ibid., chap. 7.

7. *The Martyrdom of Polycarp*, 2.1, trans. William R. Schoedel, *The Apostolic Fathers*, ed. Jack Sparks (Nashville: Thomas Nelson, 1978).

8. Ibid., 2.2.

9. Ibid., 2.3.

10. Ibid., 5.2.

11. Ibid., 9.1.

12. Ibid., 9.3.

13. Ibid., 17.3.

14. Ibid., 18.2–3.

15. Davies, *The Early Christian Church*, 78.

16. *The Martyrdom of the Holy Martyrs*, chaps. 2, 4.

17. *The Martyrdom of Perpetua and Felicitas*, 1.3; 2.3–4; 3.1–3; 4.1

18. Ibid., 5.2; 6.3.

19. Tertullian, *Ad Martyras*, chap. 3.

20. Ibid., chaps. 4–5.

21. Tertullian, *De Fuga Persecutione*, chap. 1.

22. Ibid., chap. 5.

23. Ibid., chaps. 7, 12, 14.

24. Ibid., chap. 14.

25. Davies, *The Early Christian Church*, 115–18.

26. Gregory of Nyssa, Panegyric, quoted in Davies, *The Early Christian Church*, 129.

27. Davies, *The Early Christian Church*, 129–30.

28. Ibid., 174–76.

29. Dietrich Bonhoeffer, *The Cost of Discipleship*, rev. ed. (New York: Collier, 1963), 37.

30. Ibid., 47.

31. Ibid., 69.

32. Ibid., 100–101.

33. Ibid., 64, 106–14.

34. Ibid., 264–68.

35. Ibid., 269.

36. Ibid., 273.

37. Davies, *The Early Christian Church*, 185. Davies observes, "The Peace of the Church virtually closed the list of martyrs, within the empire, and as their heirs the monks now came forward in great numbers."

38. Edward E. Malone, *The Monk and the Martyr* (Washington, D.C.: Catholic Univ. of America Press, 1950), 8; cf. Clement of Alexandria, *Stromata*, 4.4.

39. Ibid., 19.

40. Ibid., 27–43.

41. Ibid., 44.

42. Lisa M. Bitel, *Isle of the Saints: Monastic Settlement and Christian Community in Early Ireland* (Ithaca, N.Y.: Cornell Univ. Press, 1990), 10.

43. *The Lives of the Desert Fathers: The Historia Monochorum in Aegypto*, trans. Norman Russell, intro. Benedicta Ward (London: Mowbray, 1981), Prologue, 9.

44. Ibid., 40–45.

45. Ibid., 2.10.

46. Philip Rousseau, *Pachomius: The Making of a Community in Fourth-Century Egypt* (Berkeley: Univ. of California Press, 1985), 126.

47. Ibid., 58–63.

48. Owen Chadwick, *John Cassian*, 2d ed. (Cambridge: Cambridge Univ. Press, 1968), 112–13.

49. Stephanus Hilpisch, *History of Benedictine Nuns*, trans. M. Joanne Muggli, ed. Leonard J. Doyle (Collegeville, Minn.: St. John's Abbey, 1958), 1–2.

50. Ibid., 4.

51. Don John Chapman, *Saint Benedict and the Sixth Century* (Westport, Conn.: Greenwood, 1971), 147ff., 162–64.

52. See Jean Décarreaux, *Monks and Civilization: From the Barbarian Invasions to the Reign of Charlemagne*, trans. Charlotte Haldane (London: George Allen and Unwin, 1964), 27. "The prestige of the preacher, his ascetic virtues, the fame he achieved, the real or supposed thaumaturgical gifts he possessed, provided him with a halo. Their apologetics were rudimentary. The God of Clovis or the 'druid' of St. Patrick having proved themselves stronger, there was no reason why the Franks or the Irish should not join the better side."

53. Ibid., 210–11.

54. See Donald Hochstetler, *A Conflict of Traditions: Women in Religion in the Early Middle Ages 500–840* (Lanham, Md.: Univ. Press of America, 1992), passim.

55. Chapman, *Saint Benedict*, 2–13.

56. Ibid., 29ff.

57. Ibid., 24.

58. Noreen Hunt, *Cluniac Monasticism in the Central Middle Ages* (Hamden, Conn.: Archon Books, 1971), 18.

59. Cf. John S. Coolidge, *The Pauline Renaissance in England: Puritanism and the Bible* (Oxford: Clarendon, 1970). Coolidge argues that the Puritans interpreted Scripture through the eyes of Paul; Stanley P. Fienberg, "Thomas Goodwin's Scriptural Hermeneutics and the Dissolution of Puritan Unity," *The Journal of Religious History*, 10 (June 1978): 32–49, argues that Presbyterian Puritans interpreted Scripture through the Old Testament with an emphasis on reason while Independents interpreted Scripture through Christ; John R. Knott, Jr., *The Sword of the Spirit: Puritan Responses to the Bible* (Chicago: Univ. of Chicago Press, 1971), 4,

stresses the Puritan belief in "the dynamism of the Holy Spirit acting through the Word."

60. Everett H. Emerson, ed., *English Puritanism from John Hooper to John Milton* (Durham, N.C.: Duke Univ. Press, 1968), p. 27.

61. Ibid., 91.

62. Ibid.

63. Ibid.

64. W. H. Frere and C. E. Douglas, eds. *Puritan Manifestoes* (London: SPCK, 1954), 45.

65. William Bradshaw, *English Puritanisme and Other Works*, ed. R. C. Simmons (Westmead, Eng.: Gregg International Publishers, 1972), 1.

66. John Whitgift, *The Works of John Whitgift*, ed. John Ayre (Cambridge: Cambridge Univ. Press, 1851–53), 181.

67. Emerson, *English Puritanism*, 87–88; this is a point Walter Travers made clear in his appeal for the institution of a presbyterian form of church government in *A Full and Plaine Declaration:* "Yet could not England be brought to leave that form of governing the Church whereunto it had been accustomed under popery, but divided and separated as under the doctrine and discipline of the Gospel, two things which both by their own nature and also by commandment of God are to be joined together."

68. For a discussion of Perkins's casuistry, see Ian Breward, "William Perkins and the Origins of Reformed Casuistry," *The Evangelical Quarterly*, 49 (1968): 3–20.

69. Thomas Goodwin, *The Works of Thomas Goodwin* (Edinburgh: James Nichol, 1861–66), 12.94.

70. Ibid., 70.

71. For a discussion of African understandings of "power encounters," see Cyril Okorocha, "The Meaning of Salvation: An African Perspective," and Kwame Bediako, "Jesus in African Culture: A Ghanaian Perspective," in *Emerging Voices in Global Christian Theology*, ed. William A. Dyrness (Grand Rapids: Zondervan, 1994). For a Western view see John Wimber and Kevin Springer, *Power Evangelism* (San Francisco: Harper and Row, 1986).

Chapter 8

The Gift of the Holy Spirit

From the beginning of recorded time and in the most primitive societies, people have had a mixture of desire and dread over the prospect of a personal encounter with God. What Rudolph Otto referred to as the universal experience of the "Holy" finds expression in all cultural settings. Otto described the Holy as characterized by *mysterium tremendum et fascinans*: mysterious and untouchable, dreadful in capacity for instilling tremendous fear, yet fascinating in capacity to draw people.[1] Simply put, from the perspective of biblical faith, God is holy. In most religious systems of the world, whether complex or primitive, the mystical or spiritual encounter with God has a high value, though Otto complained that the more rationalistic a religious system became, the more inclined it grew to undervalue or discredit the validity of spiritual experience.

While Christians think of a spiritual experience as an experience with the Creator God and his Son the Lord Jesus Christ, across history and culture spiritual experiences might also describe encounters with demons, angels, the dead, or any of a variety of spiritual beings. Some understandings of spiritual experience among Eastern religions, on the other hand, contain no specific reference to another being or spirit, where all spiritual reality is understood as a whole and any part of the whole may move throughout the whole when released from the confines of time and space imposed by the false awareness of living in a body.

Universal spiritual experience is a given of human experience. Since the time of Schleiermacher and Otto, religious experience has been valued as self-authenticating as an end in itself within a growing corner of Western Christianity.[2] Throughout the Bible, in the life of Israel and of the early church, people unfaithful to God and people faithful to God had spiritual experiences. They are a dimension of being human, though they are not synonymous with salvation. Spiritual experiences do not necessarily represent the favor of God or a positive relationship to the divine, nor does a visitation by the Spirit of God imply eternal acceptance by God. God sent a lying spirit to the sons of the prophets, who made spirituality a profession (1 Kings 22:21–23; 2 Chron. 18:20–22). Eliphaz, the unjust antagonist of Job, had a genuine spiritual experience, but it had no effect on his character or being (Job 4:15). King Saul experienced the Spirit of the Lord, but the Spirit departed, leaving him with an evil spirit from the Lord (1 Sam. 16:14–16, 23; 18:10; 19:9). Furthermore, the Scriptures do not deny the reality of such spiritual encounters as divination, sorcery, or necromancy; they merely forbid these negative forms of spiritual experience (Deut. 18:9–14).

When Peter preached the first gospel sermon on the Day of Pentecost, he did not offer his audience eternal life. Instead, he offered them "the promise" that God had made to Israel by the prophets of old, announcing that those who turned to Jesus would "receive the gift of the Holy Spirit" (Acts 2:38–39). Jesus Christ makes possible the genuine, positive experience with God that people everywhere long to have. By the Holy Spirit, the exalted Lord Jesus maintains immediate relationship with those who have faith in him and dispenses the benefits of salvation available through him. The Holy Spirit takes possession of and occupies those who submit their lives to this Lord. Through the Spirit they then share his life, and he begins to change them.

BIBLICAL BACKGROUND

In the Old Testament, the Spirit of the Lord visited people and caused things to happen to them, for them, and through them. The Spirit acts upon the created order and causes things to transpire that accomplish the will of God. Prophets, priests, and leaders of ancient Israel had the experience of the Spirit of the Lord "coming upon" them to endow them with ability (Ex. 31:3; Num. 11:16–17; Judg. 3:10; 6:34; 11:29; 1 Sam. 16:13–14) or knowledge (Num. 24:2; 2 Sam. 23:2; 1 Chron. 12:18; 2 Chron. 15:1; 18:23; 20:14; 24:20; Neh. 9:20, 30) in order to accomplish God's purposes. In "coming upon" people, the Spirit of the Lord seized them and took control of them. Such a visitation did not cause a permanent change in the individual; rather, the individual's ability or knowledge depended on their possession by the Spirit of the Lord. When the Spirit left, matters reverted to the way they had been. Besides ability and knowledge, however, the Spirit of the Lord also wrought a change in emotions (1 Sam. 10:6, 9–10; 11:6), character (Isa. 32:15–17), and life itself (Job 33:4; Ps. 104:30; Isa. 40:7; Ezek. 37:1–14).

The word for *Spirit* in Hebrew *(ruach)* means "breath" or "wind." When God breathed into the nostrils of the clay figure he had fashioned, it became "a living being" (Gen. 2:7). The Spirit of the Lord proceeds from God like breath from a person, and he changes whatever he touches. By the time of the writing prophets, the image of breath or wind was enlarged by mixing metaphors. God promised to "*pour out* my Spirit on all people" (Joel 2:28). To the wind image was thus added the image of water (see also Isa. 32:15; 44:3; Ezek. 36:25–27; 39:29). God's Spirit would be like water to cleanse and sustain life, though that event lay in the future for the prophets. The coming of the Spirit in this way for everyone, not for just the occasional prophet, would be the central element of the new covenant God promised to establish with those who had faith (Jer. 31:31–34).

The promise that one day God would pour out his Spirit contains a profound presupposition of faith that permeates the ancient Hebrew writings: People do not by their nature possess or partake of the Spirit of God. Judaism, Islam, and Christianity all share this presupposition. Hinduism, Buddhism, and Christian Science, on the other hand, consider all reality to be an aspect of the divine. The Hebrew Scriptures describe at some length the characteristics of the human spirit, which contrasts sharply with the picture of God's Spirit.

The human spirit is the domain of the emotions, character, the intellect and will, and vitality (see Table 8A). Furthermore, a remarkable relationships exists between the physical body and the human spirit, such that they affect each other (see Table 8B). Within human emotions, character, intellect and will, and vitality occur the frailty and inevitable failure of human life. To correct this universal flaw, the technical theological term for which is sin, God promised through the prophets that he would one day send his Spirit.

Domain of the Human Spirit in Hebrew Thought

Intellect	Will	Emotions	Character	Vitality
Job 20:3	Prov. 16:32	Gen. 41:8	Ps. 32:2	Gen. 45:27
Prov. 20:27	Job 15:13	Ex. 6:9	Ps. 34:18	Ex. 35:21
Isa. 26:9	Deut. 2:30	Deut. 2:30	Ps. 51:10	Josh. 5:1
Ps. 77:6		1 Sam. 1:15	Ps. 51:17	Judg. 15:19
Isa. 29:24		1 Kings 21:5	Ps. 78:8	1 Sam. 30:12
Ezek. 13:3		Job 7:11; 21:4	Prov. 11:13	1 Kings 10:5
Mal. 2:15		Eccl. 4:6	Prov. 14:29	2 Kings 2:9
		Isa. 54:6	Prov. 15:4	1 Chron. 5:26
		Ezek. 3:14	Prov. 16:2	2 Chron. 9:4; 21:16
		Dan. 2:1,3; 7:15	Prov. 16:18	Job 10:12
			Prov. 16:19	Ps. 51:10; 76:12; 77:3; 143:7
			Eccl. 7:8–9	Eccl. 8:8; 10:4
			Isa. 66:2	Isa. 57:16
			Mal. 2:16	Jer. 51:11
				Ezek. 21:7

Table 8A

Examples of the Effect of Sin on the Human Spirit

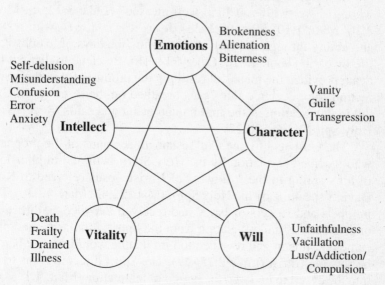

Table 8B

The Gospels

The Gospels reflect the presuppositions of Hebrew faith concerning the Spirit of God and human spirits. They also make clear that the fulfillment of God's promise to give the Holy Spirit comes through Jesus Christ. Only occasionally did John reiterate in his Gospel events included in the other Gospel accounts. But he does join the others in repeating the experience of John the Baptist, who declared by a revelation from God that Jesus is the One who will baptize with the Holy Spirit (John 1:33; cf. Matt. 3:11; Mark 1:8; Luke 3:16). Jesus taught publicly that God would give the Holy Spirit to those that ask (Luke 11:13; John 3:34), and in private he made clear that the Spirit would come in his name (John 14:16–17, 26).

Jesus plays the central role in the coming of the Spirit because of who he is in relationship to the Father and the Spirit. The birth narratives describe him as conceived by the Holy Spirit (Matt. 1:18;

Luke 1:35). At his baptism, when Jesus began his public ministry, the Holy Spirit descended and a voice declared, "You are my Son, whom I love; with you I am well pleased" (Luke 3:22; cf. Matt. 3:16; Mark 1:10; John 1:32–33). Jesus was endowed with power and ability through the Holy Spirit during the days of his physical life on earth (Matt. 12:28; Luke 4:14, 18). He came to die, but his death provided the means of fulfilling the promise, for in the resurrection John declared that Jesus breathed on the disciples as God did in the creation of the first human being and said, "Receive the Holy Spirit" (John 20:22).

The Gospels link the Old Testament accounts of the prophets, who received revelation by the Holy Spirit, with the implications of his coming to the followers of Christ. Jesus referred to King David's speaking by the Holy Spirit (Matt. 22:43; Mark 12:36). The prophets and leaders of Israel had received knowledge, direction, understanding, and revelation from the Spirit. Similarly, the Spirit came on Simeon and revealed to him that he would not die before he saw the Christ (Luke 2:25–27). The Spirit directed Jesus to go into the desert to undergo the period of temptation (Matt. 4:1; Mark 1:12; Luke 4:1). Jesus told his followers that the Holy Spirit would teach them, guide them, remind them, and testify of Christ; and when they were called to give an account of their faith in persecution, the Holy Spirit would give them words to speak (John 14:26; 15:26; 16:13–15; cf. Matt. 10:20; Mark 13:11; Luke 12:12).

Finally, John repeats the prophetic theme of the Spirit, like water, being the source of life in a barren desert. In the style of the classical Hebrew prophets, who poetically made their declaration in parallel metaphor, Jesus declared to Nicodemus that "no one can enter the kingdom of God unless he is born of the water and the Spirit" (John 3:5). Having experienced a human birth does not by nature give a person a place in the eternal realm (cf. 6:63). Having a place in heaven requires a new birth, a birth from above, a birth from the Spirit (3:3, 6–8). Jesus renewed the theme of the Spirit as life-giving water to the Samaritan woman at the well: "Indeed, the water I give him will become in him a spring of water welling up to eternal life" (4:14). Finally, Jesus promised, "Whoever believes in me, as the Scripture has said, streams of living water will flow from within him" (7:38). John, who gave particular attention in his

Gospel to the implications of the gift of the Spirit for followers of Christ, adds his own comment to this offer from Christ:

> By this he meant the Spirit, whom those who believed in him were later to receive. Up to that time the Spirit had not been given, since Jesus had not yet been glorified. (John 7:39)

General Apostolic Writings

The early church experienced the coming of the Holy Spirit as the fulfillment of a promise from God made by the prophets (Acts 2:17; cf. Joel 2:28) and confirmed through Jesus Christ, who promised that the disciples would receive the promised Spirit themselves (Acts 1:5, 8; 11:16). At his exaltation, Christ received the promised Spirit and poured it out on his disciples and on all who might become his disciples (2:33, 38). The Spirit comes to those who have faith in Jesus Christ and seals them as a possession of God (Gal. 3:14; Eph. 1:13). Whereas all of the benefits of salvation come through the living, exalted Christ, he applies those benefits to his followers by the Holy Spirit. While salvation comes as a consequence of being "in Christ," the experience of being "in Christ" comes about through the corresponding wonder of the Holy Spirit in the believer. The Spirit provides the continuity between what happened on the cross two thousand years ago and the person who experiences the effects of that death today. That is, the Holy Spirit creates the ongoing relationship between a human believer and the exalted Lord.

Indwelling by the Holy Spirit. In ancient times the Spirit of the Lord "came upon" selected individuals whom God used, and then it left again. Instead of the isolated few who have the time or means or discipline to live a mystic's life, the Holy Spirit comes to all who join their lives to Christ. The change of terminology from the Old Testament to the book of Acts reflects the significance of the gift of the Holy Spirit. By the action of Christ the Spirit "fills" those who belong to Christ. It serves as a "seal of ownership" put into the hearts of all believers (2 Cor. 1:22). The coming of the Spirit makes possible the immediate relationship with the exalted Christ because it is his Spirit that enters and takes possession of those who have faith in him (Gal. 4:6; 1 John 3:24; 4:13).

This relationship with Christ through the Holy Spirit has such importance for applying salvation that the early church in Acts spoke much more frequently of the coming of the Holy Spirit than of receiving salvation (Acts 8:15–17; 10:44–45, 47; 11:15; 15:8; 19:2, 6). Salvation was not for them a commodity to be possessed; rather, it meant that they had come into the possession of the One who could keep them. Thus, they realized they were not their own; their bodies were the temple of the Holy Spirit they had received from God (1 Cor. 6:19). They were included in Christ when they believed and received the seal of his ownership represented by their possession by the Holy Spirit (Eph. 1:13). The possession by the Spirit was full and complete, such that believers in Christ were frequently described as "full of" or "filled with" the Holy Spirit (Acts 2:4; 4:8; 6:5; 7:55; 9:17; 11:24).

Application of salvation. Jesus Christ obtained salvation by his death, and he gives salvation through his life. The one who has faith in him receives salvation, however, as a by-product of receiving the Spirit of Christ. The Spirit applies the benefits of salvation to those who believe. Receiving the Spirit involves the gift of life:

> And if the Spirit of him who raised Jesus from the dead is living in you, he who raised Christ from the dead will also give life to your mortal bodies through his Spirit, who lives in you. (Rom. 8:11)

The rebirth to eternal life promised through the prophets who proclaimed the coming of a new covenant comes to pass as a result of the coming of the Spirit (2 Cor. 3:6; Gal. 6:8; Titus 3:5).

Justification from the legal dimension of sin, which Christ accomplished by virtue of his cross and resurrection, is applied in the name of the Lord Jesus Christ by the Spirit (1 Cor. 6:11). Consequently, the Holy Spirit delivers the righteousness of Christ that comes by faith (Gal. 5:5). He adopts those for God who have faith in his Son, so that in sharing the life of the Son through the Spirit, they also share his relationship to the Father as his adopted children (Rom. 8:14–16; Gal. 4:6). The presence of the Spirit also serves as a guarantee that God will complete the work of redemption, assuring believers that they have inherited the promises of God (Rom. 8:23; 2 Cor. 1:22; 5:5; Eph. 1:13; 4:30).

Becoming holy. God assumes the responsibility for making people holy. Holiness is a unique characteristic of God and cannot be duplicated by people. We cannot lead holy lives apart from the holiness of God being in us by the Holy Spirit. He creates an alternative to sin for us, working in us to duplicate the character of Jesus Christ (Rom. 8:1–13). Holiness does not come by human effort, but by the gracious work of God through his Spirit (Rom. 15:16; 1 Cor. 6:11; Gal. 3:2–5; 2 Thess. 2:13; 1 Peter 1:2). He performs a work of transformation that bit by bit changes a Christian gradually into the likeness of Christ:

> Now the Lord is the Spirit, and where the Spirit of the Lord is, there is freedom. And we, who with unveiled faces all reflect the Lord's glory, are being transformed into his likeness with ever-increasing glory, which comes from the Lord, who is the Spirit. (2 Cor. 3:17–18)

The Holy Spirit carries out the implications of salvation for someone who has died with Christ through faith and seeks to follow him. He makes it possible to live the Christian life, for through him Christ lives his life in the Christian. In this way, the Spirit produces the emotional and character qualities of Christ that make life beautiful even in adversity—qualities such as love, joy, peace, patience, kindness, goodness, faithfulness, gentleness, self-control, purity, understanding, and hope (Acts 13:52; Rom. 5:5; 14:17; 15:13; 2 Cor. 6:6; Gal. 5:16–25; 1 Thess. 1:6). The effect of this work of sanctification of a believer in Christ is that they come to have the quality of a "letter from Christ" written by the Holy Spirit, "not on tablets of stone but on tablets of human hearts" (2 Cor. 3:3; cf. Jer. 31:33).

Revelation and direction. The early church understood that God revealed things to the prophets of ancient times through his Spirit (Acts 1:16; 4:25; 28:25; Heb. 3:7; 1 Peter 1:11; 2 Peter 1:21). They experienced this same phenomenon themselves as the Holy Spirit gave revelations and guidance in their daily conduct. Christians experienced the Spirit's guidance in the decisions of life, particularly those related to faith and ministry. They often described the experience as the Spirit speaking to a person or group (Acts 8:29; 10:19; 11:12; 13:2; 20:23; 21:11; 1 Tim. 4:1; Rev. 2:7, 11, 17, 29; 3:6, 13, 22; 14:13; 22:17). In other cases, the church experienced the Spirit as teaching, testifying, revealing, witnessing, or in some way showing them the things of God that people could not know if the Spirit did not make them known (Acts 5:32; 1 Cor. 2:10–14; Eph. 3:5; Heb. 9:8; 10:15; 1 John 5:6).

Whereas the people of the ancient world customarily sought omens and consulted oracles before beginning an important venture, Christians relied on the guidance of the Holy Spirit in the conduct of their lives and in the administration of the church (Acts 13:4; 15:28; 16:6–7; 1 Cor. 7:40). In cases of conscience, they experienced his leading toward the truth (Rom. 9:1). They had the peace of knowing that God would guide them in the business of day-to-day life.

The Spirit supplies the continuity of life between the believers and the exalted Christ. Through him, believers have immediate access to God (Eph. 2:18). The Spirit helps them through forming a link or intercession with God (Rom. 8:26–27). Through experience in the Holy Spirit, Christians have open to them a mystical experience of prayer that admits them into the presence of God (Jude 20; Rev. 1:10).

Power and ability. A major theme of Scripture involves the way God empowers the unlikely to do both the mundane and the magnificent. Whether the shepherd boy who became a king, the stuttering fugitive who gave voice to the pleas of a nation in bondage to Egypt, or the coward who conquered with an army even more unlikely than himself, the Bible throbs with stories of God's enabling people to function in a meaningful way. Jesus promised his followers that "you will receive power when the Holy Spirit comes on you" (Acts 1:8). The early chapters of Acts describe how Christians, when filled with the Holy Spirit, had the ability to speak in other tongues, to stand before hostile rulers and proclaim Christ, to speak the word of God boldly, and to confront whoever needed confrontation (2:4; 4:8, 31; 13:9). Christ used some apostles to perform miraculous wonders through his Spirit, by which God testified about the salvation found in Christ (Rom. 15:19; Heb. 2:4). These demonstrations of the Spirit's power confirmed the truth of the claim that Jesus Christ was Lord over all powers and forces (1 Cor. 2:4; 1 Thess. 1:5). The early believers also discovered that the Holy Spirit did not manifest the same powers and abilities in all Christians; rather, God provided the powers and abilities needed in a given time and place to accomplish his ministry through the church (Rom. 12:1–8;1 Cor. 12:1–31; Eph. 4:1–16).

Observations. The Spirit expresses the unity of God in accomplishing salvation. The apostles understood that there was only one Spirit (Eph. 4:3–4). Commonly referred to by the apostles as the Holy Spirit, whom the prophets of Israel had referred to as the Spirit of the Lord, the Spirit was also described as the Spirit of Jesus, the Spirit of Christ, or the Spirit of the Son (Gal. 4:6; Phil. 1:19; 1 Peter 1:11; 1 John 3:24; 4:13). The interrelationship of Father, Son, and Spirit appears regularly in the apostolic writings without any attempt to resolve how the Spirit of the Father and the Spirit of the Son can be the same Spirit. The sublimity of the relationship may be seen, however, in passages that describe the way in which the benefits of salvation come to those who have faith in Christ—such as Paul's prayer for the Ephesians that the Father "may strengthen you with power through his Spirit in your inner being, so that Christ may dwell in your hearts through faith" (Eph. 3:16–17).

HISTORICAL/THEOLOGICAL DEVELOPMENT

For the first several centuries of its life, the church regarded the Holy Spirit as a familiar figure who made faith in Christ an experiential reality. No great controversy surrounded the church's experience of him. Christians understood salvation as involving the coming of the Spirit. Montanus and his followers stressed the ecstatic experiences of the Holy Spirit, but their primary focus related to their expectation of the return of Christ, as will be noted in the next chapter. The doctrine of the Holy Spirit became a primary element in evangelism and a focus of controversy only after the collapse of the Western empire as the Eastern and Western Churches drifted further apart.

The Filioque Controversy

At Chalcedon, the universal council had settled on a formula to describe the relationship of the Father, Son, and Holy Spirit. A controversy later arose, however, that threatened the orthodox understanding. In their conflict with the Arian Goths, the orthodox Christians of the West spoke of the Holy Spirit as proceeding from the Father *and the Son*, in order to stress the deity of Christ. This way of speaking appeared in the Athanasian Creed, so named to honor the defender of orthodox Christology. The problem came, however, when the Western Church began to add the phrase "and the Son" (*filioque*) to the Nicene Creed as well, though without benefit of a universal council. This alteration in the Nicene Creed probably began in the late sixth or early seventh century.[3] As has commonly happened in the West, popular practice preceded official policy, for the papacy did not adopt this practice until the eleventh century.

The church in Spain in disquieting measure held to the adoptionist Arian Christology favored by the Goths. Charlemagne called a synod at Frankfort in 794 to deal with the issue, which resulted in the condemnation of the view, though the large part of the church in Moslem territory paid no attention to the synod. The *filioque* addition proved to be an effective way of combating adoptionism in Spain, however, and the custom of speaking of the Holy Spirit as proceeding from the Father and the Son gained popularity there. In this context Charlemagne, now crowned emperor, gave his support for the approval of the addition to the Nicene Creed at a synod meeting in Aachen in 809.[4] He further commissioned Theodulph of Orleans to compile a registry of quotations from the early fathers that might support the addition.[5] This move made perfect sense to the Latin Church in their struggle with Arianism over Christology, but to the Greek Church, which had not taken part in that struggle, the confusion of the Trinitarian formula seemed inappropriate.

The Greeks accused the Latins of confusing the idea of "proceeding" with the idea of "being sent." While the Son may be the one *through* whom the Spirit is sent into the world, the Spirit does not *proceed* from the Son.[6] To them, the *filioque* addition violated the doctrine of the Trinity, which allows for one nature but distinct characteristics of each member. If the Spirit proceeds from Father and Son, then the two share the same characteristics and the Spirit is left as inferior.[7] The Eastern Church insisted that for a true unity of Godhead, the Trinity must have its source, cause, and principle in one member, not two. Patriarch Photius of Constantinople insisted that anything else would be polytheism.[8]

Because of deteriorating political realities, the Roman empire no longer existed, though theoretically the Holy Roman emperor was accepted as joint emperor with the Byzantine emperor, just as in an earlier time Rome had both an emperor of the West and an emperor of the East. Lacking political unity, speaking different languages, possessing different worship traditions, belonging to different cultures, the Eastern and Western Churches had no context in which to resolve the *filioque* controversy. While liturgical pluralism has its place and posed no serious threat to unity at that time between the two churches, the doctrinal implications of the *filioque* issue posed a grave obstacle that other issues served to heighten.[9]

When the crisis of ecclesiastical wills came in 1054, in the conflict between Leo IX of Rome and Michael Cerularius of Constantinople, a number of matters in the conflict had more to do with the personalities involved than with the whole church, but the *filioque* issue was one that could not be overlooked.[10] Though the Orthodox could probably have accepted an understanding of the *filioque* phrase that meant that the Holy Spirit proceeded *out of* the Father *through* the Son, the doctrinal issue soon became lost in the ecclesiastical issue of the Latin Church changing the creed without consulting the Greek Church in ecumenical council.[11] The *filioque* addition joined with the papal claim to supremacy to impede normal relations between the East and the West, though negotiations did continue for the next several centuries (as the meeting at Nicea in 1234, the council of Lyons II in 1274, and the meeting at Ferrara in 1438).[12]

Eastern Orthodox

The Eastern Orthodox Church bears the stamp of a conscious awareness of the presence of the Holy Spirit in its liturgy and life. Rather than calling attention to the Holy Spirit as a distinct emphasis of faith, however, the Eastern Church has tended to stress the Spirit as a member of the Trinity, as the liturgy proclaims:

> We have seen the true light;
> We have received the Holy Spirit;
> We have found the true faith.
> Let us worship the inseparable Trinity,
> for it has redeemed us.[13]

The role of the Holy Spirit in redemption, however, has an ever-present dimension that involves the mystical relationship to God.

In contrast to the systematic approach to theology in the West, which has tended to stress the legal dimension of faith (i.e., justification, atonement, guilt, forgiveness, and satisfaction), the theology of the East has avoided rationalistic systems like those of Aquinas or Calvin and stressed the mystical dimension of faith (i.e., sanctification, rebirth, re-creation, and transfiguration).[14] Orthodoxy showed no interest in the Western debate about justification during the Reformation since they regarded the legal issues of sin as a minor theme compared with the major theme of the restoration of what was lost in the Fall.

Sergius Bulagkov, one of the most important interpreters of Orthodoxy in the twentieth century, began his work on *The Orthodox Church* by describing the church as new life in Christ guided by the Holy Spirit and "the domain where the Holy Spirit lives and works."[15] The Holy Spirit creates the church and mediates the Trinity. He makes Scripture accessible as the Word of God[16] and creates the tradition of the church.[17] While the Latin mass regards the words of institution, "This is my body," as the critical moment in the sacrament, the invocation of the Holy Spirit during the prayer of *epiclesis* serves as the critical moment in the Greek Eucharist.[18] The liturgy creates the atmosphere of other worldliness that communicates to the human spirit, though it relies on the senses to create an openness or awareness of the presence of the Holy Spirit. Among the Orthodox, it is the Holy Spirit who uses the liturgy to open the way to the celestial realm. According to tradition, this mystic experience of worship represented the critical element in the acceptance of Christianity by the Russians.

The mystical theology of the Eastern Church does not concern itself so much with knowledge about God, which tends to be the case with the systematic theology of the West, as it does with aiming at union with God.[19] In sympathy with Pseudo-Dionysius, the Eastern Church has recognized that the positive assertion of theological systems (cataphatic theology) inevitably suffers from imperfection.[20] Thus, the Eastern Church tends toward the mystical theology of negation (apophatic theology), which arrives at God by stripping away concepts that strive to define the incomprehensible God. Having given up what one presumes to know, Lossky explains that the mystic can then find God: "For God makes His dwelling there where our understanding and our concepts can gain no admittance."[21] None of this happens in a void, however, as in Hinduism or Buddhism, but is a result of the Holy Spirit who brings union with God.

The Orthodox Christian aims at bearing the Holy Spirit, by which one lives in Christ. Through him the image of Christ shines in a Christian and gives direction for life.[22] While the monastic life offers the path of mystical union with God through complete renunciation of the world, Eastern Orthodoxy also teaches that one may also pursue this union in the midst of life's circumstances.[23] Those who have exhibited this infusion of the Spirit in Russian Orthodox life have attracted the attention of pilgrims, who grow aware of heavenly reality by being in their presence. This attention to the mystical has been a feature of Russian Orthodox life from early times.

St. Anthony (983–1073) introduced monastic life to Russia soon after the acceptance of Orthodox Christianity by Vladimir, ruler of the Kievian state, who was baptized in 987. The mystic element of monasticism took on a new emphasis with the Hesychast movement that spread through the Byzantine empire in the fourteenth century. Named for Hesychius of Jerusalem and fostered by St. Gregory the Sinaite (d. 1346), St. Nilus (1433–1508) introduced the movement to Russia. Gregory taught that the repetition of the prayer of Jesus, "Lord Jesus Christ, Son of God, have mercy upon me, a sinner," enabled a Christian to experience purification and illumination by the Holy Spirit, which makes an experience with God possible.[24] This experience gives victory over temptation to sin and makes holy living possible.

St. Nilus taught that in prayer the mind should be free of good thoughts as well as evil thoughts since the good often turns to bad; therefore, he advised the constant repetition of the Prayer of Jesus with the mind focused within the heart while breathing slowly.[25] He left his spiritual directions on mystic contemplation in the *Tradition*, which became a guide for many monasteries. Mary of Mikhalitsky, a mystic nun, also wrote her *Memoirs* about this time, which record a number of her visions.[26] With the conquest of the Trans-Volga, Kazan, Astrakhan, and Western Siberia, the Hesychast movement declined as monks shifted their attention to mission work in those new regions of the empire and to ritualistic observance, though monastic mysticism would enjoy revival in the nineteenth century.

Western Mysticism

The Western mystics of the Middle Ages were concerned with themes of joy, love, the will, light, truth, and liberty. These themes all relate to the activity of the Holy Spirit, whom the mystics did not necessarily differentiate from the Father or Son as they sought a deeper experience with God. The mystics demonstrated different concerns and characteristics of their spiritual experiences, but these diverse emphases correspond to the areas of activity of the Holy Spirit in the New Testament as discussed earlier in this chapter.

Hildegard of Bingen (1098–1179) reported a lifetime of visions from God before she also received the call to record the visions and preach her prophetic message. While the Holy Spirit did not represent the focus of her concern or message, he did provide the visions and the calling. When she was forty-two, she had the visionary experience that began her public ministry:

> Heaven was opened and a fiery light of exceeding brilliance came and permeated my whole brain, and inflamed my whole heart and my whole breast, not like a burning but like a warming flame, as the sun warms anything its rays touch.[27]

As a result of her experiences, Hildegard claimed to have received understanding of the Scriptures and confidence in their interpretation.

Joachim Fiore (d. 1202) influenced the "Spiritual Franciscans" of the thirteenth and fourteenth centuries. His understanding of the "Eternal Gospel" stressed the direct revelation of God through the presence of the Holy Spirit.[28] The movement was suppressed in 1254 when it took an apocalyptic turn (see chapter 9), but it had a strong influence on the contemplative life of the Middle Ages.

Mechthild of Magdeburg (1210–1297) represents that sort of remarkable woman of the Middle Ages whose mystic experiences and writing had a powerful influence on the church when European society no longer provided a means for women to have influence. At age twelve she had an experience of the Holy Spirit that altered her life by giving her a vision of the world in relationship to God.[29] Mechthild became known for the revelations she wrote down on loose sheets of paper, which Heinrich of Halle, a student of Albert the Great, circulated as *The Flowing Light of the Godhead*. At a time of decadence and corruption in the church, her visions called the clergy back to holiness.[30] For Mechthild, her visionary experience converged on a theme of love that overpowered her self-condemnation and made her acceptable even to herself.

These three mystics suggest different emphases that one's experiences could take. Among others Bernard (1090–1153) emphasized love, Hugh St. Victor (1096–1141) understanding, Richard St. Victor (1123–1173) the relation of reason and emotion, Bonaventure (1221–1274) the illumination of the mind, Ramon Lull (1232–1315) the movement from knowledge to love, Henry Suso (1295–1366) long-suffering, and Nicholas of Cusa (1401–1464) faith and love. Throughout the period of high scholasticism, the mystics found in their experience with God a satisfying alternative to speculation about God.

Protestant Awakenings

After the initial spiritual fire of the Reformation turned to religious wars and conflict among the Reformers over doctrine, a group within Protestantism began to long for an expression of faith that went deeper than theological formulas. John Arndt (1555–1621) renewed a medieval tradition of mysticism that moved beyond theological debate and mere scholastic understanding of faith to a faith that touched the heart. He wrote *True Christianity* to expound this heart religion. Arndt had a profound affect on Philip Jacob Spener, who lamented the spiritual poverty to which German Lutheranism had fallen by the mid-seventeenth century.

In an effort to deal with the problem, Spener began prayer and Bible study groups, which he called *collegia pietatis* in order to cultivate personal holiness among laypeople, especially students. Out of these gatherings grew the Pietistic Awakening. Spener published *Pia Desideria* (*Pious Desires*) in 1675 to explain the failings of the church of his day and to describe how Christians could live a holy life that touched the heart and not just the head. After the dogmatic scholasticism into which the Reformation churches had devolved after years of theological conflict and religious wars, Spener and the Pietists called for a renewed experience of the Holy Spirit.[31] Thus, they did not stress the Reformation emphasis of justification as it related to salvation so much as regeneration. In calling on Christians to return to a Pauline emphasis on the Holy Spirit rather than theological systems as the guide to Scripture, Spener declared,

> This means that Paul derived his knowledge not from human ingenuity but from the illumination of the Spirit, and these are as far removed from each other as heaven is from earth.[32]

This same emphasis appeared in the Moravian Awakening. The Moravian refugees, seeking asylum on the estate of Count Nikolas von Zinzendorf, suffered a division over the shape their church should take. As the remnants of the *Unitas Fratrum* of fourteenth-century Hussite origin, the Moravians through persecution had sunk to a weakened state. The division ended, however, through the experience of a spiritual awakening that began August 13, 1727, during a communion service at Berthelsdorf.[33]

In the group's apprehension of Christ in his atoning death and his present nearness to them, the Moravians had a corporate experience that drew them together and recreated their church. Referred to as a baptism of the Spirit or another Pentecost, the awakening of the community became the defining experience of the Moravians. They considered their experience the result of an outpouring of the Holy Spirit, which instilled in the eighteenth-century Moravians a conviction that their life as a church depended on the empowering presence of the Holy Spirit.

Through Count von Zinzendorf the Moravians received the influence of the Pietists' emphasis on the heart. He taught that

> our Savior has declared that the little ones, the children, believe in Him (Matt. 18:6): From which we can well observe that faith has its seat not in speculation, not in thought, but in the heart.[34]

The emphasis on the heart, and especially the emotional or affective domain, has created the impression of the Moravians as antirationalists, which is not an entirely unfair assessment. If antirationalist during the Age of Reason, however, they were not anti-intellectual, for they placed great stress on education, including higher education for women.[35]

Unlike the medieval mystics but like the Pietists, the Moravians did not practice an individualistic mysticism. Their experience of the Holy Spirit and the manifestation of his fruit in their lives always had a community emphasis. Thus, they developed a highly organized communal way of life, with special forms of worship and fellowship, such as the love feast.[36]

The First Great Awakening saw a repetition of much of the experience of the Moravians on a much broader scale in Britain and North America. The conversions of Whitefield and the Wesleys centered in their experience of the new birth and the operation of the Holy Spirit, to which they attested throughout their ministries. This concern with the emotional dimension of salvation alarmed a number of the clergy. Charles Chauncey, for example, pastor of the old First (Congregational) Church of Boston, registered strenuous opposition to the phenomenon of "Passion or Affection" as opposed to reason and rationalism.[37]

Jonathan Edwards defended the direction of the Awakening in New England as he described its course in several books: *A Faithful Narrative of the Surprising Work of God* (1736), *Some Thot's Concerning the Revival of Religion in New England* (1743), and *A Treatise Concerning Religious Affections* (1746). Edwards taught that the human will was helplessly bound in moral matters as a result of the Fall. People could only respond appropriately to God under the empowering influence of the Holy Spirit, whom Edwards credited with the phenomenon of the revival of religion in New England.[38] In *Freedom of the Will* (1754), Edwards elaborated his views on the work of the Holy Spirit in conversion and revival. The great concern over the unconverted within the Congregational, Dutch Reformed, and Presbyterian churches from New Jersey to Massachusetts all happened in the theological milieu of Calvinism. Concern for conversions in this context meant concern that the Holy Spirit would act.[39]

Revivalism as an institutionalized method has frequently been regarded as the heir of Pietism in that it stressed the heart rather than the head.[40] The appeal to the emotions that has characterized revivalism had its origin in the evangelical awakenings of the seventeenth and eighteenth centuries. The Baptists had a hundred years of precedent for the kind of uneducated clergy who led in the Southern revival of the mid-1700s. Without formal preparation for the ministry, men like Shubael Stearns and Daniel Marshall claimed the Holy Spirit as teacher and authenticator. This brand of preacher rejected the kind of formal sermon preparation followed by the trained clergy, preferring to preach under the influence of the Holy Spirit. In contrast to the religious concerns of the Pietists, the Moravians, and the separatist groups of seventeenth-century New England that had stressed community covenants, the Great Awakening gave people the freedom of individual religious experience.[41] By the time of the Second Great Awakening, personal experiences assumed some unusual forms. At Cane Ridge (1801) in Bourbon County, Kentucky, for example, religious experiences during the revival included the falling exercise, running, jerking, rolling, dancing, and barking.[42]

No one represents the transition from the Awakenings of the seventeenth and eighteenth centuries to the revivalism of the nineteenth century more than Charles Finney. His entire ministry and influence on countless others arose from his conversion experience, which involved a profound sense of guilt credited by him to the Holy Spirit. The final crisis of his conversion lasted several days and involved what seemed to him an inner voice that prompted him. In a ragged state emotionally as the experience dragged on, Finney began to recall passages of Scripture that gave him comfort and led him beyond intellectual assent to a trusting faith in Christ for salvation. His feelings ebbed and flowed during the crisis, and he went from confidence to dejection until he had a mystical experience of Christ accompanied by great emotion.[43] Finally, Finney experienced what he called "a mighty baptism of the Holy Ghost":

> Without any expectation of it, without ever having the thought in my mind that there was any such thing for me, without any recollection that I had even heard the thing mentioned by any person in the world, the Holy Spirit descended upon me in a manner that seemed to go through me, body and soul. I could feel the impression, like a wave of electricity, going through and through me.[44]

From that time on Finney spoke of his ministry and the local awakenings that occurred in communities where he preached as products of the work of the Holy Spirit's speaking to Finney, providing power for preaching, convicting the congregations, and filling people.

Finney followed more in the Arminian tradition of Wesley than the Reformed tradition of Edwards. This same tradition also gave rise by the middle of the nineteenth century to the Holiness movement in the United States, which would be associated with divine healing and Christian perfection. Phoebe Palmer began to use the phrase "baptism of the Holy Ghost" as a synonymous experience with "entire sanctification" as early as 1857.[45] The Higher Life movement sought to make the doctrine of Christian perfection interdenominational, with an emphasis on experiencing "baptism of the Holy Spirit" subsequent to conversion.[46] The Holiness movement received its major impetus, however, in 1867, when a group of Methodist Episcopal ministers, deploring the low state of spirituality following the Civil War, conducted a camp meeting in Philadelphia for the purpose of seeking a powerful visitation of the Holy Spirit. Within forty years of this meeting, the Holiness movement resulted in the founding of over a hundred Holiness denominations around the world.[47]

Another significant awakening began the twentieth century—the Welsh Revival of 1905, which had an influence far beyond that tiny country. Evan Roberts, the twenty-six-year-old leader in the revival, emphasized that the power for the revival had come from the Holy Spirit, who supplied him with a message. In his testimony about the revival, Roberts declared, "His Spirit came to me one night, when upon my knees I asked Him for guidance, and five months later I was baptized with the Spirit."[48] Roberts also believed the experience would be duplicated across the face of the earth among Christians who had grown silent and powerless.[49] Power characterized this revival among a people who, caught up in the Industrial Revolution of coal-mining Wales, often felt powerless. This power manifested itself in such ways as the power to control oneself, which thereby resulted in a decrease in violence and drunkenness. The fruit of self-control drew attention to this revival more than any other phenomenon. Without organization or method, the spontaneous occurrence of this revival drew 20,000 new members into the churches of Wales in a five-week period.[50]

The Welsh Revival had an impact on several groups in the United States, Pentecostalism having the most long-term effect. F. B. Meyer, while on a preaching mission to Los Angeles in April

1905, described the impact of the Welsh Revival, and several localized revivals broke out in the wake of his visit.[51] William Seymour, a black minister, began conducting cottage prayer meetings to pray for an outpouring of God's Spirit, and on April 9, 1906, the group had their experience.[52] They secured an old building on Azusa Street, where the meetings continued until 1909. The most prominent feature of the experience of the Holy Spirit in the Azusa Street revival was speaking in tongues. Out of this revival the worldwide Pentecostal movement quickly emerged.

Early on the revival divided into camps over the issue of sanctification. Seymour taught that Christian experience involved three distinct stages: conversion, entire sanctification, and the baptism of the Holy Spirit. William Durham taught that sanctification involved a lifelong process and did not happen as a "finished work."[53] Eventually the Assemblies of God followed Durham while the Apostolic Faith and many of the Pentecostal Holiness groups in the South followed Seymour.

An important awakening also came to Asia in the early 1930s. The Shantung Revival came to that province of China following a time of discouraging reports in the evangelistic ministry of the mission there. This situation prompted a yearning for spiritual power among several missionaries, who began to study the biblical teaching on the work of the Holy Spirit, particularly related to evangelism. Between September 1931 and June 1932 at least twenty-four missionaries of the North China Mission and a vastly greater number of national leaders and new converts experienced what they termed "the baptism in the Holy Spirit."[54]

The Shantung Revival focused on the Holy Spirit and manifestations of his power exhibited through Christians. The "baptism of the Holy Spirit" or the "fullness of the Holy Spirit" came with personal feelings of joy, holy laughter, surrender, peace, conviction of sin, grace, and assurance. In the context of Buddhist China it might be called bliss.[55] In the face of the Chinese preoccupation with and dread of spirits of all kinds, the Holy Spirit made himself known, particularly through healings, exorcisms, dreams, and visions. These experiences of the Holy Spirit became the occasion for a dramatic increase in conversions on the eve of the Japanese invasion.[56]

By the early 1930s, mainline Protestant groups in the United States had developed a fear of anything that smacked of Pentecostalism, and the missionaries of the North China Mission acknowledged this fear:

> For fear my reader should take doctrinal exception to the term "Back to Pentecost" let us notice that we are not going back to before Pentecost, but only waiting upon the Lord to prepare our hearts to RECEIVE what He has so graciously given. We believe that the Holy Spirit came at Pentecost, but very few believers have experimentally received Him in His fulness.[57]

While the Pentecostal movement spread rapidly among working-class people on the fringe of mainline Christian society in the United States, the charismatic movement of the 1960s and 1970s spread just as rapidly through the middle class of mainline churches and Catholicism. From its beginnings at St. Mark's Episcopal Church of Van Nuys, California, the charismatic movement, with its emphasis on experiencing the ecstatic gifts of the Holy Spirit, cut across denominational, educational, and sociological boundaries of American Christianity.[58]

THE GIFT OF THE SPIRIT AS GOOD NEWS

The Holy Spirit enables people to experience God personally. People may know *about* God through creation and revelation, but they know God personally through his Holy Spirit. While Jesus Christ is the fullest revelation of God, we only know him through the Scriptures and the living testimony of the Holy Spirit. Spiritual experience does not necessarily mean emotional experience, for the human spirit also involves the intellect, character, ability, and life itself. While the Holy Spirit affects all of these dimensions of the human spirit, in responding to the gospel some people are more concerned about one dimension than another.

Transformation

The materialist says that people die. Christianity affirms this same position, with a few significant qualifications about what happens after death that will be discussed in the next chapter. Some of

242 • The Gospel and Its Meaning

the Eastern religions and New Age thinkers believe people are a part of the whole and undergo a transformation at death that takes different forms (depending on the religion). People who believe they will die but would like to live on with a personal, self-conscious existence intuitively know that some sort of transformation must take place for them to go from a physical existence to a spiritual existence. The gospel declares that the Holy Spirit creates that transformation in a person before they die. This transformation is alternatively called a new birth, a new creation, or regeneration.

In a society that has a strong sense of right and wrong, the predominant spiritual issue relates to such legal issues as forgiveness, justification, and punishment. In an amoral society that has abandoned the old taboos of behavior, such as England and British North America after Puritan restraint was replaced by Restoration decadence, the predominant issue became how one might be made able to enter heaven. With the collapse of values in the late twentieth century in the United States and the abandonment by postmodernism of the old preoccupation with the physical world, people are concerned with how they relate to the spiritual world. Apart from some transformation that involves a change to compatibility with the divine nature, people will not experience God in the spiritual world. In contrast to Eastern and New Age thought, Christianity teaches a basic incompatibility between the unregenerate human spirit and God. Yet for the person who desires eternal companionship with God, the gift of the Holy Spirit offers good news that God will change the human spirit and cleanse it of the corruption that forms a barrier to experiencing God.

Holiness

This transformation affects people not only by changing the human spirit to provide for eternal life, but also by changing the spirit with respect to character and emotions. The "fruit" of the Holy Spirit refers to this effect on the human spirit. People gain new capacities for dealing with the situations of life. Christ does not keep Christians from the range of negative experience, but his Spirit equips them to respond in a holy fashion, which may mean joy in some circumstances and patience in others. Pavel Savchenko, a Russian Baptist pastor, speaks of this experience as being "transfigured by Christ." Christ's character begins to transform our own as our emotions begin to correspond to his. He takes our character flaws and begins the slow process of restoring us into his image. He takes emotions that have become fragile or hardened, superficial or inappropriate, and slowly makes them genuine and useful again. When people grow weary of who they have become and of how little capacity they have for dealing with life, the gift of the Holy Spirit offers good news that such lives can be restored to the divine image.

Empowerment

The restoration of the divine image also means that the Holy Spirit brings power to live and ability to act. The widely observed phenomenon of "felt" powerlessness occurs at different levels of several societies—a company employee feels caught in the web of a vast corporate machine; a peasant who owns no land feels powerless, which debilitates him; people feel unable to act or speak in their normal human relationships because of fear, intimidation, manipulation, insecurity, or a variety of other related psychological chains. By empowering people, the Holy Spirit not only gives people the freedom of Christ to act, but also the ability. Empowerment does not mean that the forces that led to the original feeling of powerlessness have ceased. It simply means that the Holy Spirit gives people the power to live in spite of their condition. It also means that people receive gifts and abilities from God that they have never experienced before.

In Latin America, where liberation theology has had its most articulate expression in the civil struggles of that area of the world, this theology has had an extremely successful rival for the theological reference point of the people. The churches that have grown most dramatically are the Pentecostal churches, which emphasize the power of the Holy Spirit in the lives of Christians. The issues that liberation theology addresses do not go away, but people have the power to live in the face of their reality. In North America, empowerment may mean the discovery of the inner power to raise children and provide for a family when an irresponsible father forsakes his marriage vows and abandons his first responsibility under God. The power of the Holy Spirit extends to the level at which the need for power to live is felt. It transcends theological agendas and socio-cultural barriers. For people who feel powerless, the gift of the Holy Spirit offers good news that God desires to fill people with the power they lack, which can only come from above.

Guidance

The presence of the Holy Spirit also affects people in the intellectual and volitional realms of spiritual life by providing them with the guidance they need to make decisions and act on them. Deciding right from wrong in a world that lacks clear markers, deciding about a career, deciding how to raise teenage children, and deciding so many other questions of life have implications that affect many people for a lifetime. The Holy Spirit comes to help the mind as much as the emotions. Holistically, he gives peace to the emotions so that the mind may think.

While the form of guidance may take a form as extraordinary as a dream, vision, or voice, the Spirit normally gives insight, clarity, wisdom, and understanding. Guided by the Holy Spirit, even something as irrational as the human mind has the capacity for rational thought. Because the Holy Spirit has also created the church, people are not left on their own when faced with difficult choices. They may find that the Spirit speaks to them through other people. For people shipwrecked by the wrong choices of life, who have established a pattern of disastrous judgment that seems irremediable, the gift of the Holy Spirit offers good news that God will give guidance to them as they abide in Christ and seek his counsel.

Application of Salvation

The Holy Spirit provides the personal contact between the saving activity of Christ on earth, his present authority as Lord of lords, and the person who turns to him in faith. The Holy Spirit brings the life of Jesus Christ into the one who will receive him. He brings salvation and begins the work of changing someone into the image of Christ.

I once spoke with a retired army top sergeant who had taken an interest in religion. I visited him with a pastor, who explained to him how the blood of Christ atoned for his sins. The man responded that he could not follow Jesus until he knew he could live a Christian life. The pastor said that he did not have to live a Christian life because Jesus would forgive him. The man replied that he did not want to be a hypocrite, to which the pastor replied that the blood of Jesus was sufficient to cover any sin the man might commit. The man remained steadfast in his resistance: He was not going to follow Jesus unless he knew he could live up to what that commitment involved. He went on to say that he believed in God, the Bible, prayer, miracles, Jesus, his death for our sins, the resurrection, and the Second Coming. He also believed he was going to hell because he would not let Jesus save him. I then realized that this man knew nothing of the role of the Holy Spirit in making it possible to follow Christ. Christ changes us and begins to live his life through us. This was the sergeant's real spiritual issue, and when he understood the good news of the gift of the Holy Spirit, he began to cry, for he had found his Savior.

NOTES

1. Rudolph Otto, *The Idea of the Holy*, trans. John W. Harvey (New York: Oxford Univ. Press, 1979).

2. See Friedrich Schleiermacher, *On Religion: Speeches to Its Cultural Despisers*, trans. John Oman, intro. Rudolph Otto (New York: Harper Torchbooks, 1958).

3. Kenneth Scott Latourette, *A History of Christianity*, rev. ed. (New York: Harper & Row, 1975), 1:303.

4. Ibid., 359–60.

5. Jaroslav Pelikan, *The Spirit of Eastern Christendom (600–1700)* (The Christian Tradition 2; Chicago: Univ. of Chicago Press, 1977), 185.

6. Ibid., 193.

7. Ibid., 194.

8. Ibid., 197.

9. John Meyendorff, "The Liturgy: A Lead to the Mind of World Wide Orthodoxy," in *Orthodox Theology and Diakonia*, ed. Demetrios J. Constantelos (Brookline, Mass.: Hellenic College Press, 1981), 83. Since 1054, however, liturgy has become increasingly important for Orthodoxy. For the Eastern church, orthodox does not mean correct belief but correct praise.

10. J. M. Hussey, *The Orthodox Church in the Byzantine Empire* (Oxford: Clarendon, 1986), 135.

11. Ibid., 181.

12. Ibid., 215, 276.

13. Ernst Benz, *The Eastern Orthodox Church*, trans. Richard and Clara Winston (Chicago: Aldine, 1963), 37.

14. Ibid., 43–48.

15. Sergius Bulgakov, *The Orthodox Church* (Dobbs Ferry, N.Y.: American Review of Eastern Orthodoxy, 1935), 10.

16. Ibid., 22–23.

17. Ibid., 41.

18. Hussey, *The Orthodox Church*, 279.

19. Vladimir Lossky, *The Mystical Theology of the Eastern Church* (London: James Clarke & Co., 1957), 28.

20. Ibid., 25.

21. Ibid., 162.

22. Bulgakov, *The Orthodox Church*, 172–74.

23. Lossky, *Mystical Theology*, 17–19.

24. Sergius Bolshakoff, *Russian Mysticism* (Kalamazoo, Mich.: Cistercian Publications, 1977), 28.

25. Ibid., 35.

26. Ibid., 41–45.

27. Columba Hart and Jane Bishop, trans., *Hildegard of Bingen* (Classics of Western Spirituality; New York: Paulist, 1990), 59.

28. Rufus M. Jones, *The Eternal Gospel* (New York: Macmillan, 1938), 1–2.

29. *The Revelation of Mechthild of Magdeburg*, trans. Lucy Menzies (New York: Longmans, Green and Co., 1953), xviii.

30. Ibid., xx.

31. Philip Jacob Spener, *Pia Desideria*, trans. and ed. Theodore G. Tappert (Philadelphia: Fortress, 1964), 9.

32. Ibid., 57.

33. John Greenfield, *When the Spirit Came*: *The Amazing Story of the Moravian Revival of 1727* (Minneapolis: Bethany, 1967), 11.

34. Gillian Lindt Gollin, *Moravians in Two Worlds*: *A Story of Changing Communities* (New York: Columbia Univ. Press, 1967), 10.

35. Ibid., 11–12.

36. Ibid., 20.

37. Clarence H. Faust and Thomas H. Johnson, eds. *Jonathan Edwards*: *Representative Selections* (New York: American Book Company, n.d.), xix–xxiii.

38. Earle E. Cairns, *An Endless Line of Splendor: Revivals and Their Leaders from the Great Awakening to the Present* (Wheaton, Ill.: Tyndale, 1986), 45–46.

39. Edwin Scott Gaustad, *The Great Awakening in New England* (Gloucester, Mass.: Peter Smith, 1965), 57, 59, 138.

40. William Warren Sweet, *Revivalism in America: Its Origin, Growth and Decline* (Gloucester, Mass.: Peter Smith, 1965), 24–25.

41. Ibid., 40.

42. Ibid., 124.

43. Charles G. Finney, *Charles G. Finney: An Autobiography* (Old Tappan, N.J.: Revell; reprint of 1876 edition, entitled *Memoirs of Charles G. Finney*), 12–20.

44. Ibid., 20.

45. Richard M. Riss, *A Survey of Twentieth-Century Revival Movements in North America* (Peabody, Mass.: Hendrickson, 1988), 18.

46. Ibid., 19.

47. Ibid., 20.

48. Arthur Goodrich, et al, *The Story of the Welsh Revival* (New York: Revell, 1905), 5.

49. Ibid., 6.

50. Ibid., 44. This report came from G. Campbell Morgan, a highly respected skeptic of the revival, who went to Wales to investigate the stories he had heard.

51. Riss, *Twentieth-Century Revival Movements*, 49.

52. Ibid., 48.

53. Ibid., 82–83.

54. Mary K. Crawford, *The Shantung Revival* (Shreveport, La.: Revival Association, 1933), 39–40.

55. Ibid., 40–48.

56. Ibid., 23–38.

57. Ibid., 55.

58. Riss, *Twentieth-Century Revival Movements*, 147–48.

Chapter 9

The Return of Christ

A religious idea found the world over relates to the notion of a final judgment of individuals to determine their state after death. A related idea concerns the notion that the world will one day be destroyed. These concepts occur in tribal religions, in the ancient religions, in the three monotheistic religions, and in Hinduism. The dreadful and fearful Day of Judgment involves both punishment and reward, though the ultimate religious quandary concerns the basis on which the judgment will be made and who will do the judging.

The Hindu concept of reincarnation relates to this idea of judgment, insofar as an individual is doomed to a repetition of earthly incarnations in either higher or lower forms of life until that person lives a life sufficiently worthy to allow him or her to enter a state of eternal bliss. It is judgment without a judge, predetermined by karma without a determiner. If the Hindu teaching leaves many questions unanswered, it agrees with the universal recognition that the human race stands accountable for its behavior. The Hindu ethos, which allows for a variety of religious nuances that need not be systematically related (as one expects from revealed religion), also contains the idea of a final day of doom when the god Kalki dances the dance of destruction and all things in the cosmos are destroyed.

The old Norse warriors of northern Europe believed they could never enter the hall of the gods unless they died with a sword in their hands, preferably inflicting death on someone else. In other words, heaven could only be attained by fighting one's way in. Contrary to Weber's theory about the "Protestant work ethic," the origin of the work mentality probably lies much deeper in the European psyche than in the teaching of the Puritans, who actually placed their stress on grace rather than works. If the gods were as self-indulgent and treacherous as Wotan and Loge, however, the old barbarians had no choice but to fend for themselves. What god cared for them? Given the debauched pantheon of northern Europe, the old Europeans looked for a day of doom even for the gods themselves, when they would be consumed by flames.

The ancient Romans and Greeks believed that the dead journeyed to the underworld, where they received rest or punishment for their deeds in life. The tortures of hell were appropriate to the crimes of life and involved experiencing such pains and frustrations as being bitten by poisonous snakes for eternity, having refreshing water just out of reach for eternity, and pushing a boulder to the top of a hill only to have it roll back to the bottom again for eternity. To avoid the prospects of hell, Suetonius indicates that the emperors began resorting to having themselves deified by the Senate. The Roman concept of law and justice intensified the significance of a final judgment with eternal implications for reward or punishment.

Historical Islam, Judaism, and Christianity have also affirmed that each person will stand before God's judgment and give an account of their lives according to God's revealed intentions for human behavior and relationships, with respect to God and one another. Islam and Christianity teach that Jesus will be the one through whom God judges the world.[1] The three monotheistic religions also agree that God will destroy the universe and replace it with a perfect realm, purged of the corrupting influences present in the old order.

In other words, the human race shares a fearful outlook on eternity. How might one be counted worthy to enter bliss and escape just punishment? The gospel of Jesus Christ supplies an answer to this question, distinguishing itself from the other religious systems of the world.

BIBLICAL BACKGROUND

The Christian understanding of judgment and the final destruction of the present world order has its basis in the prophecies of Israel.[2]

Old Testament

The prophets of Israel and Judah spoke of a day of reckoning designated as "the day of the LORD." This Day involved both the judgment of Israel and her salvation. Cosmic upheaval, social and economic disaster, plague, and war would all accompany the day of the Lord as aspects of God's judgment on the whole earth (Ezek. 7:1–27; Joel 2:14–16, 30–31; Zeph. 1:10–18; Zech. 12:1–9; 14:4, 12–15). The wrath and punishment of God would fall on Israel and all other nations as God brought an end to wickedness in the world (Isa. 2:6–22; 13:6, 9, 13; 34:8; 63:4; Jer. 46:10; 47:4; Ezek. 30:3; Amos 5:18–20; Obad. 15; Zeph. 2:8–15). In the face of wrath and destruction, however, God would bring salvation from the oppression of wickedness for the remnant who have sought righteousness (Dan. 12:3; Zeph. 1:3). God himself would purify this remnant as a refiner smelts gold to remove the dross from what is pure (Dan. 12:10; Zeph. 3:9–20; Zech. 13:9; Mal. 3:2; 4:1, 5). Over the purified remnant, God would reign as king forever (Ezek. 43:6–9; Dan. 7:21–22, 26–27; Zech. 14:9–21).

Books such as Daniel and Ezekiel vividly portray the circumstances surrounding "the day of the LORD", and during the intertestamental period a number of writings appeared that explore the theme. This day as the Day of Judgment involves the resurrection of the righteous and the wicked—an idea that became a central concern of groups like the Pharisees and the Essenes (see Dan. 12:2). Against the background of the Jewish expectation of "the day of the LORD", the gospel speaks of the return of the Lord Jesus to judge the world.

The Gospels

The Day of Judgment represents a significant theme in the message of Jesus, who spoke frequently of the coming of the Son of Man—an event the Jews anticipated, based on Daniel's prophecy in Daniel 7:13–14:

> In my vision at night I looked, and there before me was one like a son of man, coming with the clouds of heaven. He approached the Ancient of Days and was led into his presence. He was given authority, glory and sovereign power; all peoples, nations and men of every language worshiped him. His dominion is an everlasting dominion that will not pass away, and his kingdom is one that will never be destroyed.

Jesus spoke a number of parables to stress that the Son of Man would come without warning to bring the judgment. Only those living faithfully in expectation of his coming would be prepared for the judgment (Matt. 24:37–51; 25:13–30; Luke 12:35–46; 17:26–37). In this regard, faith appears as concrete action in anticipation of the expected appearance of the Son of Man. The watchful servant fulfills the wishes of the master, regardless of how long the master delays. In light of his parables that stress keeping watch, the question of Jesus seems all the more plaintive: "When the Son of Man comes, will he find faith on the earth?" (Luke 18:8).

To be prepared for the coming of the Son of Man, one must accept Jesus, who is the Son of Man. A relationship to Christ creates the basis for admission into the kingdom and exemption from condemnation on the Day of Judgment. Only those whom Jesus knows will be allowed to enter the kingdom (Matt. 7:21–23; 25:11–12; Luke 13:22–30). The question of what standard of righteousness will permit someone to enter the kingdom forms the central theme of the Sermon on the Mount. Though few scholars argue for the authenticity of this sermon as a single piece, from the perspective of how anyone can enter the kingdom it has masterful unity that compels consideration as an authentic message from Jesus.

The Sermon on the Mount begins with an attention-grabbing litany that redefines happiness in terms of preparation to enter the kingdom (Matt. 5:3–10). The ultimate blessing in anticipation of entry into the kingdom comes through persecution because of Jesus (5:11–12; cf. 19:28). Jesus declares that goodness is the reason for which people have been placed in the world and that without righteousness, no one may enter the kingdom (5:13–20). He then explores the failure of the quest for righteousness by demonstrating how people may keep the letter of the law but fail in righteousness because of what lies within them; thus, people fail to achieve the perfection of God (5:21–48). People also strive for righteousness through acts of piety, but Jesus exposes the failure of human motive (6:1–24). People have the greatest difficulty living by faith and trusting God (6:25–7:14). The problem lies in the very nature of people, for "a bad tree bears bad fruit" (7:17). Jesus then declares that the way into the kingdom is through him; those who accept him and his words will be received by him on the Day of Judgment

(7:21–27). This thought is reinforced in John's Gospel (John 12:47–48).

Jesus paints a vivid and terrible picture of the fate of those who suffer condemnation. Apart from his words in the Gospels, the New Testament is remarkably silent about what that punishment will be like. Jesus indicates that the people of Sodom, Gomorrah, Tyre, and Sidon will fare better in the judgment than those who have seen the miracles of Jesus and still reject him (Matt. 10:15; 11:20–24; Luke 10:13–15). The Queen of the South and the people of Nineveh responded positively to the messengers by whom they heard the word of God, and they will stand at the last day to condemn those who reject him (Matt. 12:41–42; Luke 11:31–32). In parables Jesus speaks of the destruction of those who reject the invitation to come to the royal wedding feast and who reject the reign of their king (Matt. 22:1–14; 25:14–27; Luke 14:15–24; 19:27).

Those who fall under judgment will be like chaff and weeds that are gathered together and burned in a fire (Matt. 3:12; 13:24–30, 36–43; Luke 3:17). This simile speaks as much of the utter worthlessness of a life as it does about the mode of disposition. The actual disposition is one of total consumption in hell (Matt. 5:29–30; 10:28; 18:7–9; Mark 9:43–50). The experience of hell is one of torture and anguish (Matt. 5:21–22; 8:29; 18:21–35), but it is also described as darkness and isolation (8:12; 25:30).

The warnings of judgment appear as part of the total message of Jesus in his call for righteousness. Even the religious behavior of the best of people leads to destruction (Matt. 23:1–33; Luke 11:42–52), for all people are subject to the kinds of thoughts, behavior, and motives that constitute unrighteousness. Therefore, Jesus calls on all people to repent (Luke 13:5). Judgment comes as the inevitable result of a life lived apart from faith in God. Judgment will come as a result of deeds and actions in life, but at a deeper level the deeds and actions of life emerge from the essential nature of a person. Stated simply, bad trees do not produce good fruit (Matt. 3:10; 7:19; Luke 3:9; 13:6–9; cf. John 15:2, 5, 8). Even though a kind action may be good for the one who receives it, a tainted motive in performing the deed corrupts the deed so far as judgment of the person is concerned (Matt. 6:1–18).[3] A good deed does not make one righteous, though a righteous person will do good deeds.

The fundamental problem of people with respect to the judgment is the human heart. No amount of religious observance or philanthropic activity can change what is essentially corrupt. It is not the failure to be religious that makes a person unrighteous before God. In contrast to the teachings of Buddha, who held that human corruption came from the outside, Jesus teaches that human corruption comes from the human heart (Matt. 15:11–20; Mark 7:14–23; Luke 11:39). In this regard the fruit of a life characterizes the heart of a person, and Jesus indicates that his followers will be recognized by the fruit of their lives (Matt. 7:16–20; Luke 6:43–45).

The judgment as Jesus describes it is not a trial in which the defendant marshals evidence to make a case for being good enough to go to heaven. Jesus describes it more as a simple declaration of the way things are. By his definition of righteousness, no one can enter the kingdom of heaven. The problem is not lost on the disciples, who miss a great deal but understand this point (Matt. 19:25; Mark 10:26; Luke 18:26). The great separation on the Day of Judgment will occur as a result of the essential nature of things: wheat and tares, sheep and goats, varieties of fish (Matt. 13:24–30, 47–52; 25:31–46). The Judge will simply declare what people really are when the secrets of all hearts are disclosed.

This understanding of the judgment provides the context for the discussion between Jesus and Nicodemus. One might even imagine that the conversation came following a time of teaching like the Sermon on the Mount. Nicodemus begins by acknowledging Jesus as a great teacher from God—a great teacher of the Law. Jesus' response seems remarkably disjointed unless it takes place in a context like his teaching on judgment and righteousness, for he replies, "I tell you the truth, no one can see the kingdom of God unless he is born again" (John 3:3). In this conversation Jesus describes how people can experience the fundamental change of nature through the Spirit of God that will allow them to enter the kingdom. Condemnation does not come at the end of time; it hangs over the entire human race now. Eternal life is not a privilege that will be taken away from some at the judgment, rather it is an offer God gives to those who want eternal relationship with him. Eternal life will be added to those who did not have it by their nature. Thus, to the disciples' quandary over how anyone can be saved, Jesus replied, "With man this is impossible, but with God all things are possible" (Matt. 19:26; Mark 10:27; Luke 18:27).

The dynamic of one's nature manifesting itself in behavior appears in dramatic fashion in the account of the separation of the sheep and the goats (Matt. 25:31–46). The sheep do the sort of things that sheep do and the goats do the sort of things that goats do. Neither group thinks about it because each does what comes naturally. The righteous do righteousness and the unrighteous do not. All will be accountable for their actions on the Day of Judgment (Matt. 12:36–37; John 5:27–30). On the other hand, those who hunger and thirst for righteousness will receive it (Matt. 5:6); those who seek the Holy Spirit will receive him (Luke 11:13) and will thereby obtain the purity of heart that is necessary to see God (Matt. 5:8).

Jesus makes himself the central issue on the Day of Judgment. Those who acknowledge him in this life will be acknowledged by him on that Day, but those who are ashamed of him in this life he will be ashamed to acknowledge (Matt. 10:32; Mark 8:38; Luke 9:26; 12:8). Punishment comes to those who reject Jesus (Matt. 21:33–44; Mark 12:1–11; Luke 20:9–19). On the other hand, those who receive Christ receive life; they do not come into condemnation but become children of God (John 1:12–13; 3:16–21, 36; 5:21–22, 24; 6:40, 44, 54).

General Apostolic Writings

After Jesus' execution for identifying himself as the Son of Man of Daniel 7 and after his resurrection and ascension, the disciples believed he would return on the clouds of heaven in the manner described in Daniel (Acts 1:11; 1 Thess. 4:13–18; 2 Thess. 1:7; Rev. 1:7). At his appearance, he would change all of his followers instantly so that they become like him (1 Cor. 15:51–52; Phil. 3:21; 1 John 3:2). As the time drew near for his return, conditions would grow worse and worse on earth; the Antichrist would appear and nominal believers would abandon the church (2 Thess. 2:1–12; 2 Tim. 3:1; 1 John 2:18–19).

The early Christians lived with a certain tension over when the Lord would return. As the apostles died and he did not return, critics argued that there would be no return (2 Peter 3:3–4). The church held to their expectation of the Lord's return, however, even though they confessed that they did not understand the timing (3:8–10; Rev. 22:7, 10, 12).

Cosmic upheaval. The return of Christ will occur with cosmic upheaval leading up to, and coming as a result of, his return. The book of Revelation describes a time of total chaos that affects the physical universe as well as the social, economic, and political order of life on earth. Wars, famines, plagues, and economic disasters on a devastating scale will occur. This cosmic upheaval is described in three cycles of seven events in Revelation: the seven trumpets, the seven seals, and the seven bowls of God's wrath. These cycles are in parallel form; their description of the cosmic upheaval corresponds closely to the cosmic upheaval described by Christ in the Synoptic Gospels (Matt. 24:1–51; Mark 13:1–37; Luke 21:5–36). The Johannine literature, then, includes a major book that describes what is not included in John's Gospel but which the other Gospels had detailed. The detailed vision of the Lord's return appropriately comes through John, the last apostle to die, whose Gospel concludes with a question about the return, "If I want him to remain alive until I return, what is that to you?" (John 21:22).

The idea of the doom of the entire cosmos appears at other places in the New Testament as well. The entire created order will undergo a cataclysmic experience as the universe is consumed (Acts 2:19–20; Heb. 1:11–12; 2 Peter 3:7, 10). The thrust of these statements, however, is not so much God's destruction of creation as it is the coming of judgment because of humanity's devastation of God's creation. In the judgment, creation will actually be restored and renewed (Acts 3:21). Thus, it awaits eagerly the revealing of God's children at the judgment, when creation itself will be "liberated from its bondage to decay" (Rom. 8:18–22). The judgment will come when humanity has brought meaningful life on earth to an abysmal end.

Accountability. At his return, Christ will hold all human beings accountable for their lives. He himself will judge the world with justice as everyone gives an account of the stewardship of the life God has entrusted to them (Acts 17:31; Rom. 14:10–12). The apostles stress the justice, truth, and righteousness of God's judgment; he renders to each person what he or she deserves (Rom. 2:2; 3:1–8; 2 Thess. 1:5–6; Heb. 2:2–3). Everyone will appear "before the judgment seat of Christ, that each one may receive what is due him for the things done while in the body, whether good or bad" (2 Cor. 5:10; cf. Rom. 2:7–8; 1 Peter 4:5; Rev. 20:10–15). The accounting will penetrate beneath one's actions to their secret motives, so that what people consider as good God may account as corrupt (Rom. 1:18–2:16; 1 Cor. 4:4–5).

Paul stressed the surety of the Day of Judgment, particularly in his proclamation of the gospel to the Gentiles. He spoke with Felix about "righteousness, self-control and the judgment to come" (Acts 24:25). On Mars Hill in Athens he declared to the crowd that God the Creator had set a day to judge the world by Jesus Christ and that the resurrection proved the judgment was coming (17:31). Against the background of Roman law and Paul's incarceration by Felix and against the background of the Areopagus Court of Mars Hill (which had sentenced Socrates to death several centuries earlier), the prospect of judgment by the supreme God raised sobering thoughts.

Wrath and the problem of evil. At the return of Christ, God's wrath will be poured out on the godless and wicked who refuse to repent and receive the gospel (Rom. 1:18; 2:5; 2 Thess. 1:8–9). Because Jesus came to rescue people from the consequences of the judgment, those who oppose the gospel will experience the destructive nature of God's wrath (Rom. 5:9; 1 Thess. 1:10; 2:16). Only those prepared for the Lord's return will escape his anger (1 Thess. 5:3, 9). God's wrath will come for disobedience (Rom. 4:15; Eph. 5:6) and will do away with all that is wrong with human nature; therefore, Paul urged people to put to death through union with Christ's death all that belonged to their human nature (Col. 3:5–6). Those who have toyed with Christ only to abandon the faith may expect the vengeance of God (Heb. 6:4–8; 10:26–31).

In the New Testament, the wrath of God settles the problem of evil. In its classic form the problem of evil concerns reconciling the idea of an all-powerful good God with the existence of evil. But evil does not exist as a self-existent reality; it only exists as an aspect of people. God has allowed the human race to exist for the benefit of those who repent of evil and turn in faith to God. In the end, however, God will destroy everyone who works against his righteousness (Jude 5–7, 14–15; Rev. 6:10, 16; 14:14–20; 15:1–16:21; 19:1–21). Because of the universality of sin, condemnation is deserved (Rom. 3:8; 5:16), though Jesus Christ came to deliver people from condemnation (Rom. 8:34; 2 Thess. 2:12; cf. John 3:17–21).

Salvation through Christ. Though Christ will return as Judge, he will come to rescue his own people from any experience of God's wrath (Rom. 5:9; 1 Thess. 1:10; 5:9). He himself will keep his people blameless and holy on the Day of Judgment (1 Cor. 1:7–8; 1 Thess. 3:13; 5:23). Christ took possession of those who have faith in him through his Holy Spirit, and by his Spirit he keeps his own until his return (Eph. 4:30; Phil. 1:6; 2 Tim. 1:12). When he returns, he will claim as his own all who await his appearance with faith, and on them he will bestow the promises of salvation (1 Cor. 15:23; Eph. 2:6–7; Col. 3:4; 1 Thess. 4:14; Heb. 9:15, 27–28; 1 Peter 1:13). Those who have faith in Christ will have nothing to fear on the Day of Judgment, because in this life they have become like him (1 John 4:17). Since nothing impure can enter the presence of God, "only those whose names are written in the Lamb's book of life" will enter the new Jerusalem, the abode of God (Rev. 21:27).

Righteousness and faith. As indicated earlier, righteousness serves as the standard for judgment. The critical question for individuals concerns how they might achieve righteousness. The apostles declared that the righteousness necessary to stand before God comes through one's assimilation into Jesus Christ, who defines righteousness (Rom. 5:15–21; Phil. 3:9–11). By his sacrificial death, Jesus satisfied the righteous requirements of the Law for all who through faith are crucified with him (Rom. 8:1–4). Those who continue in faith until his appearing will share in the promise made to Abraham, whom God counted righteous on the basis of his faith (3:21–6:23; Gal. 3–4). The gift of righteousness comes not so much as a possession to those who have faith as a spiritual transformation that comes with being a new creation in Christ (Eph. 4:24). Thus, believers live with the expectation that they will be counted righteous on the Day of Judgment by virtue of their relationship in Christ (2 Tim. 4:8). In the imagery of Revelation this experience of imputed righteousness is represented by "fine linen, bright and clean" garments of the bride of Christ, which is the church (Rev. 19:6–8). These clothes have been made white in the blood of the Lamb and represent the righteous acts of the saints (7:14; 22:14).

Perseverance. While the apostles wrote many things about the return of Christ that had implications for salvation, they wrote to believers to encourage them to persevere because Jesus would return for his church. For those going through trials, suffering, and persecution, the return of Christ offered an encouragement to persevere in the faith (2 Thess. 2:13–17; Heb. 10:32–39; 1 John 2:28; Jude 17, 21; Rev. 2:7, 11, 17, 26; 3:5, 11, 12, 21) and to endure whatever they were facing, for when Christ appeared he would bring life, vindication, joy, and glory (James 1:12; 1 Peter 1:7; 2:23; 4:12–19; 5:1–11). The knowledge that the Lord would return instilled in the early Christians a need to persevere in holy living until that Day (Rom. 13:12; Gal. 6:8–9; Phil. 1:10; 1 Thess. 5:1–11; Titus 2:12–13; Heb. 11–12; 2 Peter 3:11–12). His return also stimulated the church to persevere in the work of ministry, in fellowship, in worship, in prayer, and in a lifestyle that led others to faith (2 Tim. 4:1–2a; Heb. 10:25; James 5:7–12; 1 Peter 2:12; 4:7).

Church discipline. Discipline within the church also has a relationship to the theme of judgment. The saints hand someone over to Satan to suffer physical harm in order that his or her spirit might be saved (1 Cor. 5:5). Though judgment will come on the world, the church has the obligation to judge itself within, to exercise appropriate discipline, and to settle disputes, because one day they will judge the world with Christ (5:9–13; 6:2). God himself exercises discipline over his children for the purpose of ensuring their place with Christ (Heb. 12:4–13; Rev. 3:19). On the other hand, because of the positive force of discipline in the context of a caring fellowship, Christians will boast of one another on the Day of the Lord (2 Cor. 1:14; Phil. 2:16; 1 Thess. 2:19–20; 2 Thess. 1:4). In the context of fellowship and self-examination as Christians gather around the table of the Lord, they do so in anticipation of the Lord's return (1 Cor. 11:26).

The age to come. On the other side of the Day of the Lord is the age to come. Alluded to throughout the New Testament, it embodies the full expectation of what salvation means. With all the references to the kingdom of God in the Gospels in terms of how one enters it, the apostles speak very little about the age to come.

They held to the certainty of a new heaven and a new earth and the new Jerusalem (Heb. 13:14; 2 Peter 3:13; Rev. 21:1–27). Christ has the exalted place with God in the age to come even though he does not appear to exercise dominion now (Eph. 1:9–10, 20–21; Heb. 2:5). Finally, the apostles know that all who love him will have a place in the kingdom when Christ returns (Eph. 2:6–7; James 2:5).

Observations

In his teaching about the Day of Judgment, Jesus identifies himself as the Son of Man. He indicates that people will be responsible for a higher standard of righteousness than mere adherence to the Law and that judgment will be rendered on the basis of a person's basic nature as manifested in their behavior. He presents himself as the One who supplies the key to receiving the righteousness needed to appear before God.

The apostles considered the return of Christ as a central article of faith, and they warned the world of the coming cosmic upheaval. All will be accountable to God for the stewardship of their lives, and those who have lived in disregard to God will experience his wrath. Christ, on the other hand, offers salvation from wrath through the gift of righteousness that comes by faith. On the basis of the expectation of the return of Christ, the apostles urge Christians to persevere and provide mutual support and discipline for one another as they await the age to come.

HISTORICAL/THEOLOGICAL DEVELOPMENT

Despite the fact that Christ did not return immediately, the church never gave up its expectation of the Second Coming. In times of ease, it was a minor matter of faith to which Christians assented, but which played no significant role in the life of the church. In times of crisis and social change, however, the church remembered the prophecies and wondered if this might be the time.

The Montanist Movement

The Montanist movement began during a period of persecution in the East (170–180). Jerome suggested that prior to his conversion Montanus had been a priest of the Cybele cult, which stressed divine possession as well as an excessive, frenzied, ecstatic form of prophecy.[4] At his baptism, Montanus began to speak in tongues and prophecy. He had one basic message to deliver: The end of the world was near and the new Jerusalem would descend in his native land of Phrygia.

While Montanus stressed the ecstatic gifts of the Spirit as part of his ministry, that feature was not unique to him at the time. The dominant feature of his movement revolved around the expectation of the Lord's return, which included the practice of celibacy and high standards of ethics and morality. A feature of life in the last days included the acceptance of women in the role of prophet. At that early period, the church continued to believe that the Holy Spirit spoke through prophets.[5] In the Cybele cult women had also played a dominant role. Priscilla and Maximilla shared the prophetic ministry of Montanus, and their words were recorded with his concerning the descent of the new Jerusalem and the thousand-year reign of Christ. These women left their husbands to await the Second Coming.[6]

Montanus and his followers offered a model for the church in which Christians did not need the hierarchy of the developing church because they had direction from God, mediated by prophets whom the Holy Spirit inspired.[7] The Montanists in turn were attacked by the developing church structures, not as heretics but as a danger to order. With the return of Christ expected at any moment, and with prophets to reveal the will of God from the Holy Spirit, church structure, bishops, and clergy seemed unnecessary. In the face of pagan persecution and Christian opposition, the Montanists experienced the kind of suffering one would expect from reading Revelation about troubles for Christians just prior to Christ's return.

The Montanist movement played a significant role in discrediting the office of prophet in the church as bishops saw the claim of divine inspiration as a threat to order and doctrine. Thus, the church began to adopt the view that inspiration through prophets ended with the apostles.[8] The excesses of the movement encouraged the church to move away from its prophetic and ecstatic tradition conspicuous among the martyrs and toward a more hierarchical and ordered mode of institutional life. It also influenced the development of an allegorical method of biblical interpretation that did not take Scripture literally, as the Montanists had done with Revelation.[9]

Montanism became a widespread movement in the empire through the persecutions of 177 on. While the expectation faded of the descent of the new Jerusalem in Phrygia, the persecutions fueled the expectation that Christ would not wait long to return.[10] The strict morality of the Montanists, at a time when church discipline seemed lax by forgiving sins even as severe as apostasy, may have contributed to the popularity of the movement for those who desired high standards.[11] Tertullian accepted some Montanist teachings and propagated a view of asceticism based on his expectation of the Lord's early return. Montanism had a strong following in Egypt, which may have influenced the direction of the Desert Fathers, who lived their ascetic, hermit existence in expectation of the early return of Christ.[12]

Montanism faded with the end of persecution and the acceptance of Christianity in the empire, though it persisted in Montanus's native Phrygia, where Justinian used violent measures to suppress it four hundred years after Montanus. Even among those who did not hold Montanist views, the Second Coming was important during the persecutions. The expectation of the great overthrow of everything in heaven and earth at the end of time composed a significant piece of the evangelistic message to the Gauls from the time of Irenaeus in the second century until Lactantius in the fourth century.[13] With the emergence of Christendom as the new order in the West, however, Augustine's theology of the Millennium replaced the earlier view of a dramatic interruption of history. He taught that the book of Revelation should be understood allegorically, for the Millennium was coming to pass through Christ's reign in the church.[14]

The Middle Ages

The Sibylline oracles appeared during the last days of the old Roman empire, following the ascendancy of Constantius, the son of Constantine, who favored the Arian party. The *Tiburtina* foretold a future golden age when an emperor would appear to reunite East and West and bring an end to the tyranny of heretics. The people of Gog and Magog would then rebel, precipitating the final crisis before the rise of Antichrist and the Second Coming.[15] The Christian Sibylline literature rested on a tradition of pagan oracles, of the same Cybele cult to which Montanus had belonged, and of Jewish manipulations of the Sibylline oracle form for proselytizing purposes.[16]

In the seventh century, a second Sibylline oracle appeared, *Pseudo-Methodius*, purporting to have been written by the fourth-century martyr, Methodius of Patara. It contained a similar prophecy about a great emperor who would appear, but this time to conquer the Ishmaelites (Muslims) who had seized one Christian territory after another.[17] Then the final conflict would begin before the Second Coming. This Sibylline tradition would have continuing influence for a thousand years in the politics of emperors and kings both in the East and the West, who had ambitions of greatness.

The Sibylline oracles seem to have provided background for the tone of the first crusade, which Pope Urban II intended in order to bring some relief to Byzantium in Asia Minor and in so doing to gain acknowledgment of papal supremacy in the East. A crusade would also provide an outlet for the energies spent on innumerable feudal conflicts of the time. But the crusade was largely usurped by the masses of poor who, inspired by the apocalyptic messages of preachers like Peter the Hermit, committed all manner of atrocities against Muslims and Jews. The masses saw the crusade as the last great battle, which would reveal the last great emperor from among the eligible Christian princes.[18]

Even the apocalyptic ministry of Savonarola had roots in the Sibylline oracles of the end times. It was in Florence, the humanist capital of the world, that Savonarola's warnings of impending doom struck their mark. Charles VIII of France represented himself as the long-expected last emperor of Sibylline fame, who would conquer the world in preparation for the return of Christ. He began his adventures by invading Italy in 1494, aiming for Florence. In this atmosphere, Savonarola preached about the coming judgment, and the people of Florence responded by driving out the ruling Medici family. Savonarola negotiated a peaceful submission to Charles and set about erecting a godly republican government. The monk's prophetic warnings turned more optimistic as Florence now became the vehicle for the dawning of the Millennium following the defeat of Antichrist.[19] The message was optimistic, however, only for those who repented and turned to God, for judgment was near:

> I have said to you: "The sword of the Lord will come upon the earth swiftly and soon." Believe me that the sword of God will

come in a short time. Do not laugh at this "in a short time," and
say it is the "short time" of Revelation which needs hundred
of years to come. Believe me that it is soon.[20]

In 1495 Savonarola wrote a *Compendium of Revelations* to demonstrate the accuracy of his prophecies. By 1498, however, Charles
had withdrawn from Italy, and the Medici pope, Alexander IV,
intended to bring Savonarola's influence to an end. In the face of
changing political and economic realities, the citizens of Florence
turned against the Dominican and burned him at the stake in the
public square.

A second major theme in the Middle Ages related to the return
of Christ concerns the study of Joachim of Fiore (c. 1135–1202).
This man gained a wide reputation as a biblical scholar with great
insight into the interpretation of the prophecies about the end times.
He divided human history into three dispensations: the age of the
Father, the age of the Son, and the age of the Holy Spirit.[21] He taught
that the history of the world from creation to the time of Jesus comprised seven periods and that the time forward from the time of
Jesus to the Second Coming would also involve seven periods. He
identified the first dispensation of seven periods with the Father and
the second with the Son. But this scheme created a problem in providing the Holy Spirit with a temporal sphere of influence. Joachim
resolved the problem by assigning to the Holy Spirit the seventh
period of the Son's dispensation. As the seventh period, or Sabbath,
it need not have the same fixed duration as the other six periods.[22]

Joachim expected Christ to come, intervene in history, and
destroy the Antichrist. He calculated the coming of Christ based on
Daniel 12:7, 11, 12 , which speaks of 1260, 1290, and 1335 "days"
respectively. Joachim took the days to mean years, which he numbered from the birth of Christ, concluding that the return would
occur in 1260, 1290, or 1335.[23] He saw a correlation between contemporary events and the rise of Antichrist, who had followers alternatively considered to be Saladin, Emperor Frederick II, and
Alfonso of Castille.[24]

Though widely respected and sanctioned by the Pope, Joachim
was condemned by the Fourth Lateran Council (1215). His scheme
provided intellectual credibility to the conviction that God is not

remote from Christians but intimately present through the Holy Spirit. The system set up conflict, however, between those who accepted it and saw themselves as model people of the final age of the Holy Spirit, and those who rejected it and therefore had to be considered agents of Antichrist.[25] Joachim's concept of three dispensations could not be reconciled with the officially accepted Augustinian understanding that there would be no millennial reign of Christ on earth except through the church, but his scheme certainly fit the popular theology influenced by the Sibylline oracles.[26]

Despite the condemnation of Joachim, he continued to be popular, particularly among the mendicants, who believed his references to the two orders of spiritual men who would bring in the kingdom referred to the Dominicans and Franciscans. The "Spiritual" Franciscans in particular saw the transition to the third dispensation as coinciding with the ministry of Francis of Assisi. In 1254 Gerard of Borgo San Donnino wrote *Introduction to the Eternal Gospel*, in which he declared that the last age, the dispensation of the Holy Spirit, would begin in 1260. Following Joachim's scheme, he taught that the Spiritual Franciscans, who followed the original intent of St. Francis, would be the instruments for the coming of the new age.[27] The publication of this book caused such a stir that the church removed John of Parma from office as Minister General of the Franciscan Order and replaced him with Bonaventure. For his part Gerard suffered life imprisonment.

The Reformation Ease

The Second Coming formed a motif that ran through the Reformation from the time of the Hussites to the disintegration of the Puritans. The radical wing of the Hussite movement became millennial in the Joachite tradition when opposition to them increased in 1419, viewing the institutional Roman Church as the Antichrist. Having established a fortress settlement as a center of activity, they prepared to take up arms against the Antichrist. Naming their settlement Mount Tabor (after the place where Christ foretold his second coming), they became known as Taborites. They waged successful warfare until a major defeat in 1434 at the hands of the more conservative Hussites, the Ultraquists.

The Reformers' view of the Roman Church led them to reject the Augustinian understanding of the Millennium. The Taborite view of Rome or the pope as the Antichrist generally prevailed during the Reformation period with an underlying expectation that Christ would soon return to establish his kingdom. As the major concern of the Reformers, however, this theme only predominated among fringe groups.

Melchior Hoffman, an Anabaptist, prophesied that he would return with Christ in 1533, following his imprisonment and execution. Christ would establish the new Jerusalem at Strasbourg. Apocalyptic concern heightened over Hoffman's prophecy because 1533 was regarded as the fifteen-hundredth anniversary of the death and resurrection of Christ. When 1533 came and went, Jan Matthys, an Anabaptist baker from Haarlem, declared that Münster would be the real site of the new Jerusalem in 1534.

The city of Münster had a population of about 15,000 when its troubles began. Religious deviation began in 1531 when Bernard Rothmann, a young Catholic priest, began preaching Lutheran doctrine. Despite opposition by the bishop, the guilds supported Rothmann and forced the town council to install Lutheran ministries in all the churches. Rothmann's religious pilgrimage did not end there, however, for by 1533 he had become an Anabaptist. His sympathizers on the town council granted liberty of conscience to Anabaptists, setting the stage for a massive influx of Anabaptists. They flocked to Münster, expecting to be saved in the new Jerusalem while the rest of the world was being destroyed sometime before Easter 1534. As a result, the Anabaptists won a great victory in the town council election of February 23, 1534.[28]

The Anabaptists then expelled the Lutherans and Catholics to cleanse the city. In return, the Lutherans and Catholics lay siege to the city, beginning on February 28. Within the walls Jan Matthys assumed theocratic control, executing enemies and abolishing private ownership of money and property. He died leading an assault on the besiegers. Jan Bockelson succeeded Matthys and soon introduced polygamy to the community before arranging his accession as King of the new Jerusalem. He enforced his apocalyptic rule with frequent executions. This episode finally ended June 24, 1535, with a successful assault on the city. The conquering army exterminated virtually all those still alive in the city.

During the rise of Puritanism, with the English church party intent on completing the Reformation in England, Joseph Mede (1585–1638) attracted attention for his study of Revelation and his conclusions about the coming Millennium. Concerns about the end of time were ripe during the Reformation period because for a thousand years the church in the West had followed Augustine's view that the Millennium coincided with the church. If Satan was bound in the fifth or sixth century, then the political, economic, social, and religious chaos of Europe a thousand years later was evidence that Satan was once again loose and the end of the world was drawing near. Mede broke with this scholarly tradition, however, and taught that the Millennium had not yet begun.[29]

From the time of Henry VIII's break with Rome, the English government and church had encouraged identifying the pope as the Antichrist. The memory of the Lollards who had made the same identification no doubt aided in popularizing the view. Besides Mede, several other scholars promoted millennial speculations. Thomas Brightman published a commentary on Revelation in 1609. Johannes Alsted taught that the first three vials of Revelation were poured out between 1517 and 1625, with the last judgment expected about 1694. John Napier, the Scottish inventor of logarithms, calculated the fall of Rome as 1639 and the end of the world about 1688. By the 1630s and early 1640s the Puritans had decided that the reign of the beast and the Antichrist included the despised Archbishop Laud and the Church of England.[30]

In contrast to earlier millenarian works, Thomas Goodwin's sermon *A Glimpse of Zion's Glory* was preached by someone who stood close to the new power brokers of Civil War England. Goodwin's reading of Revelation had influenced his move from Presbyterian thought to Independency activism. No mere demagogue, Goodwin came to a strong conviction about the congregational form of church government, which he regarded as the beginning of the kingdom of Christ.[31] Millenarian themes like those sounded by Goodwin became a main feature of sermons preached before the Long Parliament, setting the tone for their deliberations. As the Parliamentary Army became increasingly independent in its ecclesiology, the millennial views made respectable by scholars the caliber of Goodwin, who became both president of Magdalen College and chaplain to Cromwell, had a ring of respectability. Prophetesses like Lady Eleanor Douglas and Mary Cary joined divines like John Owen in viewing the execution of King Charles I as a necessary move to make way for the reign of Christ.[32]

By the early 1650s millenarianism had developed a radical streak that sought the overthrow of all remnants of the "fourth monarchy." Among the Independents during the Civil War and Commonwealth, a number of soldiers accepted the view that the four world empires of Daniel 2 and 7 had ended. The fourth empire, Rome, had apparently lived on in its constituent parts, but the "fifth monarchy" or the reign of Jesus would soon begin.[33] These fifth monarchists differed from the earlier Puritan millenarians in three respects: They believed that they had the responsibility to clear the way for the fifth monarchy rather than waiting for God to do so; they identified by name contemporary figures in English life whom they believed were mentioned in biblical prophecy; and they developed a plan for the structure of Christ's coming kingdom.[34]

When Cromwell dissolved the Barebones Parliament in 1653, the fifth monarchists also consigned Cromwell's government to Antichrist and plotted its demise. Thomas Venner, one of the most brilliant among them, planned to overthrow the government, but the plot was discovered and Venner went to the Tower until 1659.[35] After the Restoration, Venner attempted a second rising, which the government put down violently. John Bunyan's imprisonment and the severe persecution of all non-Conformists followed on the heels of the abortive fifth monarchy rising.[36] The failure of the armed rising influenced the Quakers to abandon their earlier radicalism and adopt a policy of pacifism, for which they became well known.[37]

The Third Rome

In the East, the continuation of the empire had as much importance for the divine plan of salvation as the existence of the church. Everyone knew that Rome was the fourth and last empire of the book of Daniel and that it would witness the return of Christ. With the fall of Byzantium to the Turks in 1453, however, Eastern Christianity entered a crisis. The expectation arose that the end of the world would come in 1492, seven thousand years after the accepted date of the creation of the world.[38] So convinced was it that the end of the world would come in that year that the Russian Church did not prepare a calendar beyond 1492. The end of the seventh millennium had particular import, coinciding as it did with the end of the empire, since there had only been seven councils, seven sacraments, seven days, and seven pillars of wisdom.[39]

When the end did not come, Metropolitan Zosimus prepared new Easter tables for the calendar and declared the dawn of a new Christian era with a new Constantine and a new Constantinople. Just as the political and spiritual legacy of Rome had passed to Constantinople, the Russians believed that Rome continued in Moscow. This understanding of Moscow as the third Rome was first articulated by Starets Filofey of Pskov. The view quickly gained acceptance as the only possible interpretation of events. Thus, Grand Duke Ivan III of Moscow (1462–1505) became Tsar of Russia, the Russian equivalent of Caesar. He married the niece of the last Byzantine emperor and claimed the insignia of Byzantium, the two-headed eagle, as the standard of the new Rome.[40] On the basis of this understanding of the prophecies of the end times, the metropolitan of Moscow assumed the office of patriarch, which the four patriarchs of the Orthodox Church confirmed in 1589.[41]

Moscow became the only city of Eastern Christianity ruled over by a Christian prince after the fall of Byzantium. The reorientation of Orthodox Christianity from Constantinople to Moscow occurred during the same hundred-year period as the Protestant Reformation. The Russian empire, newly independent of the Tarter yoke, began with a perceived divine mandate to continue the life and work of the Byzantine empire with specific reference to the defense and advance of the faith. To explain the disastrous fall of Constantinople, the seat of Christianity, the Russian Church concluded that God had punished the emperor and the patriarch of Constantinople for entering into communion with Rome at the Council of Florence (1439) in a bid for military aid. Though God had punished Constantinople for this, he had not ended the fourth empire but had transferred it to Moscow, because of the Russian devotion to God.[42]

So strong was the belief in Moscow as the third Rome, both politically and spiritually, that a great schism occurred in 1653, when

Patriarch Nikon ordered a revision of the Russian liturgy and customs to conform with those of the Greek Church. Regarding the Greek Church as corrupt, proven by its punishment by God for its relations with Rome, the "Old Believers" broke with the patriarch and refused to make changes. Archpriest Avvakum, who led the initial opposition to the reforms, concluded that the "time of suffering" had come.[43] To accept reform meant rejecting Moscow's place as the third Rome. This being the case, the third Rome had fallen and there was no empire left to be a fourth Rome; therefore, the end of the world must be coming soon. For supporting the reforms and inspiring the new social order, Tsar Alexis earned the epithet of Antichrist.[44]

In his initial reforms, Nikon gave instructions that the sign of the cross should be made with three fingers instead of two, as had been the Russian custom. In preliterate peasant society, the liturgy and the customs were the doctrine of the church. To change either was to abandon the true faith as imbedded in its ritual.

In 1667, a council that included both Russian bishops and several Orthodox patriarchs deposed Nikon. Instead of nullifying his reforms, however, the council condemned all who refused to follow the changes. The important monastery of Solovki refused the instructions, which resulted in an eight-year siege, from 1667 until 1676. The Tsar's forces killed all but fourteen of the two hundred monks when the siege finally ended. The government action only increased the conviction of the Old Believers that the reign of Antichrist had begun.[45]

It was a time of apocalyptic expectation. The hermit Kapiton had gained a wide following at the beginning of the seventeenth century through his teaching that since the Antichrist was already ruling, the world would soon end.[46] Under the regency of Sophia, elder sister of Peter the Great, Old Believers routinely suffered death as enemies of the state and its church. Some of the more militant Old Believers, in following Kapiton's teaching, not only sought martyrdom, but even committed suicide. The 2700 Old Believers who seized the Paleostrovskii Monastery set the chapel afire and died in the flames. A similar incident happened at Berezovna Volok. In place after place, Old Believers burned themselves alive for fear that their faith would fail if captured by the forces of Antichrist. This episode finally ended through the influence of Evfrosin, who taught that Christ provided the faithful only two options in persecution: flight or martyrdom. Suicide was not an option, for it betrayed a lack of faith.[47]

Old Believers did not comprise a monolithic movement but involved numerous sects that splintered from the common experience of rejecting the reforms of Nikon. By the time of the Bolshevik Revolution, Old Believers numbered in the millions. They formed communities in isolated regions of the vast empire in which they preserved their old liturgical forms and Russian customs during the period of radical Westernization introduced by Peter the Great.

American Christianity

Concern about the Second Coming had figured prominently in American Christianity since the time of the Puritans. Jonathan Edwards held to a postmillennialism that taught that Christ would create the Millennium through his church before his return.[48]

Dispensationalism. By the end of the tumultuous nineteenth century, however, a growing number of evangelicals began to reject postmillennialism for a premillennial view. The most widespread transdenominational premillennial movement of the nineteenth and twentieth centuries is dispensationalism. John Darby (1800–1882) developed the dispensational framework of history with its eight covenants and seven dispensations or ages.[49] Among the unique and controversial features of this system are the pretribulation rapture of the church, whereby Christians will escape the persecution and suffering of the Tribulation, and the separate ways God deals with Israel and the church.[50]

Dispensationalism spread quickly through the Bible conference movement of the late nineteenth century, beginning with the Niagara Bible Conference of 1875. These gatherings led to conferences on Bible prophecy, which dispensationalists dominated. Dwight L. Moody adopted dispensational views early in his ministry, and most of the major evangelists of the next hundred years followed his lead. Seminaries, on the other hand, viewed dispensationalism with alarm. James Snowden's survey of seminaries in 1919 found that only seven of the 236 professors surveyed in twenty-eight seminaries held dispensational views. Rather than discrediting dispensationalism, however, this study tended to discredit seminaries among believers in the growing fundamentalist-dispensationalist camp.[51] Schools like Moody Bible Institute, Columbia Bible College, Dallas Theological Seminary, and Bible Institute of Los Angeles (BIOLA) were founded in large part because of the growing disenchantment with the old seminaries and divinity schools.

The crowning achievement in the spread of dispensationalism probably came with the publication of C. I. Scofield's reference Bible, with copious notes explaining the Bible in terms of its covenants and showing the continuity of Scripture from one dispensation to the next. This Bible plus the visual aids that dispensationalists produced, such as timelines and charts, made the Bible understandable to the average layperson at a time when seminaries had become enamored with a critical approach to Scripture, which made the Bible either more obscure or more mundane. The wars of the twentieth century and the establishment of an independent Jewish state after nearly two thousand years have encouraged serious consideration of dispensational teaching, especially at the height of the Cold War. Dispensationalists also pointed to the theological liberalism of the American Protestant establishment as a fulfillment of the biblical warning of the proliferation of false teachers in the last days.[52]

Cult groups. While dispensationalism operates across denominational lines within orthodox Christianity, several significant religious groups have emerged that depart from the orthodox faith over an initial concern about the Second Coming. Mother Ann Lee gained a following through the teaching of revelations she claimed to have had, beginning in 1770. The Shakers believed the Second Coming was actually a second incarnation, with Ann Lee as the second visitation of the Messiah. They believed that the Millennium began in 1792, through the foundation of the Shakers.[53]

Joseph Smith claimed that he received the Book on Mormon as a preparation for the second coming of the Messiah. Organized April 6, 1830, the Church of Jesus Christ of Latter-Day Saints came into being to gather the saints for the thousand-year reign. Smith told his followers that they would live to see the Second Coming, but that the saints must first create a colony worthy of the Lord.[54]

William Miller, a Baptist preacher without formal training, developed his own understanding of biblical prophecy, concluding that the Second Coming would occur October 22, 1844. Through a series of conferences, preaching tours, and periodicals, his teachings became well known. He gained both a following and an opposition. After 1844 passed without incident, the Adventist group developed out of his followers.[55] Charles Taze Russell was influenced by the Adventists to start a Bible study group to determine God's plan for the world and humanity. In 1876 he became pastor of the group that became the nucleus of Jehovah's Witnesses.[56]

THE RETURN OF CHRIST AS GOOD NEWS

The fear of death, anxiety over one's state in eternity, and dread about the end of the world have faced cultures since the beginning of recorded time. Oral tradition suggests that the concern goes back into the mists of prehistoric times. This concern is not limited to primitive societies. During the Cold War, the technological powers created a probable scenario of total thermonuclear war that would destroy the world. Diplomatic paranoia also developed the need for a "doomsday" bomb. Now environmentalists fear that a greenhouse effect caused by global warming will lead to the eventual extinction of life. Underlying all of this concern rests the gnawing fear resulting from our finitude, in that we cannot control cosmic events. The gospel teaches that into this fragile world Christ will return.

Chaos

The return of Christ addresses the chaos that afflicts the world. This state of chaos afflicts all realms of human experience, though not necessarily to the same degree at the same time in all cultures. Political, social, economic, cultural, and religious systems all fall prey to this chaos, and they in turn spread the chaos to the environment. Environmental chaos proceeding from human chaos can affect entire ecosystems, global weather patterns, and biological disasters.

The chaos that afflicts "this present evil age" already stands condemned. At his return, Christ will exercise judgment over the chaos. For those who live as victims of the chaos at whatever level, or for those who grieve over the chaos, the return of Christ offers good news that God cares and has already set a time to set things in order.

Accountability

Rather than providing an excuse to withdraw from the world or live complacently with the satisfaction that God will eventually work everything out, the return of Christ demands that his followers be about his business until it occurs. If he reigns at present and his Spirit indwells his people, then no efforts in his name will be futile. With injustice seething through societies all over the world, the accountability that demands Christians live responsibly also creates a standard of justice. When the world seems so unfair and the weak little ones seem to bear the brunt of the injustice, the return of Christ offers good news to those who cry for justice.

Evil

The cry to God also comes in the plaintive cry "Why?" How can evil abound when God exists? Why does God allow evil? Why do bad things happen to good people? People do not merely ask the question intellectually; they experience the question emotionally. The Bible discusses the issue in numerous places, such as the Psalms, Job, Romans 8, the story of Joseph, and to a certain extent the entire history of Israel. The sufferings of innocent Jesus culminate the problem with respect to the sovereign Creator, for God himself stood in the position of those who must sit and watch the one they love suffer.[57] People experience the problem at the micro level, the level of their personal experience, in all of eternity. God resolves the problem at the macro level, the point at which time and space are rolled up like a scroll. At the return of Christ, evil will be no more. Rather than supply a philosophical explanation until then, the gospel simply affirms that evil and its causes will be consumed. For those who suffer and those who must watch, the return of Christ offers good news that God will wipe it all away along with the tears.

Rescue

From beginning to end, Christian faith revolves around a Savior who rescues. Unlike the civil religion of America that stresses self-reliance, the Christian faith stresses a dependency on Christ that will culminate in rescue when he returns. Unlike a morbid psychological dependency that robs people of their independence, dependence on

Christ frees people to act responsibly until his return. Instead of the idolatry of human dependence, dependence on Christ frees one from defending the chaos of the world. Instead of the fear of death, destruction, and oblivion, the gospel teaches that Christ will return to rescue those who love him from the final judgment of the present world order. For those who see the end coming and recognize that human initiatives to create great world orders only intensify the problem, the return of Christ offers good news that God will intervene to rescue the beloved.

Justification

Many people struggle to justify their existence. They have had a chance at life, but have they made the most of it? Was their life valid and worthwhile? Do they have a right to exist? The problem of justifying one's existence is complicated if one also has a conscience that still functions well enough to generate guilt and fear over past actions. As a result, the idea of a final accounting can fill people with great dread. The gospel teaches that at the return of Christ, the lives of his followers will be justified on the basis of his life instead of their own.[58] In other words, those who fear the judgment because of their sin can escape condemnation on the basis of the righteousness of Christ. Sin was condemned and destroyed on the cross for all those who died with him; therefore, they will stand justified at the judgment.

When I was a pastor, a teenage boy told me that he lay awake one night, unable to go to sleep. All he could think about was what would happen to him when he died. He felt sure that he would go to hell. His story surprised me because neither I nor the previous pastor had used "scare tactics" about the terrors of hell to manipulate the teenagers. Instead, the feelings emerged from deep within him. As it turned out, he had a great deal about which to feel guilty. That night in his bed alone, he trusted Christ as his Savior. Twelve years later he has grown to maturity as a teacher and deacon. Fear does not play a part in his theology because Christ freed him from that fear when he realized he would stand justified before him at the judgment. At that time I realized I was derelict in not dealing with the fear of judgment with teenagers in an intentional, albeit responsible way. Just as a counselor need not fear raising the idea of death with a suicidal person, one need not fear raising the issue of judgment with a teenager. Their consciences still work. For those who fear the prospect of judgment and condemnation, the return of Christ offers good news that he will justify us.

Perseverance and Reward

The return of Christ culminates in the reward of the kingdom. All that eternal life with God will bring, which no mortal can fathom, lies out before those whom Christ gathers to himself at the judgment. Christianity is not a world-denying religion like Hinduism, nor does it deny the reality of suffering as Buddhism does. On the contrary, Christ promises his followers that they can expect suffering in this world. On the other side of judgment, however, lies the reward of faithfulness to Christ. Eternity with him is the reward for wanting to spend eternity with him. Those who do not want to spend eternity with Christ will not have to do it.

Some criticize a faith that is derisively referred to as "pie in the sky by and by when I die." While this may be a legitimate concern about wealthy Christians who live in ease and use the prospect of eternal reward as an excuse not to follow Christ in this life, the criticism sounds awfully spiteful when hurled at those poor souls who face nothing but misery in this life. A woman in Russia whose husband was not a believer told me that her joy will come in another world. This woman has a profound faith, for she lives her life as an offering to Christ. She perseveres in her faith because she trusts the One who has given her the promise of a new world. For those who have nothing in this life as well as for those who recognize the hollowness of what they do have, the return of Christ offers the good news of great reward for those who persevere in their faith.

NOTES

1. In Islam, the judgment will be carried on by a tribunal that also includes Moses and Mohammed.

2. This issue intensified during the late intertestamental period when such works as the *Book of Jubilees*, the *Parables of Enoch*, and the *Testaments of the Twelve Patriarchs* appeared.

3. The issue of motive greatly concerned T. S. Eliot after his conversion. He placed on the lips of Thomas in *Murder in the Cathedral* these words: "The last of these is the greatest treason, to do the right thing for the wrong reason."

4. Michael J. St. Clair, *Millenarian Movements in Historical Context* (New York: Garland, 1992), 80.

5. Kenneth Scott Latourette, *A History of Christianity: Beginnings to 1500*, rev. ed. (New York: Harper & Row, 1975), 1:128–29.

6. St. Clair, *Millenarian Movements*, 82.

7. Theodore Olson, *Millennialism, Utopianism, and Progress* (Buffalo: Univ. of Toronto Press, 1982), 93.

8. Latourette, *History of Christianity*, 1:134.

9. St. Clair, *Millenarian Movements*, 85–86.

10. Norman Cohn, *The Pursuit of the Millennium*, rev. ed. (London: Maurice Temple Smith, 1970), 25.

11. Latourette, *History of Christianity*, 1:138, 216.

12. Ibid., 1:225.

13. Cohn, *The Pursuit of the Millennium*, 29.

14. Ibid., 29.

15. Ibid., 31.

16. Bernard McGin, *"Teste David Cum Sibylla:* The Significance of the Sibylline Tradition in the Middle Ages," in *Apocalypticism in the Western Tradition* (Brookfield, Vt.: Variorum, 1994), 4:7–16. McGin gives an overview of the career of the Sibyle from pagan times.

17. Cohn, The *Pursuit of the Millennium*, 32.

18. Ibid., 61–88.

19. Bernard McGin, *Visions of the End: Apocalyptic Traditions in the Middle Ages* (New York: Columbia Univ. Press, 1979), 277–78.

20. Ibid., 280.

21. St. Clair, *Millenarian Movements*, 100.

22. Olson, *Millennialism, Utopianism, and Progress*, 112–16.

23. Ibid., 120 n.17.

24. St. Clair, *Millenarian Movements*, 101.

25. Olson, *Millennialism, Utopianism, and Progress*, 125, 127.

26. Cohn, *The Pursuit of the Millennium*, 109.

27. Rufus M. Jones, *The Eternal Gospel* (New York: Macmillan, 1938), 3.

28. Cohn, *The Pursuit of the Millennium*, 258–62; St. Clair, *Millenarian Movements*, 172–73.

29. Olson, *Millennialism, Utopianism, and Progress*, 199–200.

30. B. S. Capp, *The Fifth Monarchy Men* (London: Faber and Faber, 1972), 27–36.

31. Tai Liu, *Discord in Zion: The Puritan Divines and the Puritan Revolution 1640–1660* (The Hague: Martinus Nijhoff, 1973), 4–7.

32. Capp, *The Fifth Monarchy Men*, 50–51.

33. D. H. Kromminga, *The Millennium in the Church* (Grand Rapids: Eerdmans, 1945), 180–81.

34. B. S. Capp, "Extreme Millenarianism," in *Puritans, the Millennium and the Future of Israel*, ed. Peter Toon (London: James Clarke, 1970), 68.

35. Ibid., 84.

36. Christopher Hill, *A Tinker and a Poor Man* (New York: Alfred A. Knapf, 1989), 105.

37. Christopher Hill, *The World Turned Upside Down* (New York: Viking, 1972), 194.

38. Nicholas Zernov, *Eastern Christendom* (London: Weidenfeld and Nicolson, 1961), 140.

39. Ernst Benz, *The Eastern Orthodox Church: Its Thought and Life*, trans. Richard and Clara Winston (Chicago: Aldine, 1963), 181.

40. Ibid., 181–82.

41. Zernov, *Eastern Christendom*, 141; see also Nicolas Zernov, *Moscow the Third Rome* (New York: AMS Press, 1971), 48.

42. Zernov, *Moscow the Third Rome*, 31–35.

43. For an account of Avvakum's life, see Serge Zenkousky, ed., *Medieval Russia's Epics, Chronicles, and Tales* (New York: Dutton, 1963), 322–70.

44. Robert O. Crummey, *The Old Believers and the World of Antichrist* (Madison, Wis.: The Univ. of Wisconsin Press, 1970), 14.

45. Ibid., 4, 19–20.

46. Ibid., 7.

47. Ibid., 45–47, 56. See also Sergius Bulgakov, *The Orthodox Church* (Dobbs Ferry, N.Y.: American Review of Eastern Orthodoxy, 1935), 210.

48. Timothy P. Weber, *Living in the Shadow of the Second Coming* (New York: Oxford Univ. Press, 1979), 13–14.

49. C. I. Scofield, ed., *The Scofield Reference Bible* (New York: Oxford Univ. Press, 1945), 1, 3 n.4–5.

50. Weber, *Living in the Shadow*, 21.

51. Ibid., 27–33.

52. Ibid., 87.

53. J. F. C. Harrison, *The Second Coming* (London: Routledge & Kegan Paul, 1979), 166.

54. Ibid., 177–81.

55. Ibid., 194.

56. See Melvin D. Curry, "Jehovah's Witnesses," in *Cults and Non-conventional Religious Groups*, ed. J. Gordon Melton (New York: Garland, 1992), passim.

57. I am indebted to Frank Tupper for this insight.

58. N. T. Wright explored the theme of justification at the judgment in his Gheens Lectures at The Southern Baptist Theological Seminary, April 25–27, 1995.

Chapter 10

Human Response

Every religion of the world holds out the expectation of the appropriate human response to its perception of the divine. The appropriate response of the religion of ancient Israel differs markedly in form from the appropriate response expected within modern day Judaism. Even within modern Judaism, variations of the response exist among the groups in the family of Judaism. Orthodox, Reformed, Conservative, and Hasidic Jews have varying ways of carrying out the form of their response to God while belonging to the same family of faith. Likewise, Islam has several groups within its family, including the Sunnites, Druse, and Shiites. The family of Hinduism has as many "denominations" as it has regions of the subcontinent who reverence patron deities. Buddhism has three main groups: the Theravada, the Mahayana, and the Vajrayana. While each group within these families have distinctives that set them apart from their brothers and sisters, these distinctives in no way nullify the essential characteristics of the particular religions. Despite the varieties of expression of Christian responses to God in light of the gospel by the various major denominational groups and many minor groups, all share a central core response that sets Christianity apart from the other religions of the world.

BIBLICAL BACKGROUND

The appropriate response to God presented in the New Testament has a basic pre-Mosaic origin, which appears at the same time both simple and highly demanding. Its simplicity leaves critics asking "Is that all?" But it is this very simplicity that shreds all of the superficiality that too easily clings to religion, which leaves others protesting, "The cost is too high."

The Gospels

As this book has argued, the New Testament presents Jesus as the central factor in humanity's relationship to God. While many religions have great central figures, Jesus functions in a radically different way for Christians than those central figures do for other religions. The function of Jesus, in fact, forms the essential scandal of Christianity. Jews have profound respect for Moses and Muslims for Mohammed, but neither accords to their prophet what Christians accord to Jesus. To do so would be unspeakable blasphemy. Hindus affirm the countless avatars of divinity, and Buddhists affirm oneness with the divine Buddha, but the exclusive claims of Christians for the uniqueness of the incarnation of God in Jesus Christ seems to Hindus and Buddhists like so much intolerance. Given the gospel as it has been examined in this book, it should come as no surprise that the early church defined the appropriate response to God in terms of how one responds to Jesus. He issues a call for people to come to him personally.

Following. Jesus issued a simple call for people to follow him. The simplicity of the invitation always came in relation to the consequences of accepting the invitation. The idea of following has both a positive and negative dimension, for to follow Jesus means to leave something behind. The call to follow meant a variety of things to different people when Jesus sought them. To some it meant leaving a vocation (Matt. 4:19–22; 9:9; Mark 1:17–18, 20; 2:14; Luke 5:27; John 1:40, 43), to others leaving family and friends (Matt. 8:19–22; 10:37; Luke 9:57–62; 14:26), and to still others leaving a place of belonging, property, or wealth (Matt. 19:21, 27; Mark 10:21, 28; Luke 18:22, 28). To all it meant leaving one's life as it had been (Matt. 10:38–39; 16:24; Mark 8:34–37; Luke 9:23–25; 14:27; cf. John 12:25–26).

Leaving comes as a consequence, rather than as a focus, of following Jesus. Leaving emerges as a possibility only because Jesus appears comparatively as so much more delightful than what one has left behind. In following Jesus, one discovers a life of such surpassing value that he or she will exchange anything to possess it (Matt. 13:44–45). Those who do not appreciate the value of following Jesus make their choice for the base and inferior. Jesus declares, "In the same way, any of you who does not give up everything he has cannot be my disciple" (Luke 14:33). To those who leave all and follow, however, Jesus promises the kingdom (Matt. 19:27–30; Mark 10:28–31; Luke 18:28–30) and life eternal (John 5:40; 8:12; 10:25–28).

Following does not represent an activity so much as an attitude toward life and a way of living. Following Jesus involves more than the physical activity of entering the school of an itinerant rabbi. It involves a new orientation to God and life (John 1:37, 43; 21:19, 22). Following becomes the natural orientation of life, for in following Jesus people find themselves (Matt. 20:34; John 10:1–10). Acceptability for Jesus does not depend on the length of time in following but in the fact of following, because the call of Jesus does not involve a hierarchy of followers who merit more consideration than others (Matt. 20:1–16). All who respond to the call and come to Jesus receive the gift (11:28–30).

Repentance. The Synoptic Gospels elaborate the positive and negative dimensions of following by the term *repentance*. Israel had understood repentance as the appropriate response to God, for it involved turning away from sin and turning toward God in terms of one's attitude and heart desire. John the Baptist provided the continuity with that ancient prophetic tradition by calling on people to repent (Matt. 3:2, 6, 8; Mark 1:4; Luke 3:3, 7–8). When Jesus began his public ministry, he likewise preached, "Repent, for the kingdom of heaven is near" (Matt. 4:17; Mark 1:15). In fact, at one point he identified his mission as one to call sinners to repentance (Matt. 9:13; Mark 2:17; Luke 5:32).

Jesus presented himself as the cause that should occasion repentance. His appearance presented the alternative that required choice. If Tyre and Sidon had seen the miracles of Jesus, they would have repented (Matt. 11:21; Luke 10:13). The people of Nineveh repented at the preaching of Jonah; Jesus presented himself as one greater than Jonah, whose message required repentance as the only acceptable response (Matt. 12:41; Luke 11:32). Thus, Jesus identified himself with his message, insisting on the necessity of repentance, without which people would perish (Luke 13:3, 5; 16:30–31). While repentance involves a mental reorientation, Jesus also insisted that repentance involved a change in behavior reflecting the new orientation (Matt. 21:28–32). This response to God results in rejoicing in heaven as a person accepts his or her place in creation by turning away from a way of life independent of God and turning to God (Luke 15:7, 10, 17–20).

Jesus instructed his followers to make the preaching of repentance a cardinal element of their following him. When he sent the Twelve out on their mission, they "preached that people should repent" (Mark 6:12). After the resurrection he reconfirmed the importance of repentance by instructing the apostles that they should preach repentance and forgiveness (Luke 24:47).

Faith in Jesus. John's Gospel, the last one to be written, does not mention repentance. Instead, the author focuses attention on the necessity of faith in Jesus as the appropriate response to God. In his prologue, John identifies this response as a key theme of his message, declaring that those who believe on the name of Jesus receive the power to become children of God (John 1:12). This power is the Holy Spirit, who comes to all who have faith in Jesus (7:38–39).

All the blessings of God come to those who have faith in Jesus. Through this faith people participate in the resurrection and experience eternal life (John 3:16, 36; 11:25–26; 14:1–6; 20:31). Faith in Jesus also results in an enlightenment that provides people with a way to live that is positive and acceptable to God (12:36, 44–46). Furthermore, faith in Jesus as the messianic Son of Man sets people free from the guilt of sin and the fear of judgment (9:35–38). On the other hand, those who do not have faith in Jesus experience condemnation, death, and the wrath of God (3:18, 36; 8:24).

Faith. While the Synoptic Gospels do not speak of faith *in Jesus* as the appropriate response to God, they do stress the necessity of faith. Having clearly established a personal need to follow Jesus, these Gospels elaborate the genuineness of following in terms of a life of faith. Faith represents the substance of repentance, and it arises through encountering Jesus. He utters a recurring lament for those who have little faith, for faith is not a generic commodity but a matter of confidence in him as the One who is able to help or make a difference (Matt. 6:30; 16:8; 17:17; Mark 9:19; 16:14, 16; Luke 9:41; 12:28; 24:25).

Those who do have faith experience the coming of the kingdom in their midst. When Jesus saw the faith of those who lowered the crippled man through the roof for healing, he both forgave sins and healed the man (Matt. 9:2; Mark 2:5; Luke 5:20).

Faith in Jesus resulted in the healing of many:

the centurion's servant	Matt. 8:10; Luke 7:9
a leper	Matt. 8:2; Mark 1:40; Luke 5:12
Jairus' daughter	Matt. 9:18; Mark 5:23; Luke 8:50
the bleeding woman	Matt. 9:22; Mark 5:34; Luke 8:48
two blind men	Matt. 9:28–29
Syro-Phoenician woman's daughter	Matt. 15:28; Mark 7:29
Bartimaeus	Mark 10:52; Luke 18:42–43
a leper	Luke 17:19

In the Synoptic Gospels, Jesus represents the locus of faith in God, for God exercises his power through Jesus. Those who do not have faith do not see the power of God (Matt. 13:58; Mark 6:56). But those who have even the barest of faith will experience the kingdom (Matt. 13:31–32; Mark 4:30–32; Luke 13:18–20; cf. 17:6). Jesus is the one who elicits this faith (Mark 9:24; Luke 7:50). A failure of faith amounts to a failure of trust in Jesus (Matt. 8:18, 23–27; 17:20; Mark 4:35–40; Luke 8:22–25).

In John's Gospel, many people began to believe in Jesus because of the miracles he performed (John 2:11; 4:53; 11:42, 45; 12:11). Others refused to believe unless they saw miracles (4:48; 6:30), and some of these refused to believe even when they saw them (12:37–40). Jesus put little stock in people who followed him simply because of his ability to perform miracles, for he knew the human heart (2:23). He expected faith that he is in the Father and the Father in him (14:10–14). John specifically wrote in order that people might come to that faith (20:31).

Doing the words. In the Gospels, an appropriate response always includes an appropriate resulting action; faith produces godly behavior. Jesus expects people to do his words (Matt. 7:24; Luke 6:46–49). Those who have faith in him are the ones who love him, and those who love him obey him (John 14:15–24; 15:9–12). Through Jesus people come to know the will of God, but unless they act on that knowledge, they have not received the word with faith.

Thus, Jesus can speak of obedience not as a cause of salvation, but as a sign of salvation (Mark 3:35; 4:21–25; Luke 11:28; John 3:21; 17:6, 8). Zacchaeus represents that person whose faith in Jesus manifests itself in a change of behavior that amounts to doing righteousness (Luke 19:8–9). The one who hears, understands, and acts is the one who has true faith that leads to life (Matt. 13:1–23; Mark 4:1–20; Luke 8:4–15; John 12:47–50).

Attitude. Jesus also speaks of the appropriate attitude of the person responding to God. Essentially, his message involves taking on the attitude of Christ, so that listening to Jesus forms the necessary first step to an appropriate response to God (Matt. 17:5; Mark 9:7; Luke 9:35; 10:39, 41–42). Since Jesus lived a life of humility, those who refuse to humble themselves will never enter the kingdom; but those who do humble themselves and confess their sinfulness will be accepted by God (Matt. 19:14; Mark 10:14–15; Luke 18:14, 16–17; 23:40–43). Just as Jesus forgave his tormentors, those who follow him must be willing to forgive (Matt. 6:14–15; 18:21–35; Mark 11:25; Luke 6:37; 17:3–4). Ultimately, one must desire a loving heart for God and a compassion for other people (Matt. 18:5; 22:34–40; 25:34–46; Mark 9:33–37; 12:28–34; Luke 9:46–48).

Accepting Jesus. Receiving Jesus makes it possible to become a child of God (John 1:12). By accepting him, one accepts God, while rejecting Jesus means rejection of God (Matt. 21:33–44; 22:1–14; John 13:19–20; Mark 12:1–12; Luke 20:9–18; Luke 14:15–24). Accepting Jesus involves acknowledging who he is in relationship to God and how he provides access to him. Peter, Martha, and Thomas made confessions of their faith under differing circumstances (Matt. 16:13–20; Mark 8:27–29; Luke 9:18–20; John 11:27; 20:24–29). Verbal confession and its validity must be seen in light of the other issues already discussed in this chapter. Peter's confession preceded his denial. Thomas's confession only came with empirical proof, which Scripture elsewhere suggests does not constitute faith. Some believed in Jesus during his lifetime, but they did not confess him for fear of being put out of the synagogue (John 12:42–43). In this regard, acceptance of Jesus carries with it the expectation of a willingness to be identified publicly as a follower of Jesus (Matt. 10:32–33; Luke 12:8–9).

General Apostolic Writings

In the New Testament, those who followed Jesus did not refer to themselves as Christians. In terms of their relationships to one another, they called themselves "brothers" and "sisters"; in terms of what Christ was doing for them, they referred to themselves as "saints"; in terms of their response to God and their basis for unity as a people, they referred to themselves as "believers" (Acts 1:15; 2:44; 4:32; 5:12; 9:41; 10:45; 11:2; 15:2, 5, 23; 16:1, 14–15; 21:25; 1 Cor. 6:5; 7:12–14; 9:5; 14:22; 2 Cor. 6:15; Gal. 6:10; 1 Thess. 1:7; 2:10; 1 Tim. 4:12; 5:16; 6:2; James 2:1; 1 Peter 2:17); in terms of defining themselves and establishing the boundaries of their community, Paul distinguished those who belonged to Jesus from "unbelievers" (1 Cor. 6:6; 7:14–15; 10:27; 14:23; 2 Cor. 4:4; 6:14–15).

Generic faith. Faith or belief often appears as a generic expression for the appropriate response to God, but these instances seem to lack any concrete content. Sometimes the context means faith in God (Gal. 3:6–9; Col. 2:12; Heb. 6:1; 11:1–40; 1 Peter 1:21). Frequently it describes the attitude of someone who receives the benefits of relationship to God (Acts 15:9; Gal. 3:14; Eph. 1:18–19; Heb. 4:3; James 2:5; 5:15). Faith itself arises as a consequence of the gracious initiative of God (Acts 14:27; 18:27). It forms the foundational quality for experiencing an appropriate relationship to God, and out of faith arises the ability to endure and become beneficial to God (Acts 19:18; Rom. 11:20, 23; 13:11; 1 Cor. 3:5; Eph. 2:8; 6:16; 1 Thess. 5:8; 1 Tim. 4:10; 2 Tim. 1:5; 1 Peter 1:9; 2 Peter 1:5). Rather than a generic quality without specific content or object, faith in the New Testament always has an understood object. Even the generic usages of "faith" occur in the context of a community that placed their faith in Jesus Christ.

Faith in Jesus. When the apostles preached and called on people to respond appropriately to God, they spoke in terms of faith, trust, or intimate knowledge of Jesus Christ. Salvation comes to those who have faith or trust in Jesus Christ (Acts 4:12; 10:43; 11:17; 16:31; 26:18). The apostles urged people specifically to have faith in Jesus Christ (2:38; 20:21; 22:16; 24:24). The issue at stake in the preaching of the apostles was that people would believe in the Lord Jesus Christ (Acts 5:12; 9:42; 14:23; 16:31).

The benefits of salvation do not come on the basis of generic faith, but through a faith directed specifically toward Jesus Christ. Faith in him leads to the many dimensions of salvation:

Righteousness	Rom. 3:22; Phil. 3:9
Atonement	Rom. 3:25
Justification	Rom. 3:26; Gal. 2:15–16
Adoption	Gal. 3:26–29
Eternal Life	1 Tim. 1:16
Access to God	Eph. 3:12
Indwelling of Christ	Eph. 3:17

Faith means faith that Jesus can save because of who he is as the Christ, the Son of God, the Lord of Lords (Heb. 3:1; 13:15; 1 Peter 1:8; 1 John 3:23; 5:1, 10). Faith involves that kind of knowledge of Christ that creates in one a trust that can only come from intimacy (2 Peter 1:8; 1 John 2:3, 20–21; 3:6; 2 John 1–3).

The message of faith. Faith in the New Testament explicitly refers to Jesus Christ, who is known through the gospel message: "Those who accepted his message were baptized" (Acts 2:41). The *content* of faith rests in the message about Jesus that people have accepted and thereby begun a life of following and trusting Jesus, whom they met in that message. Simply put, faith begins through believing the stories about Jesus (Acts 4:4; 8:12; 15:7; 16:14–15; 17:12; Rom. 10:17; 1 Cor. 1:21; 15:1–2, 11; 1 Thess. 1:6; 2:13; 2 Thess. 1:10; 3:1; Titus 1:9; Heb. 4:2). Faith is not a nebulous matter individually constructed and privately held. Rather, the apostles write of *the* faith, a specific and particular understanding of reality revealed in Jesus Christ from creation through his expected return (Acts 6:8; 14:22; 2 Cor. 13:5; Gal. 1:23; Eph. 4:13; Phil. 1:27; 1 Tim. 2:7; 3:9; 4:1, 6; 5:8; 6:10–12, 20; 2 Tim. 2:18; 4:7; Titus 1:13; Heb. 4:14; Jude 3). Instead of a strictly private matter, the faith or message about Jesus forms the basis for community and the binding matter of common concern for those who become the church: "All who were appointed for eternal life believed" (Acts 13:48).

Believing the testimony of the witnesses about Jesus formed the basis for accepting people into the fellowship of "believers" as well as for receiving the benefits of salvation (Acts 14:1; 17:34;

28:24; 2 Cor. 4:13–14; Gal. 3:2, 5; Eph. 1:13–14; 1 Thess. 4:14–18; 2 Thess. 2:13; Titus 1:1–4). "The faith" functioned as a synonym for "the gospel" in the apostolic writings, and both implied a particular message about Jesus as the substance of faith (Rom. 1:16; 10:14–15; 1 Cor. 15:1–2, 11; 2 Cor. 9:13; 2 Thess. 1:8; Heb. 4:6; 1 Peter 4:17–18).

Continuing faith. The apostles define faith as a continuous state of relationship with God rather than as a static experience. While faith in Christ may have a beginning, it has no end. Faith that ends is not faith but infatuation. If faith comprises the essence of the appropriate response to God, then faith involves a continuing experience of unending response to God:

> So then, just as you received Christ Jesus as Lord, continue to live in him, rooted and built up in him, strengthened in the faith as you were taught, and overflowing with thankfulness. (Col. 2:6–7)

Faith grows, as Jesus had said, like a mustard seed and results in a life that continually gives itself over to Christ (2 Cor. 10:15; 2 Thess. 1:3; 2 Peter 3:18). Salvation therefore belongs to those who continue in the faith, "not moved from the hope held out in the gospel" (Col. 1:22–23; cf. 2 Cor. 1:24; 1 Tim. 1:19; 4:3; 6:11–12; 2 Tim. 4:7; Heb. 2:1–3; 3:6, 8–12, 14; 6:12; 9:28; 10:32–39; 2 John 9). Thus, the apostles were concerned to know if faith was genuine or if it had been merely a vain, superficial expression (1 Thess. 3:5, 6–10). In the face of persecution or pleasure, the genuineness of faith is revealed as more than mere verbal assent or intellectual acceptance of theological concepts (Phil. 1:29; 2 Thess. 1:4; James 1:3; 1 Peter 1:7). The apostles observed the possibility of affirming "the faith" without having faith in the One of whom "the faith" spoke (1 Tim. 4:1; 6:10, 20; 1 John 2:19). Others departed by rejecting the message of faith or its implications for living (1 Tim. 5:8; 2 Tim. 2:18; Heb. 4:11; 2 Peter 2:15, 21).

As a result, the apostles urged the followers of Jesus to remain in him, to stand firm in the faith, and to continue to pursue the life of faith in Christ Jesus (Acts 14:22; 2 Cor. 5:7; Col. 2:5; 2 Thess. 2:15; 1 Tim. 2:15; 3:9; 4:6; 2 Tim. 1:13; 2:22; Titus 1:9; 2:2; Philem. 5; Heb. 4:14; 10:22, 23; 2 Peter 1:12; 1 John 2:27–28; 3:24; 2 John

4; 3 John 1, 3–4; Rev. 14:12). A life of faith forms the basis for doing the work of God, exhibiting the character of Christ, and knowing one belongs to Christ (2 Cor. 2:9–10; Phil. 2:17; 1 Tim. 1:4–5; 3:13; 2 Tim. 3:10; 1 John 5:13; Rev. 2:19). The test for whether one has faith or merely fascination in Christ is revealed over time, for faith continues. The only way for faith to continue is if it has as its focus the Lord Jesus Christ himself, who through faith strengthens and preserves his people (Heb. 12:1–3; 1 Peter 1:5; 2 Peter 2:2; 1 John 1:7; 2:4–6).

Repentance. While a working definition of *metanoia*, the Greek word generally translated as "repentance," usually means a change of mind, the significance of this change often goes unappreciated. It is not the sort of change of opinion that says, "I will have steak instead of roast." Instead, it constitutes change in the way one's mind perceives the nature of things and says, "I will not eat meat again because I believe it will kill me." The change of mind forms a deep-seated conviction that governs one's life. In the latter days of twentieth-century America, the term used to describe this kind of change of mind is "paradigm shift." Once the shift has taken place, it is impossible to undo it and see the world from the old perspective. Once Europeans perceived the world as round, they could not return to living as though it were flat.

Repentance describes the reorientation that comes with faith in Jesus Christ. Occasionally the apostles speak of repentance and faith together, but normally they use repentance as an alternative term to describe the appropriate response to God (Acts 20:21). Alternatively, the apostles sometimes address this same idea by calling on people to "turn" from sin or darkness to God and Christ (Acts 3:19, 26; 9:35; 11:21; 26:18; 2 Cor. 3:16; 1 Thess. 1:9; 2 Tim. 2:19). In the early sermons of Acts, Peter called on people to repent or turn to God from wickedness. He said nothing about faith (Acts 2:38; 3:19, 26; 5:31; 9:35) until he spoke to the Gentile Cornelius and his household, but in that situation he did not mention repentance (10:43). When Peter gave an account of the Gentile conversion to the church in Jerusalem, he declared that the Gentiles received the Holy Spirit just as the others "who believed in the Lord Jesus Christ" (11:17). Instead of agreeing that the Gentiles had faith, however, the members of the church replied, "God has granted even the

Gentiles repentance unto life" (11:18). In other words, the church of Jerusalem, with its Jewish heritage and dynamic understanding of the unity of faith and repentance, used the terms interchangeably as describing different dimensions of the same experience.

Repentance represents the behavioral effect of faith, for it is a reorientation that touches all dimensions of life. It should be evident in one's behavior (Acts 26:20). God expects people to respond to him in a way that repentance describes (17:30; 2 Peter 3:9). The kindness of God and genuine encounter with him through faith leads to repentance; those who lack this attitude toward God have no faith and will face wrath (Rom. 2:4–5; 2 Cor. 7:10; Heb. 6:1, 6; Rev. 9:20–21).

Obedience, faith, and righteousness. The behavior of repentance and faith is obedience; the status of repentance and faith is righteousness. Paul speaks of "the obedience that comes from faith" (Rom. 1:5). John indicates that obedience provides a basis for assurance that one knows Jesus (1 John 2:3; 3:21–24). Obedience accompanies faith in Jesus Christ (2 Cor. 9:13). For the apostles, however, obedience also meant obeying the command to believe the gospel and have faith in Christ, such that rejecting Christ constitutes disobedience (Rom. 6:17; 2 Thess. 1:8; Heb. 4:6; 1 Peter 1:22–25; 2:4–8; 4:17–18).

Faith, therefore, forms the basis for righteousness or acceptability to God. God accepts those who trust him. Those that do not have faith have no use for God. Abraham serves as the example of God's acceptance of people on the basis of their faith in him (Rom. 4:1–25; Gal. 3:6–29; Heb. 11:8–19). Instead of law, God gave the patriarch a promise, and he believed God. On the basis of this faith, God accepted him as righteous (Gen. 15:6). The faith of Abraham, however, manifested itself in a way that can only be called repentance. That is, his faith in God caused a change in his way of relating to the world. Following God meant leaving language, culture, religion, family, land, and people. God put everything else in perspective so that Abraham believed God and valued him more than anything else that had a claim on him. He manifested the obedience of faith rather than the obedience of consequences. He obeyed because of his relationship with God, not to earn a relationship with God.

This right relationship or acceptability to God comes through faith (Rom. 1:17; 3:22; 4:5; 9:30; 10:4–8; Gal. 2:15–16; 3:6–9, 11,

290 • The Gospel and Its Meaning

22–25; 5:5–6; Phil. 3:9). God himself makes the relationship right for those who have faith in his Son (Acts 13:39; Rom. 3:26–30; 5:1–2; 9:32; 10:9–10). By faith in Christ, who came from God and has returned to God, people can enter into the same type of relationship with God that Christ enjoys.

Baptism. In Acts, those who accepted the message were baptized (Acts 2:41; 8:12–13, 36; 9:18; 10:47–48; 16:33; 18:8; 19:2–5). Peter's Pentecostal sermon included a call to be baptized, as did Paul's conversion account (2:38; 22:16). Reference to baptism appears in the major bodies of the apostolic writing as the universal practice of the church. Believers were baptized (Rom. 6:3–4; 1 Cor. 1:13–17; Col. 2:12; Heb. 6:2; 1 Peter 3:21). Baptism functioned for the church as an outward and visible sign of an inner and spiritual grace, for in baptism the new convert acted out the drama of his or her faith in the Christ as Savior. Unlike the discreet baptisms of the latter twentieth century in the United States, those baptisms took place in the most public area where an abundance of water could be found. The humiliating spectacle of someone being soaked in public made the paradigm shift of faith all the more vivid and observable. The early believers became publicly marked people, suspect and unacceptable to the population at large.

Rejection of Christ. To discuss an appropriate response to God implies an inappropriate response. The early believers considered rejecting Christ as the step that would cut off access to God (Acts 4:11; Rom. 2:8; 2 Thess 2:10–12; 2 Tim. 3:8; Titus 1:14–15; 1 Peter 2:4–8). Any who refuse to believe in Jesus Christ have rejected God's initiative in relationship (Acts 3:22–23; 19:9; 1 John 2:22–23; 5:10). Those who do not believe cannot enter what God offers to those who have faith (Heb. 3:19; Jude 5). If people reject Jesus, they have no other means of access to God (Heb. 10:26–31). And those who have heard the gospel and enjoyed the community of faith only to turn to another belief system cannot reexperience repentance, for they have relegated Christ to an old way of looking at things—the old paradigm (Heb. 6:4–6).

Conclusion

The apostles experienced salvation through faith in Jesus Christ. Because of their faith in him, they viewed all of reality in a new perspective oriented toward Christ, which they called repentance. This new orientation created a basis for obedience to Christ, rooted in their relationship with him. By virtue of this relationship established by the initiative of God and received by faith, people are acceptable or righteous in the sight of God.

HISTORICAL/THEOLOGICAL DEVELOPMENT

In the apostolic period, baptism coincided as closely as possible with the conversion experience. By its symbolic nature, it expressed the faith of a convert and dramatically portrayed the experience of repentance—turning from an old way of life to a new life. In turning to Christ, a person demonstrated his or her rejection of all other loyalties through baptism. By the second century the church began delaying baptism for a period of instruction, but this delay did not alter the impact of the declaration that baptism communicated.

Baptism

Besides representing the relationship of the new believer and Christ, baptism also constitutes the ceremonial rite of incorporation whereby a person is accepted into the church. It appears evident that the patristic church considered the value of baptism to be in the sincerity of the confession made by it, as the lengthy period of instruction implies.[1] With the emergence of doctrinal disputes and the rise of heresy, faith increasingly came to be understood in terms of cognitive belief in affirmations about Christ more than in terms of a personal encounter with the living Christ.[2] The fathers of the church expressed their understanding of "the faith" in their writings. This practice eventually led to the development of the creeds, which represent the consensus of the universal church concerning the Christ in whom they believed.[3]

The questions asked of new Christians at baptism reflect the developing formulas of the faith, which coincided with the growing period of instruction prior to baptism.[4] The *Didache* describes a period of instruction that candidates for baptism had to undergo. It also describes how the ceremony of baptism grew to include symbolism and ritual that reinforced the meaning of baptism. In addition to the implicit image of burial and resurrection through the medium of the Holy Spirit represented by water, the formula of baptism in the name of the Father, Son, and Holy Spirit also occurred. The *Didache* also specified a preference for cold, running water, but made allowance for warm (stagnant) water and even for pouring, when insufficient water was available.[5]

In some regions, baptism was followed by placing a white robe and a garland on the new Christian. Such procedures emphasized that a person had accepted the seal of possession by Jesus Christ, for salvation and baptism belonged only to those who held to orthodox belief about Jesus Christ.[6] By the third century, baptism commonly occurred only once a year. In some places this happened at Pentecost, emphasizing the reception of the Holy Spirit. In other places it took place at Easter, emphasizing the resurrection.[7]

The offer of baptism to any who came went far beyond the mystery religions, which practiced forms of ceremonial washing and tended to recruit "the better sort of person." The preaching to non-Christians continued to include the challenge to receive baptism, which would bring the benefits of salvation that the gospel promised.[8] Precisely because the gospel promised a change in character, a cleansing of the spirit, and a new life that would never end, the invitation to Christian baptism had a powerful appeal, but it also earned the contempt of pagans, who reviled Christianity for the baser sort of person attracted to it.

Baptism addressed several key themes that concerned the classical mind. The theme of victory with Christ over hostile powers through the resurrection was made graphic in baptism. The cleansing, regeneration, and enlightenment that the Holy Spirit brings became experiential through baptism. The mystery cults promised knowledge and salvation in different forms through participation in a *mysterion* (Greek) or *sacramentum* (Latin). For the Christians, however, the act of baptism served as a covenant agreement whereby believers bound themselves to Christ. Unlike the mystery cults, they did not offer secret, esoteric knowledge. Instead, they proclaimed their message to any who would receive it. Baptism itself did not occur in secret grottoes as in the Mithra cult, but in public places, where all could witness the profession of faith in Christ.[9]

Concerned as he was with faithfulness in persecution, Tertullian advised people to put off baptism lest they be unable to live up to the calling. He urged parents not to have their children baptized, which suggests that infant baptism had become common by the end of the second century.[10] Hippolytus indicates that children were baptized as a matter of course from the third century on. Infant baptism comprised one of the major concerns of Augustine in his conflict with the Pelagians. The Pelagians taught that people were sinners not by nature but by choice. Infants had no need of baptism for the remission of sins, because they had not yet committed personal sin. The synods at Carthage and Milevis (416) condemned the Pelagian view, upholding the common view in the preceding two centuries of the necessity of infant baptism.[11]

The acceptance of infant baptism as the norm coincided with the new official status of Christianity and the rapid growth of the church through the inclusion of what Davies calls "semi-converts."[12] Hinson argues that after the persecutions, baptism took on a quasi-magical acceptability that drew in large numbers of people attracted by the benefits of baptism, who did not necessarily appreciate the significance of the baptismal confession of faith.[13] Such stories as the baptism of Constantine's army and Charlemagne's forced baptism of the Celts serve to illustrate how baptism had become separated from one's response to Christ as it served the same sort of function that the old sacrifices to Caesar had served in pagan days. The relationship of baptism and confession continued to exist on the frontiers of Christendom, where groups of people increasingly turned to Christ; but where the church enjoyed establishment status, instruction and confirmation replaced the old notion of conversion in practice.

Baptism marked people for life before Christianity became the state religion. One story illustrates its significance. Victorinus, a famous teacher of rhetoric in Rome, had a powerful impact on Augustine in the struggle of his own conversion. Victorinus privately confessed to Simplicianus that he was a Christian, but Simplicianus insisted that he would not believe it until he saw Victorinus in the church of Christ. Victorinus resisted this challenge for fear of how his friends and the public might respond, but a greater fear began to develop that Christ would deny him before the angels if he would not make a public profession of faith. He then sought public baptism, with all of the social implications.[14] As infant baptism became normative and Christianity assumed respectability, the radical decision of baptism was lost.

A thousand years later, baptism of consenting adults once again appeared as a major concern of the relatively small group of radical reformers known as Anabaptists. From the perspective of Catholics and Lutherans alike, the Anabaptists were rebaptizing Christians. From the perspective of the Anabaptists, however, no one truly experienced baptism unless he or she entered the water as a free moral agent. Infants could not be baptized since they could not of their own volition choose to express faith in Christ. Rather than being a united movement, a variety of groups in continental Europe and in England reached a conviction about "believer's baptism" in the sixteenth and seventeenth centuries. In theological perspective, some came from Lutheran, some from Calvinistic, some from Arminian, and some from Zwinglian traditions.

The Anabaptists of continental Europe and the Baptists of Britain did not identify the church with Christendom, but looked to Scripture for a model of a church composed of conscious believers. Their approach to church and society seemed to threaten the entire established social order. Many of those who sought to reintroduce believer's baptism to the church died as martyrs, including Felix Manz (d. 1527), Conrad Grebel (d. 1526), and Balthasar Hübmaier (d. 1528).[15]

In England, the Particular Baptists (Calvinistic) grew much more rapidly than the General Baptists (Arminian) in the period of the English Civil War, Commonwealth, and Protectorate (1644–1660). John Bunyan was converted and was baptized by immersion in the early 1650s and soon gained a reputation as a gifted preacher and writer. He also acquired a reputation as a bit of a controversialist. One of his most famous controversies found him at odds with other Calvinistic Baptists of London over the necessity of baptism by immersion for admission to communion in the church. The London Baptists held a strict view, but Bunyan insisted that the lack of immersion should not bar anyone from fellowship. Whereas the London Baptists regarded baptism as the door to the church and the Lord's livery, Bunyan held that only faith in Christ could admit someone to his church.[16] He separated from the other Baptists over this issue, and after his death his church became identified as a Congregational church.

The concern of the Puritans to maintain true churches of visible saints cannot be separated from their concern for conversion. As Puritanism disintegrated into various factions, the Congregationalists, Presbyterians, and Baptists all retained concern for these issues, though they pursued them in different ways. In New England among the Congregationalists a problem began to cause difficulty for maintaining a church of converted, visible saints. According to church teaching, only someone whose verbal profession of faith and Christian living testified to conversion could enter fully into the church covenant. The children of such people could receive baptism, but they did not become full members of the church and were not permitted to share the Lord's Supper until they made a profession of faith and acknowledged the covenant.

But what about baptized children of the converted who failed to express any evidence of conversion of their own? The Synod of 1662 adopted a new position, allowing for the baptism of the children of those who had never become full church members. This decision essentially brought to an end the attempt to maintain a church of converted saints, and the privilege of communion at the Lord's table was gradually extended to all who had been baptized as infants. This alteration in the Congregational concern for conversion became known as "The Halfway Covenant."[17]

Penance

Penance first began to develop in the life of the early church as a way of offering an expression of repentance after baptism. The *Didache* provided for public confession of sin in church, especially prior to observing the Lord's Supper.[18] Tertullian allowed only one repentance after baptism when the problem of postbaptismal sins arose.[19] He offered the possibility of a second repentance for remissible sins, but for sins like murder, idolatry, fraud, apostasy, blasphemy, and adultery he offered no hope of forgiveness after baptism.[20] He advocated acts of penance as the means of expressing this second repentance, just as baptism expressed the first repentance.[21] Both of these acts constituted the "two planks" of salvation.[22]

During the Novatian controversy the practice of forgiveness and restoration through prescribed acts of penance precipitated a crisis when a council meeting in North Africa in 251 approved penance to restore those who had offered sacrifices during the persecutions.[23] Following the persecutions, the belief developed that those martyrs who had survived their suffering had the power to declare sins forgiven. As a consequence, penitents came to them in great numbers seeking forgiveness, which the martyrs generally granted. Following the Decian persecution it became customary in the East for a special priest designated by the bishop to hear the confession of any who had sinned, to establish the terms of penance, and to grant absolution. Because of abuses, however, this practice was discontinued in the late fourth century.[24]

By the third century penance had developed a common form that included confession of sin, exercises such as prayer and almsgiving, and absolution or reconciliation.[25] The Synod of Elvira in Spain (305?) had little inclination to provide for penance when grievous sin took place. On the other hand, the Synod of Ancyra in Asia Minor (314) recognized five degrees of penance for varying offenses.[26] The growth of this system of penance corresponded to the influx of people into the church in the post-Constantine era and began to replace in function some of the initiation process that had related to baptism of adult converts in the earlier centuries.[27] It provided a way to demonstrate commitment, obedience, and the seriousness of one's profession.

Pope Gregory departed somewhat from Augustine's views on election as he followed the modified Augustinianism of the Synod of Orange, which stressed God's foreknowledge rather than predestination. In so doing, he placed more emphasis on the responsibility of people to deal with their sin. He also stressed that works of penance and intercession by the saints and martyrs would lighten one's experience of discipline and cleansing in purgatory.[28] Private confession reemerged in the Middle Ages and with it the priest's instructions for penance, which now included such options as fasting, pilgrimages, self-flagellation, almsgiving, gifts to the church, or prayers. The priest, on the basis of the theory of apostolic succession, exercised the claim to remit sin, but only where true repentance had occurred. The Fourth Lateran Council (1215) decreed that all Christians should go to confession at least once a year.[29]

Indulgences appeared during the Middle Ages in the West as an alternative to the requirements of penance. In the East, penance tended to be regarded as a thanksgiving for forgiveness rather than as a condition for forgiveness. In the West the view arose that sin not dealt with in life would have to be purged in purgatory; therefore, plenary indulgences offered an attractive way to work off part of the load for the truly repentant. Urban II made one of the earliest offers of plenary indulgences to those who took part in the first crusade.

Alongside this theory of indulgences in place of penance, the scholastics developed the theory of the "treasury of the church." According to this theory, the church had authority over the accumulated merit of the saints over and above what Christ had done. The church could draw against this treasury of merit to grant indulgences. Pope Clement VI endorsed this theory in 1343, and it soon expanded to include the view that the living could obtain indulgences for those already in purgatory.[30]

John Wycliff (d. 1384) followed Augustine's view of election and predestination. In so doing he concluded that salvation lay outside the control of the ministry of the church. He condemned the tradition that had grown up to make salvation secure, including the veneration of the saints, relics, pilgrimages, masses for the dead, and indulgences. His position cut to the heart of the spiritual control of the clergy as it had been developing in the West during the late Middle Ages. Over a hundred years would pass, however, before anyone mounted a powerful enough challenge to indulgences to split the church in the West.

As chapter 3 has suggested, Scripture provided the orienting feature of Luther's career. The end of his efforts in studying Scripture, however, rested in his discovery of the idea of justification by faith. In his efforts to please or satisfy God so that he might enjoy salvation, Luther had tried the life of a monk, practicing self-deprivation, making pilgrimages to the shrines of saints, and taking advantage of holy relics. He even visited Rome in the Jubilee Year to benefit from the indulgence attached to such a visit. Despite all of these exercises that had gradually gained credence through the centuries as a basis for forgiveness, nothing brought Luther confidence in salvation until 1515, when he came to the conviction that God expects only faith.

So strongly did Luther feel about the centrality of faith as the chief response God demands of people that he composed a list of ninety-five matters of dispute, chiefly arising from the sale of indulgences in his district to finance the rebuilding of St. Peter's Cathedral in Rome. Luther did not object to the encouragement of "works of piety and charity," but these could not form the grounds for salvation. Even more did he condemn the idea of purchasing an indulgence in order to avoid one's good works.[31] In his first proposition, Luther declared, "Our Lord and Master Jesus Christ, in saying 'Repent ye,' etc., intended that the whole life of believers should be penitence."[32] He affirmed the ongoing struggle of Christian life, which required a contrite stance toward God while relying on faith as the beginning point for the struggle.[33] Luther worked out his theology of conversion, like Augustine, largely in reflection on his own circumstances and in tandem with his scholarly exposition of Scripture.[34] In his *Lectures on Romans*, he emphasized human inability to prepare for conversion and stressed God's exclusive prerogative in preparation.[35] This stance precluded the mechanical methods that indulgences represented. The consistency of Luther's position may be seen in his criticism of attempts to convert Jews by force.[36] To him, such efforts profaned both the grace of God and justification by faith. Forced acquiescence does not constitute faith.

Grace and Choice

Sin and grace are issues that arise from the doctrine of God, and given the overriding concern of Augustine for the Creator God, these issues formed major concerns in the working out of his theology. The teachings of Pelagius on the human response to God ran afoul of these foundational concerns; therefore, Augustine engaged in a heated debate with the Pelagians. In simple form Pelagius taught that people had the freedom of will to choose to obey God, while Augustine taught that sin so dominated people as a result of the Fall that no one can turn to God apart from his initiative in grace to cause it to happen. All people have inherited a sinful nature in Adam, but God has chosen some by his mercy to receive pardon and salvation. Pelagius, on the other hand, held that people have a moral duty to exert themselves in obedience to God's law, thus denying the concept of inherited sin and an impaired will. To Augustine such a view made grace unnecessary and God a mere bystander in the saga of human self-improvement.

Though condemned by synods in North Africa, Pelagius and Caelestius, his closest associate, made statements of faith that conformed to the orthodoxy of the creeds. Since the creeds did not address the issue of human response, Pope Zosimus found the two perfectly acceptable, reprimanding instead the North African bishops who condemned Pelagius.[37] The Pelagians held right belief about Jesus, but they did not hold to faith in Jesus as the criterion for salvation. Instead, they stressed moral obedience as the basis for salvation.

The semi-Pelagianism of John Cassian held to the Eastern view that God wills that all people should be saved. Whenever anyone gives the slightest inclination toward God, God strengthens that inclination by his grace. This view seemed to place the initiative with people rather than with God. Accordingly, the Synod of Orange (529), with the approval of Boniface II, condemned this position, though it affirmed that sufficient grace is bestowed in baptism for a person to achieve salvation.[38]

During the Reformation, the issue of grace and free choice again emerged as a major source of conflict. Long before the Synod of Dort, Luther and Erasmus carried on a literary duel over the nature of the will. Erasmus advocated the humanistic understanding of free will while Luther upheld an Augustinian view of the will in bondage to sin. Erasmus approached this question largely from the perspective of moral philosophy and saw in Luther's stress on grace a dangerous antinomian tendency that might ignite the masses.[39] By his argument, he did not mean to disparage grace so much as to assert human responsibility.[40]

Having pointed out in his *Ninety-Five Theses* the impotence of indulgences to affect salvation in any way, Luther raised the issue of free choice in his *Assertion* (1520).[41] He rejected the notion that free choice or will had anything to do with attaining salvation. Erasmus, however, believed people could apply themselves "to the things which lead to eternal salvation or to turn away from them."[42] In *The Bondage of the Will* (1525), Luther responded to Erasmus and insisted that people act out of necessity. They have some limited choice with respect to the temporal world and may even choose to obey the commands of God. Performance of these works, however, do not make a person good or lead to salvation because of the failure of human motive. With respect to motive, one's choices are either motivated by God or by Satan.[43] Whereas Erasmus viewed human cooperation with God as a grounds for salvation, Luther viewed it as a consequence of salvation.

This perspective of Luther was amplified and eclipsed by Calvin and the Reformed churches, so much so that this position became known as Calvinism. The Protestants of France, Holland, Scotland, and many in England, Germany, and Switzerland championed this view. The Puritans in particular held to this view while the established Church of England became largely Arminian after the Restoration of 1660. The conflict between the great allies, Wesley and Whitefield, lies largely in the fact that Wesley held Arminian views on human free choice while Whitefield held Calvinist views. In the United States, this issue divided the evangelical wing of the church, particularly in the nineteenth century with the rise of revivalism.

With his emphasis on the Holy Spirit (see chapter 8), Charles G. Finney argued that people under conviction by the Holy Spirit can make a free decision to trust Christ.[44] He rejected the Calvinist understanding of predestination even before his conversion. Once converted, Finney passionately presented a gospel available to any who would respond, even though he was ordained a Presbyterian minister.[45] The "Old School" Calvinists, who stressed the sovereignty of God (see chapter 2), held that people could not make a free decision for or against Christ regardless of the means employed by a preacher—and Finney employed a number of means.

Finney came under harsh attack for introducing a number of "new measures" to facilitate responses to Christ. The Calvinists feared that the means he employed were manipulating the emotions of people, thus counterfeiting an experience of the Holy Spirit.[46] Finney held "anxious meetings" to counsel people on how to be saved and organized house-to-house visitation as well. He set apart a special section of pews in his services for "seekers" who were anxious about salvation. Finney prayed in public for the salvation of people by name. He also utilized "protracted meetings" of many weeks duration. These and other new measures were intended to elicit responses to Christ.

Lyman Beecher and Asahel Nettleton led the opposition to Finney and his new measures. The principal objection lay in offering the hope of salvation to everyone indiscriminately. To them, offering salvation to one not numbered among the elect constituted an affront to God. While a general armistice was reached between Finney and most of his opponents, the debate filtered into the mainstream of American theological dispute, with Calvinists generally alarmed by "public invitations" and other means designed to encourage people to decide for Christ.[47]

The importance of decision has also played a central role in the development of the Christian existentialist school of thought. Søren Kierkegaard saw the exercise of the will as the ultimate theological/philosophical concern. A person must make the undetermined choice to accept or reject God's word. In his own writing, Kierkegaard strove to confront his readers with choices. At the most fundamental level, choices had to be made without any criteria, for criteria limited and determined the choice. This most basic choice Kierkegaard called the "leap of faith." This choice creates the criteria for all other decisions as a Christian subordinates his or her will to God's word.[48] In contrast with the prevailing philosophical mood of the day, Kierkegaard rejected Hegel's notion of inevitable progress and stressed the importance of human freedom in faith and repentance.[49] He held that no amount of objective evidence can form a basis for faith. On the contrary, the leap of faith occurs as an existential encounter.[50]

HUMAN RESPONSE AS GOOD NEWS

For the sake of parallelism, this chapter requires the inclusion of this section, but this chapter is not like the others. The human response is not like the good news of what God has done. In the sense that the rest of the book has discussed good news, the human response called for by the gospel does not fall under the same category. The good news lies not in the human response, but in the invitation of God. It is good news that God has made the offer to which people may respond.

The gospel offers Jesus Christ, and people will either respond to Christ or they will not. A range of options does not exist any more than a range of options to a proposal of marriage exists. A marriage proposal is the closest analogy that the gospel message presents to human experience; it offers intimate relationship with God. Those who choose to bisect the elements of the response to Christ into rationalistic categories such as repentance, faith, obedience, and perseverance have missed the point of following Christ. Those who calculate the terms of a marriage proposal are negotiating terms for a contract.

The good news is not what Christ desires *from* us but rather that Christ desires *us*. The theological categories that describe levels of life at which response has an impact actually describe areas in which the call of Christ touches those who follow him. The gospel elicits the response to the invitation. The response does not cause salvation; it is the effect of the gospel on those who desire the relationship with Christ. The pearl of great price is not costly to the buyer because all else is valueless by comparison.

As this book has suggested, the gospel of Jesus Christ appeals to different levels and dimensions of spiritual need. It addresses the variety of human experiences. While this book has attempted to illustrate some of that variety, it by no means exhausts the subject. In truth, it may be little more than a personal testimony because of the inevitable cultural and theological filters I have brought to the study. For all its flaws, however, the study at least suggests the height and depth and width and breadth of the love of God revealed in Jesus Christ. It also suggests that the church in any age has the capacity to reduce the gospel to one narrow experience of the truth of Christ, to the neglect of other aspects that would be good news for other people.

Too often the church lies in danger of shielding the gospel of Christ from people. This withholding of Christ is not intentional, but it happens any time we present theological conclusions that spoke powerfully to a past generation instead of the living Christ who speaks anew to the specific spiritual issues of each successive generation. In order to respond legitimately to Christ, a person must clearly see Christ. In order to understand the meaning of the gospel, a person must understand how Jesus Christ answers the questions of that person's life. This book has illustrated how different elements of the gospel address different life issues. Furthermore, it has demonstrated how entire theological systems and traditions grew up around particular elements of the gospel. When we confuse the system or the tradition with the gospel, we place a veil between Christ and the one who needs to know him. By constantly returning to Jesus afresh, however, the gospel continues to speak to each successive generation after two thousand years as it addresses issues in a contemporary way that the previous generation could never have conceived. This approach does not produce a relative gospel; rather, it faithfully transmits a comprehensive gospel to the next generation of believers.

NOTES

1. E. Glenn Hinson, *The Evangelization of the Roman Empire: Identity and Adaptability* (Macon, Ga.: Mercer Univ. Press, 1981), 73–95.

2. J. G. Davies, *The Early Christian Church* (Grand Rapids: Baker, 1980), 93.

3. For examples of these early "rules," see Irenaeus, *Against Heretics* 1.10.1; Justin, *Dialog with Trypho*, 132.

4. See Justin, *First Apology*, 61.

5. *Didache*, 7.

6. Davies, *The Early Christian Church*, 104. See also Hippolytus, *Apostolic Tradition*, xxi. 12–18.

7. Tertullian, *On Baptism*, 20.

8. Hinson, *Evangelization of the Roman Empire*, 216–19; Michael Green, *Evangelism in the Early Church* (Grand Rapids: Eerdmans, 1975), 152–56.

9. Hinson, *Evangelization of the Roman Empire*, 167–81.

10. Tertullian, *On Baptism*, 18.

11. Henri Rondet, *Original Sin: The Patristic and Theological Background*, trans. Cajetan Finegan (Staten Island, N.Y.: Alba House, 1972), 123–27.

12. Davies, *The Early Christian Church*, 200.

13. Hinson, *Evangelization of the Roman Empire*, 221.

14. Augustine, *Confessions*, 8.3–5.

15. Kenneth Scott Latourette, *A History of Christianity* (New York: Harper & Row, 1975), 2:780–81.

16. For a discussion of this controversy, see my doctoral dissertation, "Evangelistic Fervency Among the Puritans in Stuart England, 1603–1688" (Louisville, Ky.: Southern Baptist Theological Seminary, 1982), 236–51.

17. Edwin Scott Gaustad, *The Great Awakening in New England* (Gloucester, Mass.: Peter Smith, 1965), 9–12.

18. *Didache*, 4:14; 14:1.

19. Tertullian, *On Repentance*, 7. Hermas also held this position.

20. Tertullian, *On Chastity*, 18–19.

21. Tertullian, *On Repentance*, 7.2.

22. Ibid., 2.9.

23. Davies, *The Early Christian Church*, 130.

24. Latourette, *A History of Christianity*, 1:217.

25. Davies, *The Early Christian Church*, 154.

26. Hinson, *Evangelization of the Roman Empire*, 124–26.

27. Ibid., 129.

28. Latourette, *A History of Christianity*, 1:340–41.

29. Ibid., 1:528–29.

30. Ibid., 1:529–30.

31. Martin Luther, "Ninety-Five Theses," in *The Harvard Classics*, ed. Charles W. Eliot (New York: P. F. Collier & Son, 1910), 262.

32. Ibid., 265.

33. Marilyn J. Harran, *Luther on Conversion: The Early Years* (Ithaca: Cornell Univ. Press, 1983), 105.

34. Ibid., 55. Harran argues that an intimate relationship exists between Luther's exegesis and his personal religious experience.

35. Ibid., 100.

36. Ibid., 103.

37. Davies, *The Early Christian Church*, 237.

38. Latourette, *A History of Christianity*, 1:173–82.

39. E. Gordon Rupp, A. N. Marlow, Philip S. Watson, B. Drewery, trans. and eds., *Luther and Erasmus: Free Will and Salvation* (Library of Christian Classics 17; London: SCM, 1969), 9.

40. Ibid., 10.

41. Ibid., 13.

42. Ibid., 47. Erasmus presented this position in his *Diatribe Concerning Free Will* (1524).

43. Ibid., 17–18.

44. Lewis A. Drummond, *Charles Grandison Finney and the Birth of Modern Evangelism* (London: Hodder and Stoughton, 1983), 111.

45. William Warren Sweet, *Revivalism in America: Its Origin, Growth and Decline* (Gloucester, Mass.: Peter Smith, 1965), 135.

46. Keith J. Hardman, *Charles Grandison Finney, 1792–1875: Revivalist and Reformer* (Grand Rapids: Baker, 1990), 104–32.

47. Drummond, *Charles Grandison Finney*, 107–23.

48. Alasdair MacIntyre, "Søren Aabye Kierkegaard," in *The Encyclopedia of Philosophy*, Paul Edwards, ed. (New York: Macmillan / The Free Press, 1972), 4:336–40.

49. L. Joseph Rosas III, *Scripture in the Thought of Søren Kierkegaard* (Nashville: Broadman & Holman, 1994), 34.

50. Ibid., 27–28.

Epilogue

This book has sought to demonstrate how the gospel has addressed the central issues of life posed by people in different cultures and times. It has also suggested how the gospel continues to address the ultimate issues of people in different cultures of the contemporary world. In terms of implications for ministry, this study suggests that the gospel should be addressed to people in terms of their spiritual issues rather than from the traditional perspective of the Christian's sharing the gospel.

Frequently, a reorientation of the church's theological perspective has resulted from the faith experience of a single individual. Furthermore, orienting the theology, worship, or practice of the church around a specific element of the gospel has often happened because that particular element spoke powerfully to the spiritual crisis of an entire generation at a particular time and place. As this orientation became institutionalized, however, the gospel had the danger of taking on a cold, scholastic tone, becoming locked in tradition. It then took a new crisis for people to find a different element of the gospel that provided a fresh vision of God through Christ. In the life of the church, the older generation has a heightened responsibility to recall that what speaks to one generation does not necessarily speak to another.

Over time the church tends to identify the gospel with that element that has dominated its experience. In fact, the gospel itself becomes veiled in the theological system, liturgical practice, ecclesiastical pattern, or devotional discipline that formed the context in which the gospel had meaning. It is then easy to transfer the meaning from the gospel to the church structure. The end result can be loyalty to tradition rather than faith in Christ. Loyalty has little to say to a new generation in crisis, but Christ offers salvation. This problem is as old as the teaching of Jesus about wineskins. The church has often had no room for people whose conversion or faith experience did not conform to the institutionalized pattern.

This problem does not belong only to those groups that place a high value on tradition. Tradition by itself is not the problem; it may actually keep the gospel message alive. Groups that decry tradition, such as Baptists and Pentecostals, are susceptible to the same danger. For when accepted norms and patterns of spiritual experience become institutionalized, then the gospel becomes veiled by the traditions of a previous generation. Those patterns may have facilitated faith in a different context, but now they inhibit the experience of Christ they once fostered.

Though specific elements of the gospel address specific issues of life, this study has also observed that by concentrating on only one aspect of the gospel to the exclusion of other aspects, the danger of heresy, error, or division arises. The gospel is not a theological system, but the story of salvation through Jesus Christ. Preoccupation with any single part of that story gives a distorted picture of Christ. This tendency turns to functional polytheism if one group stresses one aspect of the story while another group stresses a different aspect. By refusing to see all the other aspects of the story of salvation, groups can develop rival pictures of Christ set in opposition to each other. Thus, the Docetists saw an exclusively divine Christ while the Arians saw only a human Jesus. Rival pictures need not be heretical to achieve distortion. When one group focuses on social justice, as seen in the Incarnation, as the total gospel, they are as guilty of distortion as the group that reduces the gospel to a lecture on how the atonement works.

This study has also suggested that the effort to make the gospel applicable to the issues of a particular time and culture may lead to theological problems several generations later. The veneration of the saints, the Western understanding of transubstantiation, and the adoption of the *filioque* phrase in the creed all arose as part of an evangelism methodology. While these methodologies proved effective in their inception, they all led to controversies in later generations when they had lost their evangelistic context and grown into dogma. This phenomenon therefore calls into question the notion of pragmatism as the test for evangelism. New teachings inevitably result from evangelistic methodologies, and these teachings eventually become institutionalized. In this regard, success may not be the best test. The church does not have unlimited freedom to conform the meaning of the gospel to the attitudes and values of a culture for the purpose of gaining adherents.

Certain aspects of this study will seem to add new depth to the idea of superficiality. My biblical treatments are conspicuous for their avoidance of some of the more obvious critical questions employed in twentieth-century biblical criticism in the West. Unfortunately, the schools of biblical criticism have not yet settled on the proper method of study. The twentieth century has spawned more approaches to the truth than the last twenty centuries combined. From the approach I had initially begun of examining the context of particular letters, the theologies of particular writers, and the other distinctions that the prevailing theories of criticism help expose, I shifted to a rather simplistic method. As I looked at all the distinctions, I was struck by the remarkable similarity of themes regardless of author or context. Thus, the study suggested an overarching consensus of the apostles about the implications of the gospel.

In the area of church history, extremely complex dynamics have been reduced to rather simple narratives that will leave scholars of the different epochs aghast. Those concerned with the practice of ministry, on the other hand, may wonder why so much space was devoted to things that happened so long ago. One is left with the dilemma of pursuing church history as an end in itself in order to reconstruct what happened, or of attempting to make some judgments in order to appropriate the work of church historians for the benefit of those who must lead today's churches in the proclamation of the gospel. While the treatment of the historical settings in which the gospel has been explained will not satisfy the scholars who debate what really happened in those settings, it nonetheless suggests the diverse applications of the gospel over twenty centuries and the power of the gospel to touch lives.

The preceding comments concerning biblical studies and historical studies should not be taken as a rejection of critical scholarship. Rather, they represent a bit of the frustration that one must feel when moving from the tools of examination to the task of theological reflection that leads toward informed ministry. The methods of study and examination in these classical disciplines have been in flux since the times of Origen and Eusebius, and they are not settled yet. The methodology must fit the questions being asked. The effort to integrate classical disciplines with the practice of ministry requires the kind of interplay and mutual informing that results in a modification of the discipline for its own sake.

If biblical studies and church history studies have had a weakness in this century, it may be that they have suffered from opposite problems. While biblical studies have tended to move away from historical understandings of the gospel (*Historie*) to stories about God (*Geschichte*), church history has moved away from stories about God's involvement in the church to strictly historical understandings. This study has sought to recapture some of what each of these disciplines has sacrificed. While it may not have succeeded, it has perhaps suggested how the church must feel free to pursue faith inquiry that may not conform to the methodologies of secular disciplines that do not posit the existence of God.

Finally, this study has suggested that the church may look forward to continuing divisions over matters that ultimately relate to the gospel. Oddly, those who divide may ultimately affirm the same gospel. This one phenomenon represents both the tragedy and the glory of the church. The tragedy appears when Christians cannot recognize Christ in others whose faith arises from a different experience of the gospel. The glory appears in the gospel's continuing power to reveal Jesus Christ as the Savior and to draw people into the church, which is constantly finding a way to renew itself for new generations.

Subject Index

Scripture Index

3:28	193	3:11	66	4:10	193
4:4–5	142	3:12	191, 286	4:13	193
4:4	117	3:16–17	229	4:23	194
4:6	225, 226, 229	3:17	286	**Colossians**	
5:5–6	290	4:1–16	229	1	41
5:5	226	4:3–4	229	1:1	196
5:16–25	227	4:4–16	194	1:2	195
5:16–23	172	4:11	196	1:3	192
6:2	195	4:13	286	1:5–6	39
6:8–9	258	4:24	257	1:10	195
6:8	226	4:30	226, 257	1:13	142
6:10	285	5:6	256	1:14	142
6:14	145	5:17	196	1:15–18	191
6:18	194	5:19	192	1:15–17	63
Ephesians		5:21	195	1:18	194
1	41	5:22–24	194	1:19–22	116
1:1	195, 196	5:29–30	194	1:20	146
1:2	194	6:6–9	195	1:22–23	287
1:3–14	65	6:12–14	197	2:5	287
1:3	194	6:12	147	2:6–7	287
1:5	65	6:16	285	2:6	195
1:7	142	6:23	194	2:8	43
1:9–10	259	**Philippians**		2:10	191
1:9	65	1:1	195	2:11–12	145
1:11	65	1:2	194	2:12	171, 285, 290
1:13–14	287	1:6	257	2:13–14	146
1:13	225, 226	1:10	258	2:15	146
1:17	196	1:19	229	2:16–23	197
1:18–20	170	1:20–26	195	2:20	145
1:18–19	285	1:27	286	3:1	21, 195
1:20–23	191	1:29	287	3:3	145
1:20–21	259	2:1–11	195	3:4	257
1:20	21	2:5–8	115, 116	3:5–6	256
2:4–9	171	2:6–11	37, 40, 197	3:17	192, 195
2:6–7	257, 259	2:9–11	191	4:7	196
2:8	191, 285	2:11	35	4:12	196
2:10	65, 195	2:16	258	**1 Thessalonians**	
2:13	146	2:17	288	1:1	193, 195
2:14–16	116	3:1	193	1:3	193
2:15–16	146	3:7–11	167	1:5	228
2:18	228	3:7–8	193	1:6	227, 286
2:19–22	194	3:9–11	257	1:7	285
3:5	228	3:9	286, 290	1:9–10	21, 170
3:6	194	3:21	191, 254	1:9	35, 288
3:7–11	196	4:4	193		